VIEW OF FREDERICKSBURG, VA.

NOV. 1862.

DRAMA ON THE RAPPAHANNOCK
THE FREDERICKSBURG CAMPAIGN

Part of Burnside's Army Crossing the Rappahannock at Fredericksburg

DRAMA ON THE RAPPAHANNOCK

The · Fredericksburg · Campaign

by

EDWARD J. STACKPOLE

THE STACKPOLE COMPANY

HARRISBURG, PENNSYLVANIA

Printed and bound in the United States of America
by THE TELEGRAPH PRESS, *established 1831,*
Harrisburg, Pennsylvania

DEDICATION

To David, living heritage of the past and confident promise of the future

TABLE OF CONTENTS

ILLUSTRATIONS

Most of the old photographs used in this book were taken during the Civil War by Mathew Brady or an assistant, and have been reproduced from the Library of Congress Collection or from *The Photographic History of the Civil War,* published in 1913 by the Review of Reviews, New York. Acknowledgment is made to Mr. Carl E. Stange, Division of Prints and Photographs, Library of Congress, for assistance in locating and selecting suitable illustrations. The photos illustrating Confederate weapons and the Richmond arsenal are from the West Point Museum and Library of Congress Collections, and are furnished by courtesy of William B. Edwards, author of The Stackpole Company's forthcoming book, *Civil War Guns.* The view of Harpers Ferry was furnished by Mr. R. H. Anderson, Chief of the Visual Section, Branch of Information, National Park Service.

The numerous drawings were mostly executed during the Civil War by staff artists of newspapers and magazines who kept correspondents and illustrators in the field with the armies. These artists were Waud, Forbes, Lovie, Beard, and many others. Their sketches have been reproduced here from *Harpers Pictorial History of the Great Rebellion,* Harper & Bros., New York, 1868; *The Soldier in Our Civil War,* Stanley Bradley, New York, 1885; *Pictorial Battles of the Civil War,* Sherman Publishing Co., New York, 1885; *Battles and Leaders of the Civil War,* Century Co., New York, 1887.

The maps were prepared by Colonel W. S. Nye, editor of the text, and Mr. Ray Snow, veteran chief of the art department of The Telegraph Press. Colonel Nye secured the basic maps, prepared the preliminary drafts, and wrote the accompanying descriptive matter. Mr. Snow was the cartographer. Maps referred to were contained in the *Official Records of the Rebellion,* Volume XXI, the *Atlas* accompanying the *Official Records,* and in the following maps from the Library of Congress Collection; several topographic and situation maps prepared after the war under the direction of the Chief of Engineers and known as the Micheler maps; several maps from the

Jed Hotchkiss Collection, prepared about the time of the battle by the chief topographer of Jackson's Corps; three contemporary maps (Confederate), prepared by B. L. Blackford; and one or two maps from the Southern Historical Society. Most of these sources contain discrepancies and errors in topography and in the location of some of the troop units. All these data were, therefore, checked and corrected by a detailed study of the reports of corps, division, brigade, and regimental commanders. Since it was deemed impracticable to employ folded inserts for use in reproducing maps, it was necessary to redraw all of them in order that they might be reduced to page size without too great a loss of clarity. This involved some simplifications, including omission of various minor terrain features, roads, place names, and the like.

The valuable assistance of Mr. Richard S. Ladd, Map Division, Library of Congress, in locating and selecting basic maps, is gratefully acknowledged.

LIST OF ILLUSTRATIONS

PROLOGUE

HALFWAY BETWEEN Washington and Richmond, Virginia, at a point where the Rappahannock River makes one of its many changes of direction, the three centuries old but thoroughly modern community of Fredericksburg entertains an ever-increasing stream of visitors to an area in which four significant campaigns of the War Between the States were fought.

Virginia was the mother of eight Presidents of the United States, two of whom had their roots in Fredericksburg. George Washington spent much of his lively youth, from 1739 to 1747, on the old Ferry plantation just across the river from the town. In the city itself are a monument to George's mother, Mary Ball Washington, and her home (now a museum) where she lived out the final years of her life and died a few months after her famous son left for his first inauguration. There is also to be seen the well-appointed one-story brick structure where James Monroe built his law practice and the reputation that later brought him the highest honor which his young country could bestow. And at the lower end of Fredericksburg is the two-story white frame house in which John Paul Jones, arrived from Scotland at the age of thirteen, lived for several years with his brother.

Nor is that all! Reminiscent as it is of the very spirit of the Washington family, the atmosphere of early Colonial days can still be felt in the surprisingly large number of architecturally beautiful homes and public buildings, erected in the 1700's, which are still standing either in their original or restored condition. Two of the more fascinating relics of the early days are the Rising Sun Tavern and the Hugh Mercer Apothecary Shop.

The Tavern, one of the three oldest buildings in the city, built about 1760 on property belonging to George Washington's brother Charles, was probably a stagecoach stop as early as 1775. In the Apothecary Shop, history was made in medicine and pharmacy by its early proprietor, Dr. Hugh Mercer, a prominent citizen in the Revolutionary period who as a brigadier general lost his life in the Battle of Princeton, fighting under the command of his close friend General Washington.

Notwithstanding its valued colonial heritage, it was not until December 1862 that Fredericksburg, with a population of only four thousand, attained the distinction of being one of a comparatively small number of American cities or towns whose names are synonymous with famous battles. During the Civil War it changed hands seven times, was fiercely fought over in the campaigns of Fredericksburg and Chancellorsville, and by the close of the war had dwindled to two thousand souls. Visitors today gaze with awe at the old buildings, notably the Presbyterian Church at the corner of Princess Anne and George Streets, which was established in 1808. One of its original white columns still carries two cannon balls, imbedded in the shaft, that were fired from Falmouth Heights by the Federal artillery. It was during the first Battle of Fredericksburg that the pews of this church were torn out to serve as beds for many of the wounded after the town was captured by the Union forces on December 13, 1862.

Today Fredericksburg serves as host to travelers who if needs be can between sunrise and sunset in a single day tour a group of battlefields upon which were fought the four major engagements of the Civil War—Fredericksburg in 1862, Chancellorsville in 1863, the Wilderness and Spotsylvania Court House in 1864—all within a few miles of one another and each sharing with the descendants of a mighty host of brave men the memories of bitter fighting on and near the banks of the broad Rappahannock, in the heartland of Virginia.

There is no comparable area of like size on the American Continent, perhaps even on the face of the globe, where in a comparatively short space of time such heavy and virtually continuous fighting has occurred. Strategically located about fifty miles in opposite directions from the Federal capital at Washington and the Confederate capital at Richmond, Fredericksburg at the very beginning of the war attained a position of great military importance. Nestling at a sharp right angle bend of the Rappahannock River, which was navigable from Richmond right up to Fredericksburg's front steps, it was, more importantly, on the line of an excellent railroad which provided the shortest route to Richmond and was directly in the path of the natural invasion route from the Northern capital to the Southern.

Thus the Rappahannock River for many miles along its line of flow served as an important Confederate barrier to invasion. In that fact is found the compelling reason for the locale of the series of bloody battles, fought in the immediate vicinity of Fredericksburg, in which the Blue and the Gray together suffered over 100,000 casualties.

From time immemorial the natural features of the military theater of operations have played an influential and frequently decisive role in the movement and tactical employment of troops, whether large armies or smaller units. The more skillful commanders have always built their strategic concepts and specific battle plans on carefully constructed foundations, composed partly of known facts, partly of considered judgment—what is modernly called a military estimate of the situation, in the development of which a careful analysis of the pertinent terrain invariably played a vital part.

Rivers and bridges; railroads, roads, streams, and canals; ridges, mountains, and mountain gaps; valleys, woods, road junctions, and other terrain features were all-important to the opposing forces, although in the last analysis the experience and capabilities of the troop commanders have determined whether these inanimate tools of war were to prove an asset or a liability to their commands.

The conditions under which the Civil War was fought were

such that in every important campaign rivers and mountains were major factors in the calculations of army, corps, and division commanders—difficult obstacles to overcome on the offensive, powerful deterrents in defensive operations.

In sharp contrast to the type of warfare that has been waged since the nineteenth century bowed out, battles of the Civil War were relatively uncomplicated affairs, displaying many of the characteristics of the chivalrous contests between knights of olden days. It was customary in the sixties to take plenty of time to prepare for the shock of battle, and when the armies finally clashed, the antagonists were prone to conduct themselves in a more or less gentlemanly fashion. The hectic tempo of modern warfare was nonexistent; there were no airplanes, machine guns, self-propelled artillery, tanks, rockets, or guided missiles; the weapons available were effective only at close range, signal communications were primitive by today's standards, and battle control of the troops was accomplished chiefly by word of mouth and an occasional hastily written message.

Bridges over rivers were infrequent and easily destroyed; troops moved for the most part under their own power. Supplies and ammunition were usually conveyed by slow moving, horse-drawn vehicles. When the rains descended, roads became mud baths, so that both men and animals bogged down into immobility more often than not. Fighting usually ceased at sundown and even the temper of the soldiers cooled to the point where friendly exchange of newspapers, tobacco, and other items of temporary value took place between the lines or across streams that served as No Man's Land.

This book is the story of the Fredericksburg campaign, in which General Robert E. Lee led the Army of Northern Virginia successfully against Generals George B. McClellan and Ambrose E. Burnside, who in turn commanded the troops constituting the Army of the Potomac during the period October 1862 through January 1863. The Drama on the Rappahannock is acted out along a noble river that, like two or three others, is featured in America's history as a setting for the combat phases of the Civil War. The Rappahannock loomed importantly in the strategic planning of the generals on both sides and served repeatedly in a tactical sense to afford both comfortable security and tragic discomfiture to the hundreds of thousands of Union and Confederate soldiers who learned to know it so well.

OFF TO WAR

CHAPTER 1

THE RISE AND FALL
OF GEORGE B. McCLELLAN

ABRAHAM LINCOLN'S inauguration as President of
the United States took place in Washington on March 4, 1861,
amid the rumble of impending civil war. Six short weeks later,
on April 12, the Confederate General Beauregard gave the
signal which lit the conflagration when his artillery opened fire
on Fort Sumter from Charleston Harbor. Two days later the fort
surrendered, the Stars and Stripes were hauled down, and the
war was on.

The Spark Becomes a Flame

This first error of judgment on the part of the Confederate
States—flouting the national colors which symbolize the honor,
the dignity, and the integrity of the United States—was the
cataclysmic event that, with a powerful, historic assist from
Francis Scott Key, author of The Star Spangled Banner, solidi-
fied the Northern states in their heretofore rather casual opposition to Secession. Inflamed by the attack on the flag, the
people of the North forgot their divided sentiment and closed
ranks behind President Lincoln. The opportunity to attain their

1

THE FIRST FEDERALS
Some of Colonel Burnside's Rhode Island volunteers who fought at Bull Run.

objective by diplomatic means rather than force of arms was irrevocably lost to the leaders of the Confederacy.

Neither of the belligerents was in any sense prepared for the kind of war that eventuated. The South had the edge insofar as the basic conditioning of the individual was concerned, because it was predominantly agricultural; and horsemanship and the use of firearms were practically congenital with the white Southern menfolk. In addition to this a large number of the most capable officers of the Regular Army, graduates of West Point and the several excellent military schools which flourished in the South, threw in their lot with their own states and thus created a problem of high-level military leadership for the North which Lincoln was unable to solve until General U. S. Grant was summoned from the Western theater to fill the vacuum.

A good example of the Union's failure to appreciate the serious character of the unwanted war into which it had suddenly been plunged was Lincoln's first call for troops. Immediately after Fort Sumter was fired on, the President called on the Free States to furnish 75,000 volunteers to serve for *three months!*

The first battle, at Bull Run, was mainly an affair of blooding, with both armies composed largely of green men and officers. It was in fact a fairly amateurish effort, with many opera-bouffe aspects. The small village of Manassas was a point of strategic importance, where several highways crossed. It was also the junction point of the Manassas Gap Railroad, which ran to and through the Shenandoah Valley, and the Orange and Alexandria Railroad, which linked Charlottesville and Lynchburg to Washington. Strategically Manassas covered Richmond and threatened Washington, and it was there that the Confederacy assembled its main forces.

At Bull Run the Confederates under General Pierre G. T.

CONFEDERATE VOLUNTEERS
A group of Southern soldiers who were among the first to fight.

Beauregard had scored their first victory over the Federals under General Irvin McDowell, driving the latter in ignominious rout all the way back to Washington. After what appeared to be an easy victory, many of the Confederate rank and file thought the war was already over and decided they would like to go home. Beauregard's troops, psychologically and militarily unprepared to exploit their success, were in fact almost as badly in need of rehabilitation after the battle as were the Northern troops. The fears of the Washington Administration that the Capital was about to be engulfed were unfounded.

McClellan and Johnston

Immediately after the Battle of Bull Run General George B. McClellan was called from West Virginia to command the United States troops for the defense of Washington. Upon the November retirement of Winfield Scott as General-in-Chief, or Chief of Staff as he would be designated today, McClellan was appointed to command the several armies of the North, including that untrained armed force currently designated the Army of the Potomac, replacing McDowell. It appears, however, that

CONFEDERATE WINTER QUARTERS NEAR MANASSAS, 1861

Lincoln and Stanton learned to understand better the new general's limitations as the months wore on, because on March 12, 1862, McClellan was relieved as General-in-Chief of all the armies and restricted to command of the Army of the Potomac. McClellan had a genius for organization, his chief claim to fame resting on the superb manner in which he built his eastern army into an efficient fighting machine. His main trouble seemed to be that he never reached the point where he was ready and willing to employ freely the keen weapon that he had forged.

General Joseph E. Johnston, the highest ranking officer of the United States Army to join the Confederacy, was so recognized by President Jefferson Davis when he was given command of the Confederate forces, superseding Beauregard, after the First Battle of Manassas. Johnston was a skillful strategist and tactician, but unfortunately somewhat mercurial, and decidedly sensitive to the prerogatives of his ranking position in the hierarchy of command. In the late summer of 1861, when Davis asked the Senate to confirm five officers as full generals, Johnston's name was fourth on the list in lineal rank, preceded by Adjutant General Samuel Cooper, Albert Sidney Johnston, and Robert E. Lee. This apparent "affront," which Johnston never forgave, was the spark which led to repeated clashes with President Davis and Secretary of War Benjamin, both of whom preferred Lee's tactful ways and equable temperament. So it came about, when Johnston was wounded at Fair Oaks before Richmond in late 1862, that Davis was quick to seize the opportunity to place Lee in command. Johnston was relegated to a semi-retired status from which he was not recalled for reassignment until the closing months of the war.

The Armies Mobilize Slowly

With the Bull Run affair out of the way, both belligerents devoted the remainder of the year 1861 and the early months of 1862 to preparations for the serious battles to come. Recruiting, training, procurement of supplies, and other collateral military activities occupied the time of the two armies. Neither McClellan

REBUILDING THE ARMY OF THE POTOMAC
Drilling the 26th New York Regiment near Washington, D. C., during the
winter of 1861. A year later this unit, then in Gibbon's division, fought at
Fredericksburg, where it suffered 60 percent casualties. This photo shows
the size of a Federal regiment, and the amount of space it occupied, when
in a column of companies. In Civil War days infantry attacked in what today
is called a parade ground formation.

nor Johnston was in any particular hurry to initiate offensive
operations, seemingly being content to remain passive in their
respective areas, the former in the vicinity of Washington and
the latter at Centreville, Virginia. They marked time strategically as they molded their armies to combat stature.

An impatient Lincoln waited hopefully in the White House as
the months rolled by without any indication that McClellan ever
intended to bestir himself and his powerful army. "Little Mac,"
who looked after his men and was immensely popular as a result,
had unfortunately developed a severe case of inflated ego. He
came to regard himself as something of a Napoleon. The following extract from his report on the later Peninsular campaign
speaks for itself in presenting the general as the self-appointed
savior of his country:

> The plan of campaign which I adopted for the spring of
> 1862 was to push forward the armies of Generals Halleck
> and Buell to occupy Memphis, Nashville, and Knoxville,
> and the line of the Memphis and Danville Railroad, so as to

deprive the enemy of that important line, and force him to adopt the circuitous routes of Augusta, Branchville, and Charleston. It was also intended to seize Washington, North Carolina, at the earliest practicable moment, and to open the Mississippi by effecting a junction between Generals Halleck and Butler. This movement of the Western armies was to be followed by that of the Army of the Potomac from Urbanna, on the lower Rappahannock, to West Point and Richmond, intending, if we failed to gain Richmond by a rapid march, to cross the James and attack the city in rear, with the James as a line of supply.

So long as Mr. Cameron was Secretary of War I received the cordial support of that department; but when he resigned, the whole state of affairs changed. I had never

MAJOR GENERAL GEORGE B. MCCLELLAN
The Federal commander is shown here with a portion of his staff.

met Mr. Stanton before reaching Washington, in 1861. He at once sought me and professed the utmost personal affection, the expression of which was exceeded only by the bitterness of his denunciation of the Government and its policy. I was unaware of his appointment as Secretary of War until after it had been made, whereupon he called to ascertain whether I desired him to accept, saying that to do so would involve a total sacrifice of his personal interests, and that the only inducement would be the desire to assist me in my work. Having no reason to doubt his sincerity, I desired him to accept, whereupon he consented, and with great effusion exclaimed: "Now we two will save the country."

On the next day the President came to my house to explain why he had appointed Mr. Stanton without consulting me; his reason being that he supposed Stanton to be a good friend of mine, and that the appointment would naturally be satisfactory, and that he feared that if I had known it beforehand it would be said that I had dragooned him into it.

The more serious difficulties of my position began with Mr. Stanton's accession to the War Office. It at once became very difficult to approach him, even for the transaction of ordinary current business, and our personal relations at once ceased. The impatience of the Executive immediately became extreme, and I can attribute it only to the influence of the new Secretary, who did many things to break up the free and confidential intercourse that had heretofore existed between the President and myself. The Government soon manifested great impatience in regard to the opening of the Baltimore and Ohio Railroad and the destruction of the Confederate batteries on the Potomac. The first object could be permanently attained only by occupying the Shenandoah Valley with a force strong enough to resist any attack by the Confederate army then at Manassas; the second only by a general advance of the Army of the Potomac, driving the enemy back of the Rapidan. My own view was that the movement of the Army of the Potomac from Urbana would accomplish both of these objects, by forcing the enemy to abandon all his positions and fall back on Richmond. I was therefore unwilling to interfere with this plan by a premature advance, the effect of which must be either to commit us to the overland route,

LOADING TRANSPORTS
Transferring an army by water involved a tremendous logistical problem
even in Civil War days.

or to minimize the advantages of the Urbanna movement. I wished to hold the enemy at Manassas to the last moment —if possible until the advance from Urbanna had actually commenced, for neither the reopening of the railroad nor the destruction of the batteries was worth the danger involved.

McClellan's self-satisfaction and assurance in his own mind that he was the great soldier who alone could save the country was not shared by the President and others. This was clearly revealed in the course of time as his lack of deeds failed to support the strategic plans which he kept outlining and continually revising. In the light of history, McClellan's cavalier attitude toward the Commander-in-Chief reflects little credit on either his perspicacity or his judgment.

PORK, HARDTACK, SUGAR, AND COFFEE

This illustrates the vast amount of supplies required to feed a single regiment during a campaign of even limited duration.

McClellan Maneuvers

Finally, however, in March 1862, possibly because he had run out of excuses, but also because of increasing pressure from the President, McClellan moved his army, by water, from its camps near Washington to the Virginia Peninsula between the York and James Rivers, with the avowed intention of advancing against Richmond. His plan had been to make the move secretly to a staging area at Urbanna on the Rappahannock River, and to attack Richmond from that point, but Joe Johnston got wind of the plan and moved his Confederates overland in the same direction, to the Fredericksburg-Culpeper area, which was as close to Richmond as was Urbanna. Having failed to gain the

MAP 1. THE FIRST BATTLE OF BULL RUN (MANASSAS) AND THE
PENINSULAR CAMPAIGN

The Battle of Bull Run was fought on July 21, 1861 near Centreville, south-west of Washington. The Federals then withdrew to Washington, while the Confederates wintered south of the battlefield. On March 17, 1862 McClellan embarked at Alexandria and transferred his army by water to Fort Monroe, Virginia, preparatory to moving on Richmond. Johnston moved the Con-federate army from Centreville on March 9, and two days later was along the Rappahannock in the Culpeper-Fredericksburg area. On April 4 Mc-Clellan marched up the peninsula toward Yorktown. He attacked Confederate positions near Williamsburg on May 5, then reembarked and steamed up the Pamunkey to White House. Johnston withdrew toward Richmond. Then followed, during May and June, the Battles of Seven Pines, Fair Oaks, Mechanicsville, Gaines Mill, Savage Station, and Fraysers Farm. After winning the Battle of Malvern Hill on July 1 McClellan withdrew to Harrisons Landing on the James River, and Lee pulled back into the defense works around Richmond.

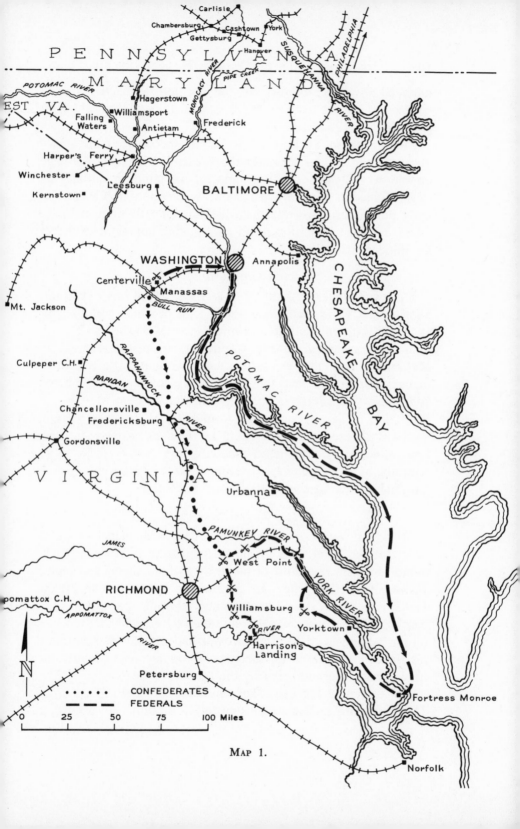

MAP 1.

intended advantage of surprise and position, McClellan landed his troops instead at Fort Monroe, then manned by a Union garrison.

Moving up to Yorktown, McClellan encountered imaginary obstacles and dallied for a month, ostensibly preparing for siege operations. When he finally made up his mind to initiate the siege, Johnston shrewdly withdrew, whereupon McClellan ineptly put his army astride the Chickahominy River near Richmond, an open invitation to an enterprising opponent to defeat his divided army in detail.

Jackson Goes Into Action

Stonewall Jackson had by this time begun his illustrious Shenandoah Valley campaign, the success of which badly frightened the Administration and prevented McDowell's 20,000-man corps, camped at the Capital, from being released to McClellan. The latter refused to move without those reinforcements, despite the fact that he already greatly outnumbered Johnston's Confederates. So Johnston attacked, on May 31, in the Battle of Seven Pines, was wounded at Fair Oaks Station, and was succeeded in command by General Robert E. Lee. Lee immediately designated his army the Army of Northern Virginia, as a symbol of his determination to operate in northern Virginia as the best way to defend Richmond.

Lee Takes the Helm

So now it was Lee against McClellan, with plenty of headaches for the latter. Lee set up fortified lines in front of Richmond, assigned one-third of his army to hold them, and called Jackson from the Valley. He perfected a battle plan to hit the Federals north of the Chickahominy, separate them from their base at White House, on the Pamunkey River, and then operate on an equality with McClellan, who had already demonstrated his timidity and could be chronically counted on to figure that he was badly outnumbered by the aggressive Lee.

Unfortunately for Lee, Jackson failed to show up on time. The Battle of Mechanicsville took place on June 26, according

to Lee's schedule, but the plan had miscarried and he met a
bloody repulse, his only satisfaction being that he was now on
the Federal line of communications. Characteristically, instead
of boldly following up his advantage, McClellan unnecessarily
retreated in the direction of the James River, ostensibly to
effect a change of base to Harrison's Landing. Fighting rear-
guard actions for six days, McClellan finally made a stand at
Malvern Hill where he administered a stinging defeat to Lee,
who then retreated to Richmond. Whereupon McClellan sat
down and repeated his interminable demands on Washington
for reinforcements.

This was nothing but the same old refrain, sung over and
over by a general who never seemed to have enough troops
and seldom employed to advantage those which he did have.
This led the sorely tried Lincoln to remark wryly on this occa-

ARMY OF THE POTOMAC IN CAMP
One of McClellan's base camps on the Pamunkey during the Peninsular
campaign.

sion: "Sending reinforcements to McClellan is like shoveling flies across a room."

Pope Rides on the Stage

As McClellan continued to temporize, Lincoln relieved him from supreme command in the Eastern theater, at the same time authorizing the constitution near Washington of a new Federal army comprising the forces of Fremont, Banks, and McDowell, with a reserve corps under Sturgis, and including Cox's division in West Virginia, all under the command of Major General John Pope. Pope's force was designated the "Army of Virginia," to the officers and men of which he published his first general order on July 14, 1862, announcing with psychologically unsound braggadocio: "I have come to you from the West where we have always seen the backs of our enemies; from an army whose business it has been to seek the adversary and to beat him when he was found; whose policy has been attack and not defense."

To that initial message to his troops he later added the widely quoted remark that his headquarters would be in the saddle, which was promptly ridiculed by the Confederates, who joked about this Johnny-come-lately who had his headquarters where his hindquarters should be.

The next move was up to Major General Henry W. Halleck,

MAP 2. THE SECOND BATTLE OF MANASSAS AND THE ANTIETAM CAMPAIGN While McClellan remained inactive at Harrisons Landing, Pope assembled a new Federal army north of the Rappahannock. Lee, who had succeeded Johnston, left McClellan to amuse himself, and moved north via Gordonsville to meet the new threat. He defeated Pope in the Second Battle of Manassas on August 29, 1862 then moved north through Leesburg on his first invasion of Maryland. Having reached Frederick, Lee decided to capture Harpers Ferry. For this purpose Jackson was sent on a circling movement to the west and south through Martinsburg thence east toward Harpers Ferry. McLaws was directed south from Cramptons Gap and Walker south from Frederick then west to Loudoun Heights. These three columns invested Harpers Ferry which promptly surrendered. Meantime McClellan reembarked, sailed back to Washington, and moved on Frederick. Lee withdrew west through the gaps. The Battle of Antietam was fought on September 17, following which Lee withdrew southwest of the Potomac, McClellan remaining in Maryland.

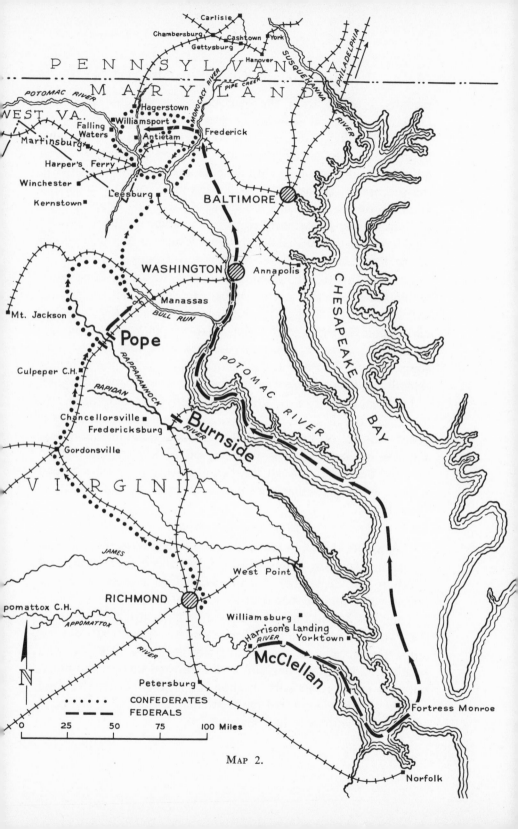

MAP 2.

recently brought from the West by Lincoln and appointed General-in-Chief of all the Federal armies. Halleck lost no time in deciding that the armies of McClellan and Pope must be united at the earliest practicable moment, preparatory to an advance on Richmond. This delicate operation would involve the withdrawal of the Army of the Potomac from its unhealthy situation on the Peninsula, concurrently with the concentration of Pope's army preparatory to marching south to the appointed rendezvous with McClellan on Aquia Creek, a few miles north of the Rappahannock River and Fredericksburg.

Lee met this threat by sending Jackson to harass Pope while he himself kept watch on the supine McClellan. When the latter still failed to move, Lee released more troops to join Jackson, whereupon Halleck ordered McClellan to join Pope. While McClellan was digesting the order, Lee led his troops to Jackson's support, defeated Pope at the Second Battle of Manassas in late August, and paved the way for his first invasion of Maryland.

Lee's strategy had by this time been fully developed. He had taken the measure of the several Federal commanders, was keenly aware of the fact that Lincoln's administration was sensitive to threats against the safety of the Capital, and figured that the best way to keep the Federal army out of Richmond was to encourage that sensitivity by pressing the threat to Washington.

Maryland is Invaded

Continuing the offensive, with his ultimate objective the Susquehanna River in Pennsylvania, Lee crossed the Potomac at Leesburg on September 4 and invaded Maryland, which he hoped would thus be won over to the Confederacy.

Pope was by this time a punctured balloon, while the Army of the Potomac was demoralized and virtually leaderless. McClellan, a Democrat with a national following to be reckoned with politically, was a popular idol to the enlisted men in the army, but had failed repeatedly to show himself an aggressive field general and had permitted the Confederate leaders to run rings around him with only half his strength.

To whom should Lincoln turn? McDowell, McClellan, Pope—each in turn had disappointed his Commander-in-Chief. Secretary of War Stanton and General-in-Chief Halleck couldn't stomach McClellan and made no bones about it. McDowell had been out of the picture since the First Battle of Bull Run and Pope had failed to measure up at the Second Battle of Bull Run, despite the fact that McClellan was partly to blame with his disappointing delay in uniting the Army of the Potomac with Pope's Army of Virginia, as he had been ordered to do. Had General Halleck been a strong man, the situation would have been favorable for him to have assumed command in person. He then could have acted promptly to consolidate the three separate armies of Pope, McClellan, and Burnside into one force of three wings under the command of the generals mentioned, and have moved resolutely to counter the growing aggressiveness of the Confederate army under Lee.

Instead of taking this logical step, Halleck virtually abdicated his position of responsibility for the conduct of the military phase of the war. He allowed a vacuum to be created by his inability or unwillingness to assume his responsibility, thus forcing Lincoln to act for him, which was one reason for the criticism subsequently leveled against Lincoln, from certain quarters, for "interfering" with his field commanders. The command situation for a time was unpleasantly fluid, as Lincoln looked vainly to Halleck to make the vital decision of choosing an acceptable field commander. Lincoln, searching for a general who would give him a victory, offered the job to Burnside, who had established something of a reputation with an independent command in North Carolina. Pope had by this time been relieved, and McClellan was not wanted, but Burnside, loyal to his good friend and doubtful of his own ability, urged the Administration to appoint McClellan. As Halleck continued to temporize, Lee crossed into Maryland. So there was no more time to be lost. Pope's defeated forces were marching back to the protection of Washington and the situation was tense, so Lincoln took the initiative, rode out to McClellan's headquarters,

THE PRESIDENT VISITS MCCLELLAN AFTER ANTIETAM

and told him personally that he was to take command of all the forces in the Eastern theater.

Robert E. Lee was on the loose in Maryland; the Army of the Union was virtually leaderless; so in desperation Lincoln once again turned to McClellan for his supreme commander. As Little Mac rode up to take over command of the now consolidated Army of the Potomac, the air rang with cheers and the rank and file took renewed heart as the master touch of the skilled organizer performed the magic of restoring the morale which Pope had so badly shattered.

The Battle of Antietam

Inspired by the heroic role in which he was now recast as the Hope of the North, and by the warm reception the army gave him on his restoration to overall field command, McClellan followed Lee into Maryland by a parallel route. The two armies met on September 17, 1862, at Antietam Creek, near the town of Sharpsburg, with McClellan again outnumbering Lee seven to four. It was here that the Union commander received a break to which he was hardly entitled, in view of his failure to exploit it. A Federal soldier had fortuitously picked up a copy of Lee's battle order wrapped around two cigars, carelessly dropped by a Confederate officer. The order was quickly relayed to McClellan, who thus derived an extraordinary intelligence advantage that rarely occurs in war.

McClellan had 70,000 men but used only 46,000 in the two-day battle. Lee had 39,000 and put all of them into the fight. In one of the bloodiest battles of the war, McClellan won on points the first day but failed to follow up his advantage on the second. Without sufficient strength to take the initiative, but still willing to accept defensive battle if McClellan should choose to renew the attack, Lee waited a bit and then returned to Virginia, while McClellan marked time and permitted the withdrawal without making any effort at pursuit.

WAGON TRAIN CROSSING ANTIETAM CREEK
Photographed shortly after the Battle of Antietam. A shattered fence and over-turned stone wall may be seen at the far end of the bridge. Note also the horse and buggy, the latter of a type still in use by the Amish folk of Pennsylvania and Maryland,

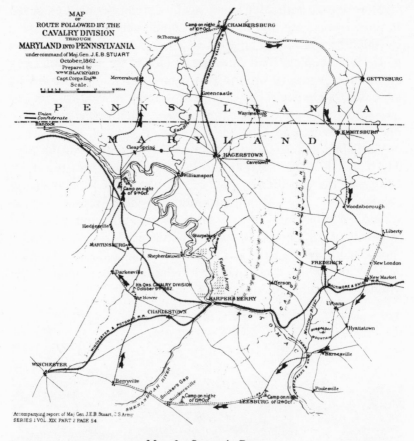

MAP 3. STUART'S RIDE

Tactically the battle may fairly be called a draw, but strategically the honors fell to the Federals. Lee had failed to win Maryland to the Confederate cause, and had lost some 8,000 men whom he could ill afford to spare. He had narrowly escaped what should have been a severe defeat, had McClellan called his bluff and followed the Lincoln precept to "put all your men in."

This was the battle for which Lincoln had been waiting; a strategic victory for the North in that Lee had been forced to put an end to his invasion and to return to Virginia. The "victory" gave Lincoln a long-sought opportunity to issue his Emancipation Proclamation, which announced to the world that slavery was abolished in the United States and would never again be tolerated. By one masterly stroke of the pen Lincoln converted the war into a Northern crusade for freedom, which gave the Union a tremendous psychological advantage both at home and abroad. Actually this was a preliminary proclamation, the official one being signed by the President on December 31, 1862, and published to the world as a fait accompli on January 1, 1863.

Stuart Rides Again

The Army of Northern Virginia spent the early autumn of 1862, after Antietam, on the banks of Opequon Creek in the lower Shenandoah Valley about 12 miles northwest of Harpers Ferry. The Army of the Potomac rested north of the Potomac in Maryland, with its base at Harpers Ferry. In order to find out what McClellan might be planning, Lee in early October sent J.E.B. Stuart with 1800 troopers on a sweeping raid around the Union army.

STUART'S RAID

Railroad buildings in Chambersburg burned during one of Stuart's rides around the Union Army.

This business of circling the Federal army was a specialty of the dashing Stuart. He had done it once before to McClellan near Richmond and now he staged a dramatic repeat performance with startling results. Crossing the Potomac at McCoy's Ford, the Confederate horsemen rode rapidly northward through Mercersburg, Chambersburg, across South Mountain and then, turning south through Emmitsburg and Frederick, recrossed the Potomac at White's Ford east of Leesburg, only a little more than two days after they had started out.

It was a fruitful expedition. Stuart's men gathered in several hundred good horses from Pennsylvania farms; wore Pleasonton's Federal cavalry to a frazzle in horse-killing marches in a continuous but unsuccessful effort to head off the Confederates and break up the raid; and shook badly the new, bright confidence that the North had reposed in the person of General McClellan. Of supreme importance to Lee, Stuart had learned during the raid that McClellan was getting set to move back into northern Virginia—an accurate intelligence report which had the added advantage that Lee was given several weeks to prepare for his opponent's return because the latter's timetable had been upset as a partial result of the exhausted condition of the Federal cavalry.

McClellan ascribed the success of the enemy raid to "the deficiency of our cavalry," and urged upon Washington "the imperative necessity of at once supplying this army with a sufficient number of horses to remount every dismounted cavalry soldier within the shortest possible time." To this the sorely tried Lincoln sent through Halleck an appropriate riposte: "The President has read your telegram and directs me to suggest that if the enemy had more occupation south of the (Potomac) river, his cavalry would not be so likely to make raids north of it."

Lincoln Jolts McClellan

As McClellan continued to stall with one excuse after another in an effort to explain why he was not following Lincoln's October 6 order "to cross the Potomac and give battle to the enemy or drive him south," the President dispatched a long letter to the general which evidently jolted him and in all truth should have caused him to blush with shame. This is what Lincoln wrote in his inimitable fashion:

Executive Mansion, Washington, Oct. 13, 1862.

My Dear Sir:

You remember my speaking to you of what I called your overcautiousness. Are you not overcautious when you assume that you cannot do what the enemy is constantly doing? Should you not claim to be at least his equal in prowess, and act upon the claim?

As I understand, you telegraphed Gen. Halleck that you cannot subsist your army at Winchester, unless the railroad from Harper's Ferry to that point be put in working order. But the enemy does now subsist his army at Winchester at a distance nearly twice as great from railroad transportation as you would have to do without the railroad last named. He now wagons from Culpeper Court-House, which is just about twice as far as you would have to do from Harper's Ferry. He is certainly not more than half as well provided with wagons as you are. I certainly should be pleased for you to have the advantage of the railroad from Harper's Ferry to Winchester; but it wastes all the remainder of Autumn to give it to you, and in fact ignores the question of *time*, which cannot and must' not be ignored.

Again, one of the standard maxims of war, as you know, is, "to operate upon the enemy's communications as much as possible without exposing your own." You seem to act as if this applies *against* you, but cannot apply in your *favor*. Change positions with the enemy, and think you not he would break your communication with Richmond within the next twenty-four hours? You dread his going into Pennsylvania. But if he does so in full force, he gives up his communications to you absolutely, and you have nothing to do but to follow and ruin him; if he does so with less than full force, fall upon and beat what is left behind all the easier.

Exclusive of the water line, you are now nearer Richmond than the enemy is by the route that you *can* and he *must* take. Why can you not reach there before him, unless you admit that he is more than your equal on a march? His route is the arc of a circle, while yours is the chord. The roads are as good on yours as on his.

You know I desired, but did not order, you to cross the Potomac below instead of above the Shenandoah and Blue Ridge. My idea was, that this would at once menace the enemy's communications, which I would seize if he would permit. If he should move northward, I would follow him closely, holding his communications. If he should prevent

LINCOLN AND McCLELLAN DISCUSS FUTURE OPERATIONS

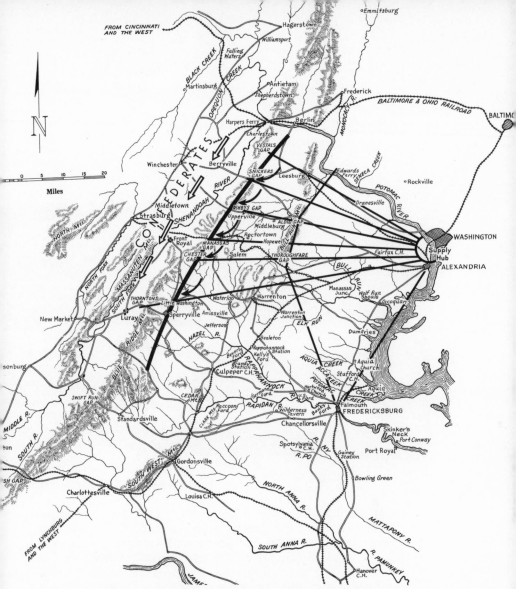

MAP 4. PRESIDENT LINCOLN'S STRATEGIC CONCEPT

In his letter to McClellan dated October 13, Lincoln suggests a master plan which was simple, sound, and workable. It cut cleanly through the tangle of imagined difficulties, the excuses, and the objections which Mc-Clellan was continually offering in place of action. It showed that by moving via the chords or inside arcs McClellan should have been able to keep his army between the enemy and Washington, attack through the mountain gaps where opportunity was offered, and still be on the shortest route to Richmond. Meanwhile McClellan could supply himself along the "spokes" radiating from the supply center at Washington, these radii generally following main roads and railroads to successive supply heads.

WHERE MCCLELLAN CROSSED THE

our seizing his communications, and move toward Richmond, I would press closely to him, fight him if a favorable opportunity should present, and at least try to beat him to Richmond on the inside track. I say "try," if we never try, we shall never succeed. If he makes a stand at Winchester, moving neither north nor south, I would fight him there, on the idea that if we cannot beat him when he bears the wastage of coming to us, we never can when we bear the wastage of going to him. This proposition is a simple truth, and is too important to be lost sight of for a moment. In coming to us, he tenders us an advantage which we should not waive. We should not so operate as to merely drive him away. As we must beat him somewhere, or fail finally, we can do it, if at all, easier near to us than far away. If we cannot beat the enemy where he

POTOMAC AT BERLIN, MARYLAND

now is, we never can, he again being within the intrench-
ments of Richmond.

Recurring to the idea of going to Richmond on the
inside track, the facility of supplying from the side, away
from the enemy, is remarkable, as it were by the different
spokes of a wheel, extending from the hub toward the rim,
and this, whether you move directly by the chord or on
the inside arc, hugging the Blue Ridge more closely. The
chord-line, as you see, carries you by Aldie, Haymarket
and Fredericksburg, and you see how turnpikes, railroads,
and finally the Potomac, by Aquia Creek, meet you at aid
points from Washington. The same, only the lines lengthened a little, if you press closer to the Blue Ridge part of
the way. The gaps through the Blue Ridge I understand
to be about the following distances from Harpers Ferry, to

wit: Vestal's five miles; Gregory's, thirteen; Snickers, eighteen; Ashby's, twenty-eight; Manassas, thirty-eight; Chester, forty-five, and Thornton's, fifty-three. I should think it preferable to take the route nearest the enemy, disabling him to make an important move without your knowledge, and compelling him to keep his forces together for dread of you. The gaps would enable you to attack if you should wish. For a great part of the way you would be practically between the enemy and both Washington and Richmond, enabling us to spare you the greatest number of troops from here. When, at length, running for Richmond ahead of him enables him to move this way; if he does so, turn and attack him in the rear. But I think he should be engaged long before such point is reached. It is all easy if our troops march as well as the enemy, and it is unmanly to say they cannot do it. This letter is in no sense an order.

Yours truly,

Maj. Gen. McClellan.   A. LINCOLN

More than ample time had now elapsed for McClellan again to put his army in fighting trim. The morale of the troops was good, they were well supplied and equipped, and they easily outnumbered Lee's army two to one. Federal cavalry reconnaissances had informed McClellan that the two wings of the Confederate army were now 60 miles apart, Longstreet's First Corps at Culpeper and Jackson's Second Corps in the Shenandoah Valley.

McClellan Fades Out of the War

In late October McClellan moved. Advancing with his usual caution, and in accordance with his plan to attack Longstreet and drive him back or at least keep him from forming a junction with Jackson, the Army of the Potomac crossed the Potomac at Berlin and on November 6 reached Warrenton, Virginia.

In view of McClellan's vast numerical superiority, Lee decided to employ maneuver rather than force. In conformity with that decision he left Jackson in the Valley to threaten the Union flank and rear. This was a dangerous calculated risk on Lee's part, but the sort of thing for which he was famous.

By this time, however, McClellan's luck had run out. Stuart's second free-wheeling raid around the Army of the Potomac, each time with impunity, had left a decidedly unfavorable impression on the public mind. Lincoln had carefully read the Antietam battlefield reports and accurately interpreted them as reflecting an unexploited opportunity because of McClellan's lack of aggressiveness. Secretary of War Stanton and General-in-Chief Halleck had evaluated McClellan and found him wanting. So once again, and this time for good, on November 7, 1862, George B. McClellan was removed from command.

McClellan's inadequacy as a fighting general was rather pungently portrayed in a twenty-nine page *Report of the Congressional Committee on the Operations of the Army of the Potomac,* which fully covered the campaigns from shortly after the First Battle of Manassas in 1861 through November 6, 1862, when McClellan was relieved, to the end of the Fredericksburg campaign. Over the signatures of United States Senators Ben F. Wade and Z. C. Chandler, and Representatives D. W. Gooch, John Covode, G. W. Julian, and M. F. Odell, the report embodied letters and telegrams passing between President Lincoln, General-in-Chief Halleck, and General McClellan, and afforded an illuminating insight into the mind of a field general whose flair for procrastination, for dreaming up imaginary obstacles where none existed, and for gratuitous placing of the blame on Lincoln and Halleck for his own shortcomings has no parallel in the military history of America.

In cold, clipped sentences, the report realistically summed up the committee's considered appraisal of General McClellan in these words: "The same mind that controlled the movements on the Peninsula (Yorktown) and the Seven Days Battles before Richmond controlled those in Maryland (Antietam), and the same general features characterized the one campaign that characterized the other. In each may be seen the same unreadiness to move promptly and act vigorously; the same desire for more troops before advancing; and the same references to the great superiority of numbers on the part of the enemy."

JACKSON ATTACKS HARPERS FERRY
Union camp as seen from Walker's position on Loudoun Heights.

CHAPTER 2

THE VIRGINIA THEATER OF OPERATIONS

THE VITAL ROLE of the glamorous State of Virginia, "Mother of Presidents," and one of the more influential of the thirteen original colonies, in the War for Independence from British control was played out mainly through the personalities and actions of prominent Virginians operating on the national stage. Virginia did, however, furnish the combat theater in which the seven-year-long Revolutionary War was finally terminated in October 1781, when Lord Cornwallis surrendered to General Washington at Yorktown.

An Historic Battleground

It was during the War Between the States, 1861-65, that Virginia achieved enduring fame as an historic battleground.

The Old Dominion was abundantly endowed at the start of the Civil War with most of the qualifications essential to the prosecution of a gentlemanly war save industrial sinews and adequate manpower, the combined lack of which proved ultimately

30

to be its Achilles' heel. Situated as it was in geographic proximity to Washington, the seat of government of the United States, it was not surprising that Virginia should become the principal eastern amphitheater wherein most of the crucial battles of the War Between the States would be fought. These occurred during the period from the initial meeting engagement between the forces of the North and the South at the First Battle of Bull Run (called the Battle of Manassas by the Confederates), about thirty miles southwest of Washington on July 21, 1861, to the final battle at Appomattox Court House, about one hundred miles west of Richmond, where the war was officially brought to a close with Lee's surrender to Grant on Palm Sunday, April 9, 1865.

Between those two apocryphal events occurred hundreds of fights on Virginia fields between the Blue and the Gray, from hit-and-run collisions between cavalry patrols and small infantry detachments to full-scale, deadly battles of attempted extermination by large armies. With all the honors paid to the sons and daughters of Virginia by generations of Americans and those of other countries, it may be assumed that the city and country folk of Civil War days would gladly have traded part of the future homage to be paid their State for a modicum of relief from the continuous mental and physical trials and tribulations visited upon them during four years of fighting and killing over the broad reaches of northern Virginia.

Virginia is one of the few states which has nearly everything in the way of natural beauty and variety—magnificent, rugged mountains with their wealth of forests, rivers, waterfalls, subterranean caverns, woods, streams, fertile valleys, far-flung plantations with their Old World charm, sandy beaches, and ocean-blue bays and inlets. It would be difficult to find anywhere a more completely equipped amphitheater, with all the natural trappings, than Virginia was able to offer for the stirring marches and battles staged in the northern part of that distinguished State during the four years of the War Between the States.

From a high-ranging helicopter at an altitude of twenty thou-

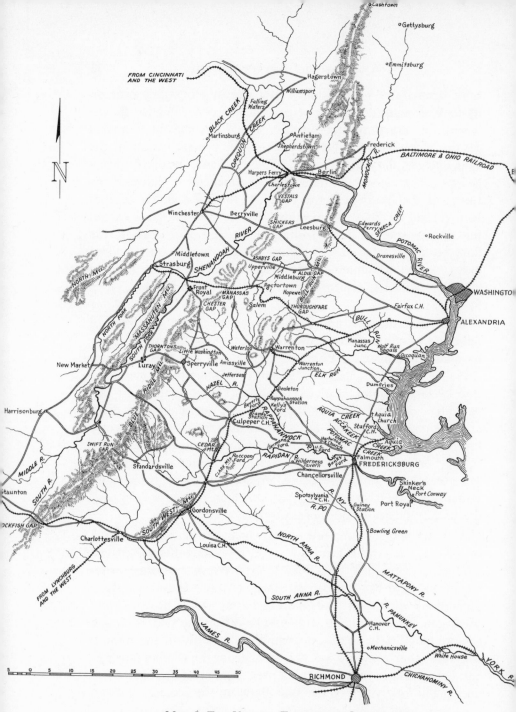

MAP 5. THE VIRGINIA THEATER OF OPERATIONS

sand feet, on a clear day an alert observer can look down on the unique pattern of terrain that is northern Virginia, from the seacoast on the east to the lofty, rugged Appalachian Mountains on the west; and from the Potomac River on the north to the James River on the south. Within that irregular, natural trapezoid, enclosing some ten thousand square miles of lush countryside, were fought all but a few of the important Civil War battles in the Eastern theater between the Army of the Potomac and the Army of Northern Virginia. A keen observer who knows his Virginia geography and has learned to interpret aerial photographs would have no trouble spotting historically famous places such as Manassas, Harpers Ferry, Winchester, Culpeper, Richmond, Petersburg, Fredericksburg, the Wilderness, and many others, while the Potomac, Rappahannock, York, and James Rivers would stand out like narrow, dark ribbons weaving their unbroken courses to the sea.

The four large rivers, all navigable for part of their attenuated lengths, wind snaky, parallel, southeasterly paths from the foothills of western Virginia across rolling country to the level tidelands, where they empty into Chesapeake Bay. Historic rivers all, for the Civil War story of Virginia is inseparably linked with the Potomac, the Rappahannock and its tributary the Rapidan, the York, and the James. Rivers were major obstacles in those days, not only because of their breadth and depth, but for the unpredictable speed with which they were wont to rise on occasion, usually at the worst possible time for the commander whose strategic decisions might fail to take their changes into sufficient account. Most of them had fords at much traveled crossing points, upstream of their navigable stretches, which were of course unusable at flood-time, so the army that was well served by its engineers was fortunate if that arm operated efficiently its pontoon companies with their hard-to-handle, heavy bridging equipment.

A noticeable change has taken place in these rivers in the intervening years. In 1862 they were difficult obstacles for troops to surmount; today they have in many places silted or dried up as a result of power dam installations, with the result that they are much more shallow than they were during the Civil War.

Today tourists whiz along Virginia's concrete highways and hard-topped byways, through cities and towns, noting briefly the historic markers but little realizing what a great change has come over the landscape since the boys in Blue and those in

LIEUTENANT GENERAL THOMAS J. JACKSON

Gray tramped the roads and the fields in the 1860's. Most of the roads in the state were then sand-and-clay. The soil varied from the clay of the Piedmont on the west, changed to sandhills as one moved to the east, and merged finally into the sand-and-pine flats of the tidewater country. The towns and cities of today were at that time villages, hamlets, and crossroads with a few frame houses thrown in for good measure.

The Shenandoah Valley

War in Virginia in 1862 was almost synonymous with action in the Shenandoah Valley, the very name of which conjures up visions of Lieutenant General Thomas Jonathan Jackson. Better known as "Stonewall," that austere, dedicated, pious but thoroughly masculine soldier-professor ranged up and down the Valley almost at will, striking terror into Northern hearts, and manipulating by his rapid marches, maneuvers, hammer blows, and psychological warfare the shifting tactics of the war departments in both Washington and Richmond. As though by the process of hypnotic suggestion Jackson succeeded in immobilizing Union divisions, corps, and even armies on more than one historic occasion.

The Shenandoah Valley, a natural theater of operations if ever there was one, formed a protective corridor, easily accessible to the Confederates. By their posture and actions in the Valley, the Confederates threatened Washington and the two important east-west communications of the Union—the Baltimore and Ohio Railroad, and the Chesapeake and Ohio Canal, both of which crossed at the northern end of the Valley. The Shenandoah was the best route for a Confederate invasion of Maryland and Pennsylvania, and conversely the logical approach for Union forces seeking to relieve Washington and the North from the deadly peril continuously posed by Jackson's fast marching "foot cavalry." Moreover, the Shenandoah was supremely important to the Confederacy for its capacity to produce and store large quantities of foodstuffs vital to the Army of Northern Virginia. This may indeed have been the compelling reason why it was so vigorously defended by the Southerners.

Both flanks of that narrow corridor, which averaged less than twenty miles in width, were protected by mountain ridges, the Shenandoah Mountains on the west, the Blue Ridge on the east, which could be crossed only at the several gaps, easily blocked by small detachments. The Valley was joined to eastern Virginia through its most important pass by the Manassas Gap Railroad on the north, and the Orange and Alexandria Railroad through Rockfish Gap on the south, while in between were a half-dozen other gaps which carried the familiar names—Vestals,

HARPERS FERRY IN 1862
In the left foreground is the burned United States Arsenal.

Gregorys, Snickers, Ashbys, Chesters, and Thorntons. All were
within fifty miles of Harpers Ferry. The land was fertile and the
roads afforded ample opportunity for rapid maneuver by an
enterprising and aggressive commander. The main pike through
the Valley ran north from Staunton to Martinsburg, a distance
of one hundred and twenty miles, via New Market and Winchester. The Valley was split down the middle by the Massa-
nutten Ridge. The two branches of its major river, the Shenandoah, traveled their watery route northward on either side of
this ridge, to unite at Front Royal and ultimately to empty into
the Potomac at Harpers Ferry.

It is notable that Jackson's force in the Valley never exceeded
18,000 men, yet with that comparatively small number of troops,
mostly infantry and artillery, and with a contributory assist by
way of the almost complete lack of Federal unity of command,
this one great captain managed at one time or another to
neutralize four or five times his own strength among the Union
corps under Banks, Shields, McDowell, Fremont, and Milroy.

One doubts that the history of warfare records a more brilliant account of effective strategy and almost invariably successful tactics than Jackson's Shenandoah Valley campaign in the first six months of the year 1862.

Glamorous Harpers Ferry

Travelers through the beautiful Shenandoah Valley are remiss if they dash unseeingly across the broad Potomac River bridge at the Valley's northern extremity without turning aside to visit Harpers Ferry, one mile to the west at the spot where the Shenandoah merges with the Potomac and three states, Maryland, Virginia, and West Virginia converge. Few are the places where Nature has carved out a juxtaposition of mountains and rivers of such breath-taking beauty or of such commanding stature as a crossroads of history. The quiet town of Harpers Ferry is historically one in a million, but as seen today its rich tradition is about all that remains to a small community that once boasted over four thousand workmen and their families.

Hovering above the gap in the Blue Ridge Mountains which overlook the junction of the two rivers, buttressed on all sides by majestic, towering mountains of giant rock, the ghosts of the Harpers Ferry townsfolk of the mid-nineteenth century can with a bit of imagination be observed reminiscing over the exciting and tragic events which took place in that neighborhood almost one hundred years ago.

It was here that John Brown of Kansas moved in with his small band of followers in October 1859, seized the United States armory and arsenal, and barricaded his little group in a defiant gesture against the authority of the Government in his fanatical effort to free the slaves. Robert E. Lee, then an Army colonel, and Lieutenant J. E. B. Stuart were the officers who directed his capture, and the outlines of the foundation of the historic armory in one of whose buildings Brown was captured before he was hanged, can still be seen along the shoreline of the Shenandoah River just a few yards above the point where it joins the Potomac.

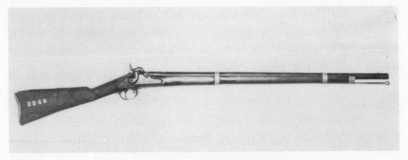

FAYETTEVILLE CONFEDERATE RIFLE
Built with machinery and parts captured by Jackson at Harpers Ferry.

The John Brown affair was of course a mere incident preceding the outbreak of war, but it served to focus public attention on Harpers Ferry, whose chamber of commerce head, had there been one, could have asked for nothing more lurid as a means of putting his town on the map.

Harpers Ferry came by its name when Robert Harper in 1747 purchased the rights of Peter Stephens, the first trader-settler. The new owner was a millwright from the Shenandoah Valley who recognized the opportunity inherent in the use of water power, and when he built his mill and ferry it turned out to be the start of a small town which quickly grew up in the unique triangle of land between the two broad rivers.

George Washington was familiar with the area and its possibilities. During his Presidency he encouraged Congress to purchase land at that site for a gun factory, which in a few years was turning out 10,000 muskets a year; while later, in 1819, the Hall's Rifle Works for the first time in America was manufacturing on a mass production basis an early breech-loading rifle with interchangeable parts.

The bustling town became really famous with the opening of the War Between the States. The troops that occupied Harpers Ferry on the south bank of the Potomac, the contiguous heights on either side of the Shenandoah where it empties into the Potomac, and Maryland Heights on the opposite shore, held the magic key which opened the door to invasion of enemy territory via the valley routes on both sides of the wide Potomac. Washington was only about fifty miles away. Winchester, the town which recalls Sheridan's famous ride and which changed hands so many times during the war that it took on the characteristics of a chameleon, was some thirty miles to the southwest. Sharpsburg, Maryland, was only a couple of hours' road march to the north, an important factor in McClellan's dismal failure to overwhelm Lee at the Battle of Antietam. For it was Jackson, who after capturing Harpers Ferry, hastened to Antietam to redress the balance of power and discourage McClellan from taking measures for gaining the tremendous victory which could so easily have been achieved against Lee's divided and much smaller forces.

A Triple Play Captures Harpers Ferry

This seizure of Harpers Ferry by Jackson was one of those dramatic operations which contributed to make Robert E. Lee one of the great military strategists of all time. Lee's bold but carefully calculated risks were uniformly successful until the war of attrition waged by General Grant nullified the best efforts of which the weakened power of the Confederacy was capable.

In September 1862, after his defeat of Pope at the Second Battle of Manassas, Lee invaded Maryland in a planned threat to Pennsylvania, and had reached Frederick when it suddenly occurred to him that he had better remove the threat to his line of communications and supply back to Virginia by taking Harpers Ferry, at that time occupied by something over 11,000 Federal troops. In the face of a probable clash with McClellan's greatly superior strength, Lee ventured to divide his army into four parts, three columns of which were directed to invest Harpers Ferry, eighteen miles southwest of Frederick (Map 2).

One Confederate column, commanded by McLaws, approached from the south and seized Maryland Heights across the Potomac from the town. Walker's column was diverted to destroy an aqueduct on the Chesapeake and Ohio Canal and then occupy Loudoun Heights on the south bank of the river directly across from Harpers Ferry. The third column, under Stonewall Jackson's personal direction, made one of his characteristic circuitous but rapid marches, covering sixty miles in a little over three days, from Frederick through Middletown, Boonsboro, Williamsport, and Martinsburg, herding Union detachments ahead of him and forcing them into the Harpers Ferry triangle. At the same time, Jackson circled to the rear to block the southwestern escape route of the Federal garrison at Harpers Ferry.

Under hostile artillery fire from commanding heights on both sides of the river, and with Jackson moving in from the rear, the Federal commander quickly caved in, and surrendered over 13,000 men in short order and with negligible casualties. Only the Federal cavalry, 1,200 strong, elected to make a dash for it. In a gallant effort they escaped across a pontoon bridge into Maryland to rejoin McClellan. En route they ran into Longstreet's reserve ammunition train, captured it, and to that extent added to Lee's problems at Antietam.

The quick surrender of the Federal garrison freed the main body of Jackson's force, which made a further rapid but exhausting march to Sharpsburg, leaving A. P. Hill's Division to parole the prisoners and then follow to Sharpsburg. Jackson reached Lee before the Battle of Antietam had started, while Hill, disposing quickly of the prisoners, made an equally rapid march and arrived just in time to prevent the troops on McClellan's left from pushing their way into Sharpsburg.

The Civil War brought both glory and ruin to Harpers Ferry. Its combined road and railroad bridge across the Potomac was destroyed and rebuilt nine times. The town with its factories and armory-arsenal buildings was shelled and burned and otherwise thoroughly destroyed as it came under the successive control of the opposing armies, and the tide of Blue and Gray warriors flowed back and forth over its jutting mountain ramparts and triangular town site. While not exactly a ghost town, for people still live there, Harpers Ferry today has no industry. Yet tourists are seeking it out in ever-increasing numbers. Some day, secure

MANASSAS JUNCTION
Used as a railhead by Pope. Jackson captured vast stores here on August 26, 1862.

in its romantic heritage, a new and prosperous Harpers Ferry will inevitably rise from the Civil War ashes, in one of the most magnificent natural settings to be found anywhere on the face of the globe.

Major Combat Areas

If one had the patience to work out with slide rule and compass the computations that would disclose those areas of Virginia over which the major part of the heavy fighting occurred, as distinct from marches and skirmishes, he likely would find that the Shenandoah Valley and the Fredericksburg area share the top position. There were by actual count more than five thousand separate battles or skirmishes between the North and the South in the course of the war. But the significant battles in the East, excluding Gettysburg, took place within geographical circles whose several radii of twenty miles or less fanned out in one or more directions from a mere handful of focal points: Richmond, Petersburg, Manassas Junction, Fredericksburg, Harpers Ferry, and Appomattox Court House.

The military strategist, surveying his probable theater of operations, studies the road net and the type of roads available,

THE ORANGE AND ALEXANDRIA RAILROAD AFTER A CONFEDERATE RAID

the waterways, the mountain passes, the hills and valleys, the kind of weather he will encounter, and other essential factors. He also scrutinizes such railroads as cross the theaters—where they start, the direction in which they run, their gauge and number of tracks, sidings, areas of vulnerability such as gorges and river crossings, and the like. The availability and flexibility of rail transportation to the enemy and to himself could spell the difference between victory and defeat.

The Confederacy was not too well served by its railroads in northern Virginia, in comparison with the more efficient railroading in the North, but there were several major lines which crisscrossed the State and connected the larger areas of population and such industry as the South possessed, however inadequately they may have met the supreme test by modern standards.

Richmond was the center of the principal railroad net which included main lines running south through Petersburg; north through Fredericksburg to the terminal at Aquia Landing; north and west to the Gordonsville Junction; and southwest through Amelia Court House, to Danville, Lexington, and the Carolinas.

The Baltimore and Ohio ran west from Baltimore through Harpers Ferry. The Orange and Alexandria slashed through open country in a southwesterly direction from Alexandria, through Manassas Junction, Culpeper Court House, and Gordonsville to Charlottesville. At this point branches led westward through Staunton in the Shenandoah Valley and southward through Lynchburg. These were the rail lines, together with the Richmond network, upon which the Confederacy depended for the movement of heavy equipment, food, clothing, and other supplies.

An Aerial Reconnaissance

To understand and derive maximum satisfaction from the study of a campaign or battle it is necessary to acquire a familiarity with the character of the terrain on which the maneuvering and actual fighting took place. Union and Confederate generals were restricted to a ground-locked horizon viewed from the nearest mountain peak, if any, that could be scaled on foot or horseback. The Federals, it is true, had two or three of Professor Lowe's observation balloons, but their generals were constitutionally allergic to such new-fangled gadgets, which were roadbound and quickly rendered useless by wind and weather. Besides, it required imagination of a high order to depend on a balloon reconnaissance to secure a terrain appreciation or other essential information upon which to plan a specific campaign within a chosen theater.

The ex-post-facto writer is not handicapped as were the generals in the 1860's. The airplane and the helicopter are at our disposal, and the latter will serve admirably to afford a preview of that area of Maryland and northern Virginia whose relatively small periphery encloses the country over which most of the fighting occurred from the outbreak of war in early 1861 to the end of 1862.

Because time and space factors are not binding for the purpose of this aerial reconnaissance, the reader is invited to consider himself a passenger in a 1957 helicopter anachronistically taking off from the Capital City of Washington. The time is early November 1862.

Reaching for altitude on the first leg of the journey, a short jog south brings Bull Run and the crossroad of Manassas into view. Then we turn northwest to follow the course of the Potomac and pinpoint the several fords and bridges which achieved mere distinction or real fame, depending on who crossed, and when and how. For example, we see the Williams-port area, where Lee's army, retreating in July 1863 to Virginia after Gettysburg, with its back to the swollen, unfordable Potomac, was allowed to escape from the clutches of a timid Meade who seemed to feel that his task would be completed

PROFESSOR T. S. C. LOWE AND ONE OF HIS OBSERVATION BALLOONS

Burnside received valuable information from this source concerning the roads, troop movements, and dispositions of infantry and artillery during and before the Battle of Fredericksburg. It is questionable that he correctly evaluated and used this information. The balloon was inflated by hydrogen gas produced by a portable generator. Infantry soldiers were detailed from nearby units to assist in handling the balloon.

once the Army of Northern Virginia could be herded back into its own front yard.

Here and there along the north side of the Potomac can be seen Federal camps occupied by the various divisions and smaller regiments guarding the approaches to Washington and northern territory in general, while small clouds of dust and tiny moving figures mark the passage of a cavalry squadron, a company of infantry, or an artillery battery on a mission or merely engaged in a training exercise.

Dropping to tree-top level over Sharpsburg, Maryland, the backwash of war is evident within the town itself and over the nearby countryside, for it was only a few weeks earlier that Lee and McClellan had fought each other to their respective knees, following which the Confederates had withdrawn to Virginia to reorganize and recruit to twice the strength available at the end of the battle. Meanwhile McClellan relaxed at Harpers Ferry to rehabilitate his shattered units and once more wait for Lincoln and Halleck to force him out of the "slows"—as the President characterized those dilatory processes—which usually gripped him when there was actual fighting to be done.

Turning south again, Sharpsburg is left behind, the South Mountain looms on the left as we cross the Potomac at Shepherdstown, above the bridge site where tens of thousands of Lee's legions will advance in the opposite direction next year on their way to Gettysburg.

Circling to the right for a quick look from a safe altitude, the area of Opequon Creek, at the north end of the Shenandoah Valley, comes into view. There Lee's army, less Jackson's corps, which is bivouacked farther south, has been recuperating and refitting since Antietam, but activities in the camp indicate that Longstreet's corps is preparing to leave the Valley, pass through a gap in the Blue Ridge, and march to Gordonsville, leaving Jackson in his beloved Valley for the time being. One may speculate, in passing, as to why Lee seemed always to prefer to be with Longstreet on the march and in camp—could it have been because Jackson never had to be prodded?

PART OF DOUBLEDAY'S DIVISION IN CAMP
A good picture of the Federal soldier as he appeared in the field. Note the
drummer boy.

Swinging back to the Potomac, where it takes a right angle turn to the east on the last leg of its journey to Washington and the sea, we pass over Harpers Ferry, note that McClellan's railhead and a couple of his divisions are still there, and then glide swiftly through the mountain gaps and out over the rolling country between the Blue Ridge and the shores of Chesapeake Bay.

It is time to turn south again if we are to catch sight of the Army of the Potomac, part of which by now has reached Warrenton, Virginia, at the same time that it comes under command of a new general, Ambrose E. Burnside. There they are, over 100,000 strong, campfires and all, bivouacked over a wide area and no doubt wondering where the next move will take them.

Rappahannock Country

Since this is an account of the Campaign of Fredericksburg, in which the Rappahannock River plays a leading part and throughout which it inescapably threads its way, the next lap of this air jaunt will follow the course of that river across the Virginia landscape in a preview of the battle area upon which the eyes of the world were focused during the winter of 1862.

The frequency of the fords that dotted the Rappahannock and its almost equally historic tributary, the Rapidan, was one of the factors which gave both rivers their importance in the military scheme of things.

Scarcely a mile of either river was without its shallow crossings for long distances in both directions from the point where the Rapidan loses its identity and merges with the Rappahannock; and each ford attained a measure of passing fame, the lasting character of which depended on the frequency and combat worthiness of the use to which it was put during the months and years when the opposing forces played the game of war along the banks and across the waters of those rivers.

The names of Ely, Skinker, Brooke, Germanna, Culpeper Mine, Harden, and Hall were attached to those river crossings which became familiar bywords to thousands of men in both armies. All these fords, among others less well known, led into that tangled mass of deadly woodland south of the river which was known as the Wilderness, a vast, inhospitable bit of country which gave to the Battles of Chancellorsville, the Wilderness, and Spotsylvania Court House much of their strategic and tactical significance.

Viewed from the air there is of course little to be seen of the Wilderness except an almost endless stretch of dense woods. But the roads that span it, leading to the several river crossings, and

OUTPOSTS ON THE RAPIDAN

the occasional observable open patches, have a real meaning for the mind that seeks to understand the battles that were fought in and around its dark, forbidding depths.

Flying in an easterly direction along the Rappahannock, a new succession of fords passes under our wing: United States Ford, where the river makes a broad U-turn near Chancellorsville; Banks Ford, five miles to the east, where a sharper U-turn is achieved; and Scotts Ford, a mile or so still farther down river and not much over a mile from Fredericksburg, our immediate objective. Hovering over these important watermarks in turn, the tactician will inevitably think about the ways in which the opposing commanders may utilize them in the forthcoming campaigns, to their own advantage and the discomfiture of the enemy.

Rising to somewhat higher altitude as we approach the town

MARYE MANSION

of Fredericksburg, we note with interest that the river, which has been flowing in a direction somewhat south of east over the last thirty miles of our flight, bends sharply to the right and heads almost straight south for a stretch, forming a rectangular pocket which with the help of a long, well defined ridge mass on the west holds Fredericksburg in a tight tactical corner.

The river appears to be about 400 feet wide at the bend, but too deep to ford, and on the opposite bank, about a mile north of Fredericksburg, is a small village which our map shows to be Falmouth. The bridges across the Rappahannock have been destroyed, and we recall having heard something about the Confederates putting them to the torch as additional defense against possible attack by the Union army.

The high ground west of the town is known as Marye's Heights, but the higher ridge on the eastern bank of the river, Stafford Heights, seems to have more character and strength, as a defensive position, than its opposite number. At the lower end of the rectangular pocket, in the direction of Richmond, the town of Fredericksburg feeds into an open plain paralleling the river, with woods here and there and some lowland that could be a bit swampy. The road to Richmond and the main railroad running south stand out sharply between the Rappahannock and the ridge to the west. And that's about all that we can learn from the air. We shall find however that our reconnaissance will prove useful when we get around to a more detailed study of the terrain on the ground.

WAR DEPARTMENT BUILDING IN WASHINGTON, 1862

CHAPTER 3

LINCOLN TRIES ANOTHER GENERAL

LINCOLN HAD reluctantly restored McClellan to command, after Pope's failure, in the vain hope that the Union army would be galvanized into an offensive to carry the war to Lee and accomplish something more than the dreary succession of defeats and military stalemates that had been inflicted on the Union armies in the battles of the first two years. The North had been making very little progress in its prosecution of the war, as the President cast about for a general who could demonstrate the capacity to put to effective use the men and munitions placed so lavishly at his disposal. However mistakenly, Lincoln gave McClellan one more chance to prove himself a leader capable of achieving victory, and the first imperfect fruits of that decision were garnered at Antietam.

When week after week passed without any sign of movement, McClellan received unequivocal orders from Washington, on October 6, 1862, to take immediate advantage of the dry season and resume the offensive forthwith, despite which it was not

50

until October 26, almost three weeks later, that he bestirred himself, crossed the Potomac into Virginia at Berlin and advanced southward toward Warrenton in the valley between Blue Ridge and Bull Run Mountains. Warrenton was some fifty road miles below Harpers Ferry, while Culpeper, where Longstreet was now encamped, was a good twenty miles further. Stonewall Jackson would have covered the intervening distance in four or five days, but not the slow-moving McClellan.

The two wings of the Confederate army, under Longstreet and Jackson, respectively, were separated by a distance of fifty to sixty miles when McClellan started his cautious advance in the direction of Longstreet's corps at Culpeper, with the expectation or at least hope of keeping him from uniting with Jackson's force in the Shenandoah Valley. As conceived it wasn't a bad plan at all, in fact it could have been a very good one—under aggressive and determined leadership. But the snail's pace which McClellan adopted for the march afforded little promise that it would be executed with the energy or spirit necessary for success.

For some unfathomable reason it was McClellan's strange idea that six miles a day was all that troops should be called

CULPEPER, VIRGINIA

upon to march, and he rarely required more of them. There is of course a vast distinction between an army or even a corps advancing a specified number of miles in a given period of time, and the amount of additional marching required of smaller elements of the army. Every veteran of recent wars will recall innumerable instances during training and in actual campaign when his outfit covered fifteen, twenty, or even more miles in a single day without improving his division's tactical situation or advancing the general line of the corps or army more than a fraction of the mileage covered by his own particular regiment or other unit.

Troop marches, particularly where large units are involved, require the most meticulous kind of staff and logistical preparation, a high quality of imagination, scientific application of command and staff know-how, and skillful coordination of effort from the commanding general down through the chain of command to the last platoon leader. All this is required if a march is to be conducted with maximum efficiency and minimum waste effort and deterioration of morale on the part of the troops, who are always quick to detect ineffective leadership at all levels of command.

The truth was that McClellan could have moved his army the distance from Harpers Ferry to Rectortown in half the time. He could have made normal marches with far less discomfort to his officers and men. The troops were forced to contend with seven inches of snow one day, melting snow and muddy roads the next, miserably wet woods for bivouacs, freezing nights, together with all the griping and dissatisfaction which invariably accompanies such a movement, with its road jams, supply failures, and conflicting orders. When, however, the Union commander took ten. days to move the comparatively short distance of less than fifty miles, Lincoln's temper exploded and McClellan was summarily removed to make way for another commander who just might have the intestinal fortitude to give the Army of the Potomac the kind of battle leadership it deserved.

Changing Horses in Midstream

The practice of changing horses in midstream was hardly characteristic of the man whose "horse sense" was almost legendary, yet Lincoln was guilty of doing just that on at least two historic occasions. The first was in early November 1862, when he supplanted McClellan with Burnside, and the second in late June 1863, when Meade replaced Hooker in the presence of the enemy only three days before the Battle of Gettysburg. Lincoln may not have been aware of the danger involved in such a procedure, or, if he were, he may have considered the administrative and command obstacles to be the lesser of two evils.

It was a sad blow to the enlisted men of the Army of the Potomac when the word came down that McClellan had been relieved. He was extremely popular with the men, who never failed to cheer him to the echo whenever he passed them on the road or in camp. There is no doubt that they had a blind faith in Little Mac and their feelings were probably fairly expressed in the letter of a Massachusetts soldier to his family dated November 10, 1862, in which he wrote:

> As sure as George B. McClellan leaves, the courage, enthusiasm and pluck go with him . . . it is all the talk in camp . . . it would amuse you to hear the soldiers talk about the government and the Abolitionists; "hope they will be murdered and the army defeated," etc. They can't understand it; they see no newspapers and do not know the sequel. Many of them are discouraged and swear they won't fight under any other general; besides, the cold weather is killing the men.

It is doubtful that either President Lincoln or the people of the North understood the great test of loyalty and patriotism to which the Army of the Potomac was being subjected in the summary removal of the popular McClellan, who cherished thinly veiled political ambitions of his own and was not above making significant reference to the possible consequences when he wrote: "The order depriving me of the command created a deep feeling in the army, so much so that many were in favor of my refusing to obey the order, and of marching upon Washington to take possession of the Government." This implied that McClellan and some of his headquarters staff were toying with the idea of a military coup d'etat, but thought better of it and then made it appear that there was a spontaneous grassroots movement in the army that he himself found it necessary to quell for the sake of the country. The truth is that there was just too much intelligence and hard common sense in the ranks of the volunteer regiments that made up by far the greater part of the Army of the Potomac, for such a mutinous sentiment to get very far even if it had been carefully nurtured as a planned project; and there is no real evidence that such was the case.

The McClellan supporters insisted that the President waited until after the fall elections (which went against the Lincoln cohorts) to remove McClellan. This may have been partly true, but even so there was sufficient justification for the ax to fall without further delay. Longstreet's corps, half of Lee's army, had already crossed the Blue Ridge and Lincoln had every right to conclude that McClellan's slow pace in crossing the Potomac and moving south was advertising his punch so effectively that Lee was being given time and space to maneuver in a way that could easily nullify all the advantage of Federal surprise and initiative.

McClellan's removal is easy to understand. Month after month of favorable summer and early fall weather had slipped by without visible evidence that McClellan intended to make a move of any sort, least of all an offensive one. Obviously Lincoln couldn't wait indefinitely, but it does seem strange that he delayed issuing his removal order until a few weeks after McClellan had been told in no uncertain terms to commence his offensive without further delay. Possibly the President cherished the despairing hope that this time it would be different; he would give it another try and if nothing else should be accomplished, the Army of the Potomac would at least be in motion in the direction of the

MAJOR GENERAL AMBROSE E. BURNSIDE

enemy and the new commander spared the task of overcoming the inertia of starting the ponderous machine.

An Unpromising Selection

The selection of General Ambrose E. Burnside to succeed George B. McClellan is more difficult to understand, for it was an appointment that by no stretch of the imagination could be termed full of promise. The real truth was that Lee and Jackson, Longstreet and Stuart were just too good for the Federal generals at that stage. The Administration at Washington had been unable to find the right combination to give the Confederates a taste of their own medicine, possibly for the reason that by comparison with the Confederate commanders no Union leader had emerged to stir the popular imagination by winning a notable victory.

But why Burnside? Why not Reynolds or Hooker, or Meade, or Couch, or anyone of the other corps or division commanders who had better fighting records than the man whose name seems almost to have been pulled out of a hat? The only explanation that makes any sense, and that very little, is that Burnside was closely identified with McClellan, was known to be opposed to the latter's relief by any other general, least of all himself, and was chosen in the belief or hope that his elevation to army command would cause a minimum of dislocation and disharmony in the ranks of the army. True, Burnside had a charming personality and made friends easily with his warm smile and engaging address, and as a graduate of the U. S. Military Academy was naturally presumed to have been thoroughly grounded in the military arts and sciences.

This was a faulty assumption. The law governing admission to the Military Academy of the Civil War period precluded entrance examinations on subjects beyond those taught in the rural common schools, which in most cases were reading, writing, and arithmetic. Consequently the average young man who secured an appointment to West Point would be found, at the end of his first three years, to have reached an educational level equivalent to qualifying him for the freshman year at one of the civilian colleges.

The intellectual education acquired at West Point was approximately the same as that of any polytechnic school, while that pertaining to the military arts and sciences, aside from the courses on engineering, was confined to the school of the soldier and close order drilling of smaller units.

No instruction whatsoever was given in strategy or grand tactics, in military history, or in "the Art of War," and consequently little if any incentive was afforded for individual collateral reading of the kind that would be likely to develop the qualities essential to generalship. The four-year course of study specifically covered two years work in mathematics, one in physics and chemistry, one in the construction of fortifications, to which was added a little English, philosophy, elementary law, one year of basic Spanish, and two of French.

Furthermore, the opportunity for professional improvement in the Regular Army after graduation was completely absent, because of the small size of the Army and the fact that duty with troops was restricted to the frontier posts of the West, where the normal complement of units was several companies of infantry at the most.

It is not surprising that, with a few exceptions, those graduates of the Military Academy who attained subsequent distinction as corps and army commanders had left the service shortly after graduation to find greater outlets for their energies and abilities, nor should their lack of preparation for the responsibilities of high command be solely charged to their own unwillingness to educate themselves by study and the reading of military history. They were in large part the victims of a system which failed to stimulate any real interest in the art and science of warfare, which in the last analysis had to be learned the hard way after the shooting started.

Furthermore, there was an absence in Washington of militarily well-educated officers of broad experience, capable of and assigned to the job of screening the records of the more promising officer personnel of the Army, appraising their several potentials for higher command, and giving the Administration a wider choice from which to select the all-important army commanders. Unfortunately it appears that it was by a system of trial and error that the commanding generals of the Union Army were selected and catapulted into their posts of responsibility. On occasion they didn't like it, and at least in the case of Burnside and Meade they protested to no avail.

Burnside's Background

Burnside was born in Liberty, Indiana on May 23, 1824 and graduated from West Point in 1847, one year after McClellan, whom he admired and whose friendship he cultivated. The Mexican War was in progress and his first assignment was Vera Cruz, but the war had ended before he arrived. He spent several uneventful years of soldiering, except for a brush with Apache Indians in New Mexico, in the course of which he was wounded. Having reached the conclusion that the cavalry carbine was unsuitable for warfare on the Plains, he invented a new breech-loading rifle. He became so enamored of his creation that he resigned from the Army in October 1853, organized the Bristol Firearms Company, built a plant in Rhode Island to manufacture the rifle in quantity, and went broke in the process. It seems that he had not completed his contract to supply rifles to the United States, so after an uphill fight of several years he gave up the struggle and turned everything over to his creditors, including his sword and uniform.

McClellan had also left the Army and was serving as Engineer-Vice President of the Illinois Central Railroad. Through his friendship with his former schoolmate, Burnside landed a job with the railroad, later became treasurer of the company, and was able to discharge all his old debts. Thus two kindred spirits were brought into an intimate business relationship, for McClellan had already achieved the distinction of having invented the saddle which bore his name from then on until

BURNSIDE AFTER BULL RUN
A group from Burnside's brigade in August, 1862.

changing times and mechanized warfare relegated the American horse cavalry to a final state of oblivion in the year 1941.

Possibly because Burnside's brief manufacturing experience had been in the State of Rhode Island, he re-entered the Service in 1861 as colonel of a Rhode Island regiment of infantry. On October 13, 1864 he was relieved from his command and in April 1865 resigned his commission in the military service to engage in railroad and steamship enterprises. Soon thereafter the people of Rhode Island elected him to the governorship for four consecutive terms and then sent him to the United States Senate, where he served from 1875 until his death in 1881 at the age of 57 years. Despite this evidence of politics in his blood, there is nothing in his military record to show that he cherished any political ambitions while in uniform, nor was he in any sense an intriguer. On the contrary, he was regarded by his military associates as a loyal and honest officer and gentleman. But few of them had any illusions on the score of his capacity for high command.

Burnside As a Troop Leader

In the early stages of the war Burnside commanded a brigade in the disastrous First Battle of Bull Run, with neither credit nor discredit to himself or his troops. Following this he was given the rank of brigadier general of Volunteers and directed to organize a coast division of the Army of the Potomac for an expedition to invade North Carolina. With his independent command of some 15,000 men he conducted a campaign along the coast, seized Roanoke Island, and performed other successful feats which seemed to impress the Administration with the fact that here was a general with promise of considerable ability.

Burnside's bold and aggressive campaign in North Carolina having resulted in the capture of 79 guns and 3,600 prisoners, he was rewarded by a promotion to major general in March of 1862. Further exploits in the South were prevented by the recall of his command to reinforce McClellan's army on the Virginia peninsula. After Pope's defeat at Second Manassas Burnside was given command of the Ninth Corps and subsequently of the right wing of the Army of the Potomac as it marched into Maryland in pursuit of Lee.

As a corps commander with the rank of major general at Antietam, Burnside was considered by his friend and superior McClellan to have been inexcusably slow in getting his troops into action on the second day. The Army of the Potomac was divided tactically into three wings for that battle and Burnside given command of the left wing. McClellan had, however, pulled Hooker's corps away from Burnside for action on the right, leaving the latter with but a single corps, which was adequate for the accomplishment of his mission had he moved promptly when directed. Burnside's orders were to attack across Antietam Creek against the right of Lee's line, which as it happened was lightly held, but the Confederates made the most of their artillery, enfilading the stone bridge in front of Burnside's troops, and the unimaginative general was unable to figure a way to cross except over the narrow bridge, despite the fact that several fords were available in his sector. Repeated oral orders kept coming down from Army headquarters to get going, from about nine o'clock in the morning till well past noon, with but little effect on Burnside, whose mental reflexes, never overly rapid, appeared to become even more sluggish in the heat of combat.

Finally a peremptory order from McClellan caused sufficient reaction to force him to move; with the result that two regiments from New York and Pennsylvania, respectively, dashed across the bridge, pierced the Confederate line, reached the

MAJOR GENERAL AMBROSE P. HILL, C.S.A.

heights overlooking Sharpsburg, and forced Lee to throw in his last reserves to bring the Federals to a halt.

That was McClellan's clue to throw in his unused reserves, 20,000 of them, to exploit the partial success on Burnside's front, which, typically, he failed to do. Whereupon A. P. Hill's Confederate division, arriving about the middle of the afternoon from Harpers Ferry, was thrown into the battle, drove the Federals back to the creek and saved Lee from utter defeat.

It is a fascinating and little known sidelight on that dramatic finale to the Battle of Antietam that A. P. Hill, McClellan's roommate at West Point, and unsuccessful suitor for the hand of the girl McClellan married, was the Confederate man of the hour at Sharpsburg; while Burnside, one class behind Hill and McClellan and a close friend of the latter, proved by his dilatoriness during an entire morning to be the unwitting cause of a delay that forfeited a golden opportunity for McClellan to defeat Lee decisively and lead perhaps to the early break-up of the Confederacy.

The Fredericksburg campaign, which was the first, last, and only battle which Burnside fought as an army commander, was destined to prove that Lincoln had once more bet on the wrong horse. The general's subsequent activities included command of the Department of Ohio, an inconsequential assignment where he managed anyhow to fumble in his treatment of a political hot potato known as the Vallandingham affair. His later command of a Union force in Tennessee did little to erase the impression of his bumbling unfitness for high command.

Later in the war the record seems to show that he was slow and unreliable as commander of the Ninth Corps during Grant's Wilderness campaign of 1864; and during the siege of Petersburg near the close of the war, Burnside was in command of the troops which staged the famous affair of the mine under the Confederate lines. Preparations for this project had been carefully completed, the colored troops designated to exploit the anticipated breakthrough had been especially assigned to the task and trained. But just before the zero hour, by order of a skeptical General Meade, the army commander, and without strong objection from Burnside, the assigned troops were replaced by regiments which had been given no instructions whatever on their special mission. Even worse, they were under the command of a colonel who at the time was drinking himself unconscious some distance behind the line of departure. The denouement was another tragic lost opportunity, with severe Federal casualties and the complete failure of what should have been an impressive breakthrough of the Confederate main line of resistance with incalculable results to the Federal cause.

In the retrospective light of military history, it is quite possible that the Army of the Potomac would have written its
glorious final record at a much earlier date had the two men
who invented, respectively, the practical and long-useful saddle
and the early breech-loading rifle (to say nothing of having
been the first to model those weird-looking whiskers that ever
since have borne the label "burnsides"), pooled their inventive
genius and stuck to that line of work. In so doing McClellan
and Burnside would have confined their energies to the essential
task of helping to provide the Union with useful tools of war
rather than exposing themselves to the inglorious failures which
ended their careers as army commanders.

BURNSIDE'S OBJECTIVE—RICHMOND!

CHAPTER 4

THE STRATEGY OF THE
FREDERICKSBURG CAMPAIGN

NOT UNLIKE the Latin phrase which introduces students to Caesar's Gallic wars, the Fredericksburg campaign in November-December 1862 may be divided into three parts: Burnside's strategy and Lee's counter moves; the case of the missing pontoons; and the Battle of Fredericksburg.

McClellan's temporary headquarters were at Rectortown, fifteen miles north of Warrenton, when on November 7 he and Burnside (at Orlean) received separate copies of the order for the former's relief. It was snowing heavily, as though nature were symbolically confirming Lincoln's fear that McClellan would delay his march until winter weather and bad roads should make it impracticable. Burnside's first action was to confer with McClellan. By mutual agreement the transfer of command was deferred for several days until the army could reach the Warrenton area. This gave Burnside a breather during which to collect his thoughts, consider the implications of McClellan's plan of campaign along the line of the Orange and

Alexandria Railroad, and decide whether to adopt it or develop a new plan of his own.

Burnside Adopts a New Plan

After studying the situation for several days, Burnside informed Halleck that McClellan's plan of operations was unacceptable. He stated that as soon as the concentration in the Warrenton area was completed he proposed to make a feint toward Culpeper or Gordonsville to deceive the enemy, then within a few days, after stocking up with reserves of food and ammunition, move the entire army rapidly to Fredericksburg en route to Richmond. He reasoned that by establishing a new base at Aquia Landing and taking the Fredericksburg route he could more effectively cover Washington and assure better protection for his lines of supply and communication, by land and water. Historic Aquia Creek, which empties into the Potomac River at Aquia Landing, was for ten years after the Indian War of 1676 the northern frontier of Virginia. This stream was an important supply route for the Army of the Potomac in 1862-63, during the campaigns of which it served as the army base, a logistical fact which must have influenced Burnside's plan to a certain extent.

The on-to-Richmond fallacy clearly obsessed Burnside as it had his predecessors. In his post-battle report which followed the Fredericksburg campaign he maintained that he had chosen to go by way of Fredericksburg on the premise that it was the shortest road to Richmond, "the taking of which, I think, should be the great object of the campaign, as the fall of that place would tend more to cripple the Rebel cause than almost any other military event, except the absolute breaking up of their army."

The destruction of the hostile army, it will be noted, would in Burnside's words admittedly deal the heaviest blow to the rebels, but he chose the lesser objective, Richmond, with a bit of specious reasoning that falls somewhat short of giving him an A for audacity.

Burnside argued that it would be a simple matter to move

STATE ARSENAL AT RICHMOND
Many Confederate weapons were made in this building, which is shown as it
appeared after the fire in 1865.

rapidly to Falmouth, cross the Rappahannock to Fredericksburg
on pontoon bridges, and advance on Richmond before Lee
could effect a junction of his two widely separated wings. He
failed to indicate what he hoped to accomplish by seizing Richmond while Lee's army was still intact and at large to the west,
nor did he explain why he was going at the task of crossing the
Rappahannock the hard way rather than by the innumerable
fords above Fredericksburg.

If it was simply a foot race that he envisaged, that was one
thing. But it would have been more sensible, if he was looking
for a fight, to move directly towards his opponent than to
circle around him with the objective of seizing upon the inert
mass of bricks and mortar, and the practically unarmed civilians,
which comprised Richmond. The only valid prize there, in fact,
was the principal cannon factory available to the Confederacy,
which was located in Richmond. The new route offered the
possibility that his opponent might show up unexpectedly and
belligerently before his own schedule called for the enemy's
appearance. If Burnside believed that by beating Lee to Richmond he would succeed in cutting him off from his base of
supplies, he misjudged his shrewd opponent, who had already

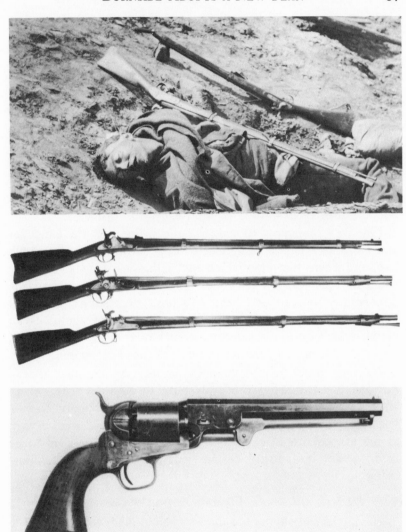

CIVIL WAR WEAPONS

Several types of small arms used by the Confederates were manufactured at the Richmond arsenal. Some were copies of foreign or United States rifles, others were assembled from captured stocks. In the top view the rifle with the broken muzzle is probably a Cooke & Bro. copy of an Enfield. Laid across the dead Confederate is a U.S. Rifle-Musket, Model 1861. The long rifles in the center view are: top, Richmond rifle; middle, Virginia musket; bottom, Palmetto musket. The lower picture shows a Colt Navy .36 caliber, Model 1851; this was the handgun most commonly used by both sides during the Civil War.

taken care of such a contingency by establishing an alternate base at Staunton in the Shenandoah Valley.

It is not likely that McClellan had shown Burnside Lincoln's letter of October 13, in which the President had suggested the line of operations that he would follow were he the army commander. That Lincoln's strategic sense had developed markedly was evident in the forementioned letter (see page 23), which displayed a surprisingly sound grasp of the logistical facts of life and which spelled out in a simple but convincing manner the several strategic moves that were open to the opposing armies and the advantages inherent in the course which he favored but refrained from putting in the form of an order.

Lincoln's theory of moving on the inside arc via Culpeper and Gordonsville was designed to bring on an early clash with Lee, and it was that plan which McClellan was slowly following when he was taken out of the game. Had Burnside had the opportunity to read and heed Lincoln's suggestions, he might have had second thoughts and felt less sure of the soundness of his own decision to discard McClellan's plan in favor of moving on Fredericksburg by the north bank of the Rappahannock.

He may have been influenced unduly by the fact that a railroad line ran from Fredericksburg to Aquia Creek, where river steamers had carried passengers on to Washington in prewar days. This line had been repeatedly destroyed and rebuilt, as the armies surged back and forth, but now it seemed to be firmly under the control of the Federals, at least for the time being.

Halleck Disagrees; Lincoln Approves Conditionally

Having already approved the McClellan plan, which Burnside now wanted to change, Halleck reacted unfavorably. On November 12 he visited Burnside at Warrenton, accompanied by two staff officers, Generals Meigs and Haupt, Quartermaster General and Chief of Military Railroads, respectively, and urged him to follow the original plan. But Burnside was unyielding, and finally, still demurring, Halleck announced that the President would have to make the decision. He then returned to

GENERAL ROBERT E. LEE

Washington, while Burnside for two days waited impatiently for the green light. The word came on November 14, in the form of a terse message from Halleck which simply said: "The President has just assented to your plan. He thinks it will succeed if you move rapidly; otherwise not."

It is always easier to judge the quality of strategic decisions after the event. But if, as appears from the evidence, Burnside's primary reason for an end run rather than a line buck was merely greater security for his supply lines back to Washington, historians may be justified in concluding that the specter of Lee's superior generalship must have weighted the scales, in Burnside's estimate of the situation, to such an extent that he chose caution rather than boldness in this his first great test as army commander. Burnside's vast superiority in combat strength should in all conscience have given him sufficient moral courage to hazard the remote possibility that Jackson would move in on his rear, which was already adequately protected by an entire corps, Slocum's Twelfth, at Harpers Ferry, in addition to strong contingents along the Potomac between Harpers Ferry and Washington, and a powerful reserve of armed manpower in the Capital itself. Certainly this danger would be a small one if the Army of the Potomac should move rapidly and aggressively to keep Lee's two wings from consolidating. By his decision to march away from his weaker opponent, rather than towards him, Burnside compounded even McClellan's perennial timidity in a proposal that was hardly calculated to elicit cheers from Washington.

Lee's Strategy

Several days after McClellan had been superseded, Lee outlined his strategy in a letter to Confederate Secretary of War Randolph at Richmond:

> As long as General Jackson can operate with safety and secure his retirement west of the Massanutten Mountains, I think it advantageous that he should be in position to threaten the enemy's flank and rear and thus prevent his advance southward on the east side of the Blue Ridge. General Jackson has been directed accordingly, and should the enemy descend into the Valley, General Longstreet will attack his rear and cut off his communications. The enemy is apparently so strong in numbers that I think it preferable to attempt to baffle his designs by maneuvering rather than to resist his advance by main force.

Debating in his own mind where best to fight Burnside, Lee seemed to prefer a position on the North Anna River, which ran east and west about thirty miles south of the Rappahannock. In a dispatch to Richmond written shortly after the Battle of Fredericksburg, he stated that his plan had contemplated a retirement to the North Anna position if the enemy should cross in force at Port Royal, which is situated about seventeen miles downriver from Fredericksburg. In this dispatch he added:

> My design was to have done so in the first instance. My purpose was changed, not from any advantage in this position, but from an unwillingness to open more of our country to depredation than possible, and also with a view of collecting such forage and provisions as could be obtained in the Rappahannock Valley. *** It will, therefore, be more advantageous to us to draw him further away from his base of operations.

Lee's strategy was clearly not to fight on the Rappahannock, but along the line of the North Anna River, where in his opinion the defensive could be turned into a counteroffensive more rapidly and effectively than at Fredericksburg, with the added advantage of causing the Federal line of communications and supply to be appreciably lengthened. Jefferson Davis, however, favored a position at Fredericksburg, and it was doubtless the Confederate President's attitude that tipped the scales in Lee's decision to make a stand there.

Lee had known by November 7 that advance elements of the Union army had reached Warrenton and that its cavalry was maneuvering along the Rappahannock. As the Federal build-up in the Warrenton area continued, Lee was undecided as to McClellan's next move, but thought he might still turn west to the Shenandoah Valley.

Longstreet has noted in his own account of the Battle of Fredericksburg that Lee knew of the Federal change in army command within twenty-four hours of the time the word reached McClellan and Burnside, presumably through spies or by courtesy of General Stuart's capable cavalry scouts. Longstreet has recorded that when the news reached Lee the latter re-

LIEUTENANT GENERAL JAMES LONGSTREET

marked that he "regretted to part with McClellan, for we always understood each other so well; I fear they may continue to make these changes until they find someone whom I don't understand."

Longstreet's Appraisal

Writing of the campaign twenty years afterward, Longstreet expressed the opinion that Burnside's initial mistake was not to have gone direct to Chester Gap, in the Blue Ridge Mountains, which was twenty miles west of Warrenton and midway between McClellan's position and the Winchester area which Jackson occupied in the Valley. Said Longstreet:

> He (Burnside) might then have held Jackson and fought me or have held me and fought Jackson, thus taking us in detail. The doubt about the matter was whether or not he could have caught me in that trap before we could concentrate. At any rate that was the only move on the board that could have benefitted him at the time he was

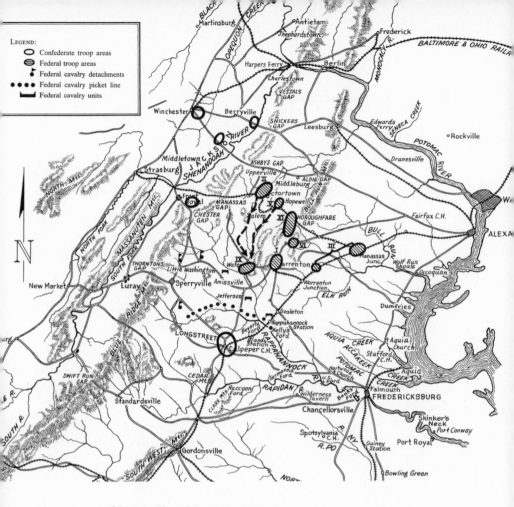

MAP 6. THE SITUATION NOVEMBER 7-9, 1862

This sketch shows the location of the opposing forces at the time Burnside superseded McClellan. The dispersion of the Confederate corps offered the Federal commander a fine opportunity to defeat them separately if he moved rapidly and struck hard. But Lee was reasonably certain that no such bold move would be made. He appears to have an inkling at this time that the Federals will continue south toward Richmond, so he has sent Longstreet to Culpeper to watch developments along the Rappahannock. Jackson prefers to remain in the Shenandoah Valley, and Lee acquiesces, feeling confident that Jackson can move rapidly to reinforce Longstreet should the occasion demand. Meanwhile Jackson's position appears to threaten Washington and the upper supply lines of the Army of the Potomac. Note the disposition of the Federal cavalry, which performed its screening mission admirably, and during the advance south from the Potomac was victorious in a number of small engagements. The Federal corps are not moving as close to the mountain gaps as Lincoln indicated was desirable. The II and V Corps continued south from the positions shown on November 7. By the 9th they had closed into areas near Waterloo.

assigned to the command of the Army of the Potomac. By interposing between the corps of Lee's Army he would have secured strong ground and advantage of position. With skill equal to the occasion, he should have had success. This was the move about which we felt serious apprehension, and we were occupying our minds with plans to meet it when the move toward Fredericksburg was reported.

When no further advance by the Federals occurred for some days, particularly in the direction of Longstreet's corps at Culpeper, the possibility of a move to Fredericksburg was more seriously considered by the Confederate strategists, whereupon Lee cautioned Jackson in the Valley to be prepared to move on short notice to effect a junction with Longstreet when the enemy plans should become clearly defined.

Composition and Disposition of the Opposing Forces

On November 9, several days after Burnside received the order from Washington relieving McClellan, the opposing forces were situated as follows:

The Union army, with a total strength of some 140,000 effectives and 320 guns, was largely disposed along the western base of Bull Run Mountains, with three corps and the Reserve Artillery near Warrenton; two corps in the New Baltimore area; one corps, the Ninth, with Stoneman's and Whipple's divisions attached, near Waterloo; Pleasonton's and Bayard's cavalry covering the army front on the line: Amissville— Jefferson—Rappahannock Station (the junction point of the Rappahannock River and the Orange and Alexandria Railroad). The Twelfth Corps remained at Harpers Ferry.

The Confederate army, numbering approximately 90,000 present for duty with 275 guns, was as previously noted widely separated. Longstreet's First Corps was at Culpeper, to which place it had moved from the Valley when McClellan crossed the Potomac in late October. Jackson's corps of almost equal strength was in the Shenandoah Valley between Berryville and Charlestown; and Stuart's cavalry was operating partly on the Rappahannock and partly in the Valley with Jackson.

Lee in addition had a small detachment, composed of a regiment of infantry and a battery of artillery, occupying Fredericksburg, while elements of Stuart's cavalry patrolled the river above the town. The Fredericksburg garrison was promptly directed to destroy the railroad between Falmouth and Aquia Creek, as insurance against the possibility that the Federals might take it into their heads to shift eastward, in which event they would need that short stretch of rails to extend their new water-borne line of supply from Washington.

Burnside Creates Three Grand Divisions

One of Burnside's first acts upon taking command was to reduce the number of generals reporting directly to the army commander by reorganizing the seven infantry-artillery corps into three grand divisions, in effect making the commanding general of the army an army group commander in today's type of army organization, with three subordinate army (grand division) commanders, each of whom was given direct control of a wing composed of two infantry corps, each corps consisting of three infantry divisions and organic artillery, with at least one cavalry brigade attached.

In naming Sumner, Hooker, and Franklin as his three chief lieutenants for the campaign upon which the Army of the Potomac was about to embark under its new general, Burnside had seemingly accepted the judgment of his predecessor McClellan. Sumner and Franklin had each commanded wings, as he himself had, during the recent Antietam campaign. Hooker, commander of the First Corps at Sharpsburg, was moved up a peg doubtless because he had by that time earned quite a reputation as an aggressive division and corps commander in the Peninsular Campaign, the battles before Richmond, Second Manassas, South Mountain, and finally Antietam, where he was severely wounded and subsequently on convalescent leave from September 18 to November 10, when he rejoined the command.

Major General Edwin Vose Sumner was the only one of the three who had not attended the United States Military Academy.

A native of Boston, he entered the Army in 1819, in the infantry, later served in the cavalry during the Indian Wars in Kansas, and was a veteran of the Mexican War. By Civil War standards he was an old man at the start of the war and despite his brave spirit clearly should never have been retained in an active combat role in competition with division and corps com-

MAJOR GENERAL EDWIN V. SUMNER

manders who were his juniors by many years, even by decades. Sumner was a loyal and devoted officer, however, a gentleman of the old school, who lacked neither character nor courage, and his superiors probably did not have the heart to shelve the old soldier.

Major General William B. Franklin graduated from West Point in 1843, was assigned to the Engineer Corps, saw action as a brigade commander in First Manassas, as division commander and later commander of the Sixth Corps in the Peninsula, at South Mountain and Antietam. In the latter fight his corps, which had been stymied watching McLaw's Confederate

MAJOR GENERAL WILLIAM B. FRANKLIN
From a photo made in 1861. Seated, left to right: Col. J. J. Bartlett, Brig.
Gen. H. W. Slocum, Gen. Franklin, Brig. Gen. W. F. Barry, and Brig. Gen
John Newton.

Division opposite Harpers Ferry, was not recalled to Antietam
until the major battle on the Federal right was over. McClellan,
having directed Burnside to take up the fight on the left,
had held Franklin's and Porter's corps in reserve for a projected
later drive through Lee's center. This final punch never mate-
rialized, however, because Burnside's protracted delaying in
getting underway permitted A. P. Hill to come up from Harpers
Ferry to save the Confederates from what should have been a
stinging defeat.

There is nothing in the record to suggest that either Franklin
or Sumner was more than an average field commander. Neither
of them had achieved distinction in the early part of the war
and it will be seen later that Franklin in particular failed to
make the most of his big opportunity at the Battle of Fredericksburg. Following that engagement he was put in cold storage
for a period of six months and then transferred to the less important Department of the Gulf where he served until the end
of the war.

The reshuffle resulted in the formation of grand divisions as follows:

RIGHT GRAND DIVISION

Major General Edwin V. Sumner, Commanding

Second Army Corps, under Major General Darius N. Couch, composed of three divisions commanded by Brigadier Generals Hancock, Howard, and French.

Ninth Army Corps, under Brigadier General Orlando B. Willcox, composed of three divisions commanded by Brigadier Generals Burns, Sturgis, and Getty.

Attached cavalry division commanded by Brigadier General Alfred Pleasonton.

CENTER GRAND DIVISION

Major General Joseph Hooker, Commanding

Third Corps, under Brigadier General George Stoneman, composed of three divisions commanded by Brigadier Generals Birney, Sickles, and Whipple.

Fifth Corps, under Brigadier General Daniel Butterfield, composed of three divisions commanded by Brigadier Generals Griffin, Sykes, and Humphreys.

Attached cavalry brigade commanded by Brigadier General William A. Averell.

LEFT GRAND DIVISION

Major General William B. Franklin, Commanding

First Corps, under Major General John F. Reynolds, composed of three divisions commanded by Brigadier Generals Doubleday, Gibbon, and Meade.

Sixth Corps, under Major General William F. Smith, composed of three divisions commanded by Brigadier Generals Brooks, Howe, and Newton.

Attached cavalry brigade commanded by Brigadier General George D. Bayard.

The Eleventh Corps, under Brigadier General Franz Sigel, constituted the reserve .corps, located first at Centreville, later at Dumfries.

The Twelfth Corps, commanded by Brigadier General Henry W. Slocum, was on detached duty guarding Harpers Ferry.

Full Speed Ahead

Burnside was full of steam and rarin' to go when Halleck's telegram arrived on November 14, putting Washington's stamp of dubious approval on the Fredericksburg adventure. The army staff leapt into action, fortunately without the aid of mimeograph machines, which would likely have burned out their bearings as the pent-up impatience of the army commander was suddenly released like a coiled spring.

Early on the morning of the following day, November 15, General Edwin V. Sumner, newly appointed commander of the Right Grand Division, took off from Warrenton like a sprinter at the bark of the starter's gun. In a surprisingly rapid march of two and one-half days his wing, which constituted almost one-third of the Army of the Potomac, covered the forty miles to Falmouth and took a position from which they could have gobbled up Fredericksburg in a matter of hours.

The march to Falmouth, averaging more than 15 miles per day, would be considered acceptable by World War I standards,

BIVOUAC ON THE MARCH

ARRIVAL OF SUMNER'S TROOPS NEAR FALMOUTH

though not in World War II when they were trained to march 25 miles per day. For the Army of the Potomac, accustomed to McClellan's five or six miles a day, it was unheard of. But it had the happy result that the North took heart, the President breathed a sigh of relief, and the men and officers themselves no doubt held their heads higher with that warm feeling of achievement that comes from doing more than anyone, including themselves, believed possible.

Lee was for a moment caught flat-footed. For once his excellent intelligence system had failed to keep up with the vital "enemy information," and Sumner's troops reached Falmouth a good 24 hours before Lee was even certain of the direction in which Burnside's army was headed. On this occasion the much maligned Federal cavalry succeeded admirably in screening the march of Burnside's army down the Warrenton pike along the Rappahannock, and it was not until the advance elements of Sumner's grand division had actually reached Falmouth on November 17 that Lee became convinced of Burnside's intentions. By that date the rest of the Union army was on the march, reaching the Fredericksburg area November 19-20.

Longstreet was immediately directed to start one division in the direction of Fredericksburg, his other two divisions and the corps artillery to follow shortly.

Jackson Prefers the Valley

Jackson's reluctance to leave the Shenandoah Valley, on the theory that his threat to Washington and to the flank and rear of the Union army would yield greater fruits than an immediate consolidation with Longstreet, persuaded Lee to allow him that discretion for the time being. One may be permitted in passing to wonder whether Jackson's earlier independent successes in the Valley and his rugged individualism may not have contributed something to his thinking in this instance, when he persuaded Lee to let him remain where he was, to play the game in his own inimitable way.

For a long period of time Jackson had been successful in pinning down enemy troops of as many as three and four times his strength, and in keeping the North off balance and in mental turmoil by his frequent maneuvering. But this time Lincoln was doing his own strategic thinking and was disposed to discount the Jackson threat.

Even after Lee had put Longstreet's corps into motion, he delayed sending for Jackson, influenced somewhat by later,

THE SHENANDOAH VALLEY

and inaccurate, information that it was only Sumner's grand division which had marched to Falmouth. However it soon became apparent that Burnside's whole army was marching eastward, so on November 19 Lee sent word to Jackson to join him at Fredericksburg. Lee himself mounted and commenced his own journey for the same destination on the 20th, the same day that Jackson's corps took off on its last long march through the familiar and beloved Shenandoah Valley, the scene of so many of his early triumphs, and which would never see him again.

Eight days of road marching brought the Confederate Second Corps on November 27 to Orange Court House by way of Strasburg and New Market, a distance of 120 miles, which still left 36 miles to travel before they would reach Fredericksburg. The Army of the Potomac had for some time been fully concentrated across the river from Fredericksburg, impatiently and strangely marking time for a solid week. This in turn led Lee to take his time in the hope that delay in effecting a junction of his two corps might lead Burnside to launch an attack that would afford the canny Southerner an opportunity to repeat the tactics which he had successfully demonstrated against Pope.

Finally, however, after allowing Jackson's weary men a much appreciated three days' rest, Lee became disturbed lest the next storm should make the roads a difficult obstacle for Jackson's corps. Accordingly Jackson on November 29 was ordered to continue the march, cover the remaining 36 miles, and take position on Longstreet's right below Fredericksburg.

HAULING THE PONTOONS FROM AQUIA

CHAPTER 5

THE CASE OF THE MISSING PONTOONS

MANY OF THE ingredients for a mystery thriller of the "whodunit" variety were present in the succession of events leading up to the Fredericksburg campaign. Although there was an absence of personalized murders to form the basis upon which to thread the story, there had been plenty of battle casualties attributable to incompetent Northern generalship; political intrigue among the military was not wanting; and the dubious appointment of Ambrose E. Burnside to lead the Army

83

of the Potomac provided the necessary element of suspense and speculation so essential to the writer of detective fiction.

The Rappahannock River served as an effective backdrop for the drama which was to be enacted along its banks in late 1862. Rising in the eastern foothills of the Blue Ridge Mountains a few miles southeast of Manassas Gap, the river wound its leisurely serpentine way across the fertile Virginia countryside on a course generally paralleling the Potomac, fifty miles to the north. Less pretentious, perhaps, but no less interesting than the Potomac and the Mississippi, which for reasons of geography and navigability were of greater national importance, the Rappahannock at least rates a high mark for sheer persistence in attracting the armies of both the North and the South.

Burnside Insists on a Pontoon Crossing

It is not clear whether Burnside had entirely ruled out in advance the crossing by the fords of Sumner's division to occupy Fredericksburg and establish a bridgehead for the subsequent passage by pontoons of the rest of the army with their trains. But there was finally no doubt in his own mind that his plan of campaign contemplated a rapid march to Falmouth and an equally prompt crossing of the Rappahannock *on pontoon bridges,* to be followed by the march on Richmond. There is likewise some evidence to indicate that he considered sending a portion of his cavalry south of the river to approach Fredericksburg from the west for the purpose of seizing the heights of the town to facilitate the crossing of the main army. The details of the program following the occupation of Fredericksburg were to be spelled out later. But Burnside was clear as to the first two steps, and was under the distinct impression that he had outlined his pontoon requirements explicitly in his conference with Halleck at Warrenton on November 12, and that Halleck understood the importance of having the bridging equipment shipped immediately to Falmouth so that it would arrive concurrently with the Army of the Potomac and be available for expeditious employment.

Sumner's grand division reached Falmouth November 17. Two days later, on November 19, Burnside himself arrived with the main body of the Union army and looked around for his pontoons, which had not arrived. As soon as Sumner had brought up his troops and examined the fords above Fredericksburg, where his men had observed stray cattle crossing the river without difficulty, he urged Burnside to let him cross at once, assuring him that he could take the town with little effort, which was obviously true at that time when the Confederates were only strong enough to offer token resistance. Burnside however had his mind fixed on crossing by pontoons, was fearful of risking the danger of threatening rains which could cause a rapid rise in the river and perhaps split his army in two, and seemed confident that the quick arrival of the pontoons would enable him to carry out his plan without a hitch.

Had Burnside displayed the mental flexibility which history associates with great military commanders, there is little doubt that he would have exploited the opportunity afforded him by the time, space, and weather factors and safely crossed the entire

FREDERICKSBURG, NOVEMBER 18, 1862
When Brady took this photo the buildings across the river were occupied by Confederate riflemen, who fired at the photographer as he hurriedly set up his tripod and exposed a wet plate.

army, less trains, before the subsequent rains made the fords temporarily impassable for foot troops. In this case the delay in the arrival of the pontoons would merely have caused some supply inconveniences for a matter of days and the engineers could have placed the bridges without the interference from the Confederates which made their task so difficult and costly later on.

Poor Burnside! The new general had gotten off to a flying start, and his army had established a speed record for the Federals in a march of which Stonewall Jackson need not have been ashamed. Lee had been given a bit of a surprise, and everything looked promising for the Union forces, with Longstreet nowhere in sight and Jackson still in the Valley.

The Lost Opportunity

Longstreet has recorded the fact that "when word was received, about the 18th or 19th of November, that Sumner with more than 30,000 men was moving towards Fredericksburg," two of his (Longstreet's) divisions, ordered down to meet him, "made a forced march and arrived on the hills around Fredericksburg about three o'clock on the afternoon of the 21st." Indisputable evidence, indeed, from the commander of the leading Confederate contingent to reach Fredericksburg, that Burnside had been given three whole days during which Sumner's divisions could with but little interference have occupied the Fredericksburg heights and established such a strong, fortified bridgehead that the story of the Battle of Fredericksburg might never have been written. But Burnside passed up that opportunity and thus lost the first round in the battle of wits between Lee and himself.

Where were the pontoons? What to do? Burnside was a good soldier, not overly burdened with brains, but a reasonably determined character when things went along as planned. His mind had been made up to cross the river on pontoons and in no other way, so—no pontoons, no crossing. Sumner's idea of going across by the fords was all right for men and horses, but that would have separated the troops from their wagon trains, which to Burnside was unthinkable. Besides, it soon started to rain, which doubtless comforted Burnside with the thought that he had been right in refusing Sumner's earlier request for permission to ford the river.

In the last analysis, however, and even after charging Halleck with the responsibility for the early delay due to lack of administrative energy, and the resultant further delay because of rain and mud and the shift from road to water-borne travel for the pontoons, the cold fact stands out that sufficient bridge equipment did actually reach Burnside on the morning of November 24. Yet it was not until December 11, two and one-half weeks later, that the move to lay the bridges was initiated. And for that no one can be blamed but Burnside himself.

It is always interesting to speculate on what might have happened had a particular general made a different decision just before or during a major campaign or battle. The imponderables are many and varied, while the history of warfare abounds with examples in which the leader who was able to think imaginatively, act audaciously, take calculated risks, and improvise ingeniously, almost invariably took his opponent by surprise and carried off the honors. Come to think of it, the preceding characterization might have been written to describe Robert E. Lee. It certainly did not fit Ambrose Burnside. Had the positions of the two generals been reversed on November 17, when Sumner made his plea, we can be sure that Lee would not have sat on his hands and let time run out as did the bemused Burnside.

The late General George S. Patton might even have gone Lee one better had he been in Burnside's shoes. Those who knew Patton well will be of one mind in agreeing that neither the threat of high water nor the lack of pontoons would have given that bold soldier a moment's pause. He would have passed Sumner's grand division across at once, and sent couriers galloping back to Hooker and Franklin, commanding, respectively, the Center and the Left Grand Divisions, with instructions to make an abrupt change of direction, cross the Rappahannock at the

TRANSPORT DIFFICULTIES BETWEEN AQUIA AND FALMOUTH

upper fords, and assemble somewhere in the Chancellorsville area west of Fredericksburg. If the trains were then unable to follow because of the rising river, Patton would have found other means of getting them across, such as rebuilding by hook or crook one of the destroyed bridges at Fredericksburg, or by ferrying necessary food and ammunition, or by living partially off the country, or even by the expedient of attacking and defeating his opponent with such dispatch that there would be plenty of time afterwards to worry about a possible shortage of supplies.

Grant played it that way before Vicksburg when he cut loose from his base and took the chance of running out of supplies. And Patton solved one of his critical supply problems in a historic way in World War II when he skyrocketed across France and had to improvise his "Red Ball Express" to keep supplies and gasoline flowing to his fast-moving armor; and again when he made the unorthodox decision to use the Air Corps to protect his right flank as he drove toward the Rhine in the closing days of the war.

Was Halleck the Villain?

Major General Henry W. Halleck was unquestionably one of the most baffling of the leading characters who played important roles in the Civil War. It must be presumed that Halleck had been an influential factor in the selection of Burnside to command the Army of the Potomac and would consequently be expected to do everything in his power to help Burnside succeed in his first campaign as army commander. It may be unthinkable even to suggest that Halleck could be so Machiavellian as to connive in a way to throw obstacles in the path of Northern success on the battlefield, but the cold facts in the case of the missing pontoons force the conclusion that Halleck was chiefly responsible for the failure to rush the bridge equipment that would have enabled Burnside to cross the Rappahannock on schedule.

Had the pontoons reached Falmouth when Burnside had every right to expect them, the Army of the Potomac would have faced Lee south and west of Fredericksburg with both flanks resting securely on the Rappahannock River above and below the town, and with little fear for supply and communications lines, despite the fact of having a river at its back. Burnside outnumbered Lee by almost 40,000 men, not counting Sigel's reserve corps, Slocum's Twelfth Corps at Harpers Ferry, or additional reinforcements from Washington upon which the Union general could call if the situation should warrant. Longstreet with about 41,000 men, approaching Fredericksburg from Culpeper, would have encountered 120,000 Federals at a time when Jackson was still 150 miles away, and even Lee would hardly have attacked under such circumstances.

But it didn't happen that way, because the pontoons had not arrived, Burnside was still cooling his heels at Falmouth, and Longstreet's corps was able to move calmly and without opposition into a strong defensive position on the heights of Fredericksburg, to the obvious relief of the townspeople who had understandably become rather nervous as they waited helplessly for something to happen.

Halleck was more of an academician and administrator than a tactical field commander. He was the scholarly type, had studied law, and while still a captain of engineers, before he resigned from the Army, had authored a successful text on International

MAJOR GENERAL HENRY W. HALLECK

Law as well as an officers' manual which he called *Elements of Military Art and Science,* which was based on a series of lectures that he had delivered before the Lowell Institute of Boston during the winter of 1845-46. The variety of subjects covered in his military text included historic examples from the Napoleonic wars which he used to illustrate the principles of war and the application of military experience to such matters as fortifications, organization, proper use of infantry, cavalry, artillery, and

engineers, and—of special interest to students of the Fredericksburg campaign—an exhaustive treatise on military bridges.

Halleck's lectures aroused such widespread interest that they
were published in 1846 by D. Appleton and Company in a book
which gained so solid a reputation that it was republished at the
outbreak of war in 1861 and was generally accepted and used
as doctrine by the Army officers of that day.

During the Civil War Halleck's only field command was in
the West as a department commander and as director of the
rather sluggish troop movement which finally wound up with
the capture of Corinth, Mississippi. His transfer to Washington
as General-in-Chief brought him to the kind of duty that had no
particular appeal to him, because he was not interested in politics
and preferred the quiet peace of his law office in California.

Halleck on Bridges and River Crossings

Halleck's treatment, in his book, of the subject of military
bridges and river crossings, seems so pertinent to an understanding of the bitter ex-post-facto controversy over the Fredericksburg pontoon episode that extracts from the book are embodied
herein, either as direct quotes or in paraphrased form for the
sake of brevity:

> The passage of a river in the presence of an enemy,
> whether acting offensively or in retreat, is an operation of
> great delicacy and danger. In either case the army is called
> upon to show the coolest and most determined courage, for
> its success will depend on its maintaining the strictest dis-
> cipline and good order.
> The passage of a river by main force, against an enter-
> prising and active enemy on the opposite shore is always
> an operation of the greatest difficulty, and not unfrequently
> accompanied with the most bloody results.
> The most effectual method of accomplishing this object
> is by strategem. Demonstrations are made at several points
> at the same time; bodies of troops are thrown across, after
> nightfall, in row boats or by flying-bridges*, to get posses-

*A floating body, propelled from one bank to the other by the current
of the stream.

sion of the opposite bank. The vanguard of light cavalry may cross by swimming. The pontoniers should have their bridge equipage in readiness near the intended point of passage, so that it can be thrown across with the greatest possible rapidity, while the advanced guards are still able to keep the enemy at a distance. Under favorable circumstances the pontoniers will have the bridge in readiness for the passage of the army before the enemy can collect his troops upon the threatened point.

Cannon balls and hollow shot are the most effectual means for destroying an enemy's bridge when our batteries can be planted within reach. When this cannot be done, we must resort to fire-boats, floating rafts, etc., to accomplish our object. Operations of this kind carried on in the night are most likely to succeed.

In another interesting paragraph on field engineering, Halleck remarks that the number of wagons in a pontoon train will be greatly diminished if it be found that "India rubber boats" may be used as supports for the bridges, and he adds that the Engineer Department of the Army was even then, in 1846, making experiments to determine the matter. Evidently the experiment failed or was abandoned, because one of the important reasons for the delay in arrival of the pontoon trains from Washington was their bulky weight, necessitating a much larger number of wagons, animals, harness, etc. than would have been required for rubber boats.

The many illustrative descriptions of successful and unsuccessful river crossings by the use or lack of pontoon bridges, as drawn from the history of the wars in Europe both before and after the French Revolution, showed clearly that Halleck had made a careful study of the subject and was fully conversant with the difficulties which were sure to confront Burnside at Fredericksburg.

Indeed the above doctrine might serve to explain Halleck's reasons for opposing the Burnside plan when it was first presented. But if that were the case, Halleck served his country badly in failing to take a stronger position at the very start, both with Burnside and with Lincoln, by insisting that the plan to cross by the fords be adhered to. He was Burnside's superior and had the necessary authority as well as responsibility for making important strategic decisions; Lincoln had assigned him to the job in Washington for that very reason; and he cannot be excused for the failure to discharge his responsibility in a more positive manner.

A careful reading of the selected passages from Halleck's book, which had become almost standing operating procedure in the army of that day, reveals a concept in marked contrast to Burnside's operational and tactical procedures at Fredericksburg, and forces one to the conclusion that Burnside either was not indoctrinated in the principles affecting a river crossing or imagined that he knew a better way to do the job.

Sumner Demands that Fredericksburg Surrender

Shortly before Longstreet's troops arrived on the afternoon of November 21, Sumner sent an officer across the Rappahan-

CIVILIANS EVACUATING FALMOUTH

nock by boat under a flag of truce from Stafford Heights, which looked down on Fredericksburg from the opposite side of the river. The letter, addressed to the mayor and common council, demanded the surrender of the town on the grounds that Confederate troops had fired on his men from the streets of the town and that its mills were manufacturing supplies for the armed forces of the Confederacy. The ultimatum stated further that if the demand was not met by five o'clock that same afternoon, sixteen hours' grace would be allowed for the removal of women and children, sick and aged, after which the town would be shelled as a preliminary to occupation by the Union forces.

It may be doubted, in view of Burnside's refusal to allow Sumner to use the fords, that the plan would have been carried out, particularly since the Confederates moved in before the deadline was reached. In any case Longstreet on his arrival was shown the letter from Sumner and advised the mayor to send a reply to the effect that the Confederates did not propose to make Fredericksburg a base of military operations and there would therefore be no justification for the Federals to shell the town. The result of the exchange of greetings was that the shelling did not then occur, possibly because the arrival of Longstreet's corps and the nonarrival of the pontoons had put an entirely new face on the tactical situation. Sumner at that time gave the mayor no positive assurance that the town would not be shelled, however, so on that night Lee advised the townspeople to evacuate their homes. On the 22nd the sad exodus of women, children, and old men started. Even the Federals were touched by the sight, to such an extent that Sumner sent word to Longstreet that the town would not be shelled so long as it remained militarily inactive.

The second favorable opportunity to take Fredericksburg before Lee's arrival thus went the way of the first. Now Burnside really was in hot water, with his schedule shot to pieces, an unfordable river yet to cross, nothing in sight to use for bridges, and a sagacious enemy improving every passing hour by adding strength both to his defensive position and to the troops to man it.

Army correspondents and soldiers alike were perplexed by the failure of the army to cross the Rappahannock as the last days of November passed. On the twenty-first an army reporter for the New York Tribune sent to his newspaper the gist of a dialogue which he had overheard the day before between two pickets on opposite sides of the river:
"Hallo, Secesh!"
"Hallo, Yank!"
"What was the matter with your battery, Tuesday night?"
"You made it too hot. Your shots drove the cannoneers away, and they haven't stopped running yet. We infantry men had to come out and withdraw the guns."
"You infantry men will run, too, one of these fine mornings."
"When are you coming over, blue coat?"
"When we get ready, butternut."
"What do you want?"
"Want Fredericksburg."
"Don't you wish you may get it?" *

If the result had not proved so tragic, the delayed arrival of the vital pontoons would have qualified as a comedy of errors. Had Halleck merely been careless or slow in carrying out his part of the plan, or if someone down the line misunderstood or was dilatory in carrying out his instructions, it would not have been the first or only time in the history of warfare. If on the other hand Halleck was annoyed by Burnside's unwillingness to be guided by his advice, an annoyance intensified by the further fact that Lincoln had overruled Halleck and approved Burnside's plan, and Halleck consciously allowed the transfer of the pontoons to be stalled for more than a week, then indeed his actions deserved the strictest kind of censure.

General Oliver O. Howard, one of Sumner's division com-

*The North Reports the Civil War; J. Cutler Andrews; (c) 1955. Univ. of Pittsburgh Press.

manders, termed the story of the moving of the bridge trains to Falmouth "a strange one."

"It seems to indicate," he wrote, "that Halleck himself was playing a part, possibly hoping to get Burnside well into winter quarters without anybody being particularly to blame. As it required thirteen days to do a piece of work which could easily

BRIGADIER GENERAL OLIVER O. HOWARD

have been done in three days, it would be a marvelous stretch of charity to impute it to mere bungling."

The Pontoon Controversy a Cause Celebré

The case of the missing pontoons subsequently became something of a cause celebre, which was fully aired in the press almost before the smoke of the Fredericksburg battle had cleared. Burnside and Halleck both came in for censure and both were strongly defended, but perhaps the most violent charges leveled at Halleck appeared in two articles published in the *Providence*

Journal on December 18, 1863 and January 6, 1864, respectively.

The writer of the article started off by criticizing Halleck's alleged habit of claiming for himself the credit for every victory achieved by the Union armies and for placing the blame for each defeat on whichever general happened to be commanding the unsuccessful army. With that introductory premise he then quoted from Halleck's report on the Fredericksburg operations, in which the general stated that Burnside's plan was to "cross his army by the fords of the upper Rappahannock, and then move down and seize the heights south of Fredericksburg, while a small force was to be sent north of the river to enable General Haupt to reopen the railroad and to rebuild the bridges."

What were the facts of the case? In chronological order, the pertinent ones were these:

November 6: An order from Halleck to Berlin, near Harpers Ferry, to move the pontoons to Washington, was dispatched, not by telegraph, but by mail, and did not reach the proper engineer officer until November 12.

November 14: Thirty-six pontoons reached Washington, and the information was immediately wired to Burnside by General Woodbury, in command of the Engineers, with the remark that "one train would start on the morning of November 16 or 17, and that General Halleck was not inclined to send another train by land" (inferring that the second train would be ferried down the Potomac to Aquia Landing).

November 17: Woodbury telegraphed Burnside that Major Spaulding (in command of the train) had not been able to get started, but would start the next day.

November 19: The train was started, but rain and mud slowed progress, and it was finally floated down the Potomac.

November 21: Half of Longstreet's corps reached Fredericksburg.

November 25: The remainder of Longstreet's corps arrived.

November 27: The pontoons finally turned up at the Lacy house, Sumner's headquarters opposite Fredericksburg, and the engineer officers in charge later testified that they could have thrown two bridges across the Rappahannock that night, without interference from the enemy, if they had been allowed to do so.

December 1: Jackson's corps arrived at Fredericksburg and the two wings of Lee's army were ready for battle.

To round out the picture, and to point up the fact that the engineers were not the ones responsible for the fiasco, General Woodbury gave the following testimony:

> Gen. Halleck's order to me of the 13th (November) made it apparent that the army was preparing to march to Fredericksburg. As to the time when the movement would be made, I never received any information. Fearing, however, that the movement would be precipitate, I went to Gen. Halleck's office, and *urged him to delay the movement* some five days, in order that the necessary preparations might be made to insure its success. To this he replied that he would do nothing to delay, for an instant, the advance of the army upon Richmond.

The newspaper article added to Woodbury's statement the bitter comment that "a single word from Gen. Halleck to Gen. Burnside would have stopped the advance of the army until the pontoon train had fairly been prepared and sent forward. Gen. Halleck refused to send that word, and allowed Gen. Burnside to go forward under the belief that the authorities at Washington were doing all they could to assist him."

CONFEDERATE SNOWBALL FIGHT

CHAPTER 6

AGONIZING INTERLUDE

THE COLLAPSE of Burnside's initial plan of operations, caused by the delayed arrival of the pontoon bridging equipment, coupled with his inability to improvise, meant that fortune was still smiling on the Army of Northern Virginia. Nevertheless General Lee had for once been out-generalled in the logistical prelude to the forthcoming Battle of Fredericksburg. Lee was again to be out-generalled by Joe Hooker in the following year, 1863, prior to Chancellorsville, but on both occasions the achievement was a temporary one, and each time the Union commander for one reason or another failed to exploit his early advantage to defeat the apparently invincible Lee.

Burnside Marks Time

Nearly two weeks had passed since Lincoln's telegram to Burnside had unleashed the new army commander. The Army of the Potomac, having completed an impressive march and neatly accomplished a change of base without the fanfare or extravagant claims to unusual achievement that McClellan

99

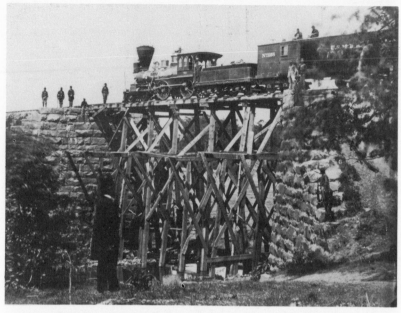

GENERAL HAUPT KEEPS THE RAILROAD IN OPERATION
Engineers repair a bridge on the Orange and Alexandria Railroad.

would inevitably have trumpeted, had for the second of those two weeks been idly passing the time doing little but fight off the cold in its camps immediately across the Rappahannock from Fredericksburg.

The winter of 1862-63 failed to measure up to the record breaking American winter of 1740, when most of the Atlantic coast harbors were frozen solid, or even the less severe Revolutionary War year of 1780 when oxen were used to haul cannon across Long Island Sound to the mainland, and Chesapeake Bay froze solid at Annapolis.* Just the same, the weather at Fredericksburg in December 1862, if not notable for unusual severity, was rugged enough for those Confederates whose shoes and overcoats, if any, required considerable imagination on the part of their unfortunate wearers to rate them as adequate against the wintry blasts, the snows, and the ice-covered ground.

*The Old Farmer's Almanac.

Burnside's soldiers on the other hand were comfortably supplied and warmly clad, thanks partly to an energetic Quartermaster General, and to an equally capable railroader general by the name of Haupt, who kept the railroads of the North in repair and running all through the war. Haupt was the kind of man who got things done and had little time for the lazy or incompetent.

Burnside's reputation for looking after the welfare of his men when he was a division and corps commander had been well established. He was noted for his habit of snooping around company messes and enlisted men's quarters, checking on his subordinates to make certain his men were being properly cared for. His elevation to the post of army commander stopped all that because he had his hands full with other duties for the short period of time that he retained the top position, virtually all of it in movement, contact with the enemy, or actual combat. After the Battle of Fredericksburg, during the winter of 1862-63, a notorious food shortage occurred in the Army of the Potomac, with disastrous effect on a morale that was already weakened by the depressing defeat and unnecessarily heavy casualties. Burnside as the Commanding General was naturally and rightly held responsible, and there were many who, convinced from the start that he was out of his depth as an army commander, were not surprised at the outcome.

It is recorded that time hung heavy on Confederate hands, after they had taken such steps as Lee directed to strengthen their defenses on the high ground west and south of Fredericksburg. So the soldiers, many of whom were teenagers, understandably helped to keep themselves healthy by engaging in snowball fights and similar youthful diversions as they waited for the Union general across the river to break the monotony of the long period of watchful waiting.

He Who Hesitates - - -!

The thoughts that passed through the active mind of amateur strategist Abraham Lincoln during this trying period of waiting have not been recorded, but they are not difficult to imagine. Burnside was meticulous in reporting to Halleck from day to day, and it must be presumed that his reports were passed along for the President to read. But action was at a standstill, vital time was slipping away, and finally, unable to stand the suspense any longer, Lincoln wired Burnside an invitation to meet him at Aquia Creek at dark on the evening of November 26 in these understanding but rather wistful words: ". . . could you, without inconvenience, meet me and pass an hour or two with me?"

The record is silent as to what passed between the two men at the Aquia Creek meeting or at the subsequent conference two days later, when Burnside journeyed to Washington to continue the discussion. Jackson's corps had not yet reached Fredericksburg, but the other half of Lee's army was strongly posted on the high ground at the western edge of the town. It is reasonable to assume that the new situation facing Burnside was

PORT ROYAL
A photo made in 1864 when Grant was using Port Royal as a base.

analyzed from every angle with a view to developing a revised plan that might promise success as soon as the bridges could be placed.

There was no question as to Union preponderance of manpower, and for a refreshing change from McClellan, Burnside did not besiege the authorities at Washington with calls for reinforcements. The strategic position of the Union army, now

MAJOR GENERAL DANIEL H. HILL, C.S.A.

directly covering Washington, did result in releasing 15,000 of the large body of troops stationed in the capital for transfer to Burnside's command, giving him a combat strength of more than 120,000 men. Burnside, aware of his overwhelming superiority, had initially held Slocum's Twelfth Corps at Harpers Ferry and Sigel's Eleventh at Centreville but on December 9 he ordered both corps, totaling over 26,000 men, to Dumfries, 20 miles north of Fredericksburg, as army reserve. There was such a thing as over-congestion of an area, and it was at this late date not at all certain that a formidable river crossing against a strongly posted veteran army such as Lee's would be the comparatively simple operation that it had promised to be only a few days earlier.

One of the considered plans that seemed to hold promise was to move a strong maneuvering force to a point opposite Port Royal, about seventeen miles south on the Rappahannock, throw one or more of the pontoon bridges across and attack upstream, on the south side of the river, concurrently with the crossing of the main body in the vicinity of Fredericksburg. This scheme would have the advantage of disrupting Lee's line of communication to Richmond and at the same time serve as the flanking left prong of a pincers movement against the Confederate position.

As the Rappahannock flows seaward below Fredericksburg it gradually widens and, with its wooded banks, presents from Port Royal south a formidable obstacle to an army wishing to cross either there or below. At Port Royal, which was first established in 1744 and subsequently developed into one of the main shipping points on the river, the Rappahannock is over half a mile wide and it is doubtful that Burnside had sufficient excess pontoon equipment to throw even a single bridge across at that point at the same time that he would be effecting a crossing at Fredericksburg. It may even be doubted that he had taken steps to reconnoiter that far south, for he certainly failed to scout D. H. Hill's Confederate Division at Port Royal. Seemingly he was content to rely on the long distance vision of his balloon observers.

Even if Burnside had decided to attempt a crossing at Port Royal, Hill's Division, concealed in the dense woods that fringed the river on the Port Royal side (now a part of the A. P. Hill Military Reservation), could easily have nullified all his efforts by concentrating merely a portion of its infantry and artillery firepower on the narrow column of Federal troops crossing the pontoon bridge. It may be questioned, indeed, that the engineers could have succeeded in laying the bridge.

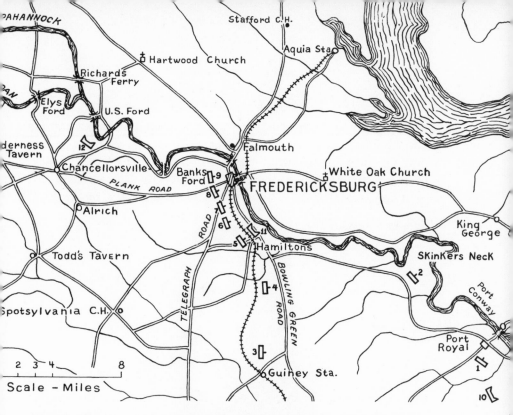

MAP 7. THE VALLEY OF THE RAPPAHANNOCK, SHOWING LEE'S DISPOSITIONS
ON DECEMBER 10

Jackson's corps is on the right, the divisions being indicated by numerals,
as follows: 1. D. H. Hill; 2. Early; 3. Taliaferro; 4. A. P. Hill. Longstreet's
corps was occupying the ridge west and southwest of Fredericksburg, from
the river on the left to Hamiltons Crossing on the right. His divisions are
indicated as: 5. Hood; 6. Pickett; 7. McLaws; 8. Ransom; 9. R. H. Anderson.
Stuart's cavalry is located as shown, the brigades being: 10. W. H. F. Lee;
11. Fitzhugh Lee; 12. Hampton; 13. Rosser. The Federal army was in camps
north and southeast of Falmouth, generally back about a mile and a half
from the river.

In addition to its importance as a shipping point on the
navigable Rappahannock, Port Royal and the small village
of Port Conway on the opposite bank had their moments in
history. The latter was the birthplace of James Madison, fourth
President of the United States. It was there, too, that Lincoln's
assassin, John Wilkes Booth, crossed the river on April 24, 1865,
as he fled from the pursuing Union soldiers, across the river
and into the Garrett barn, a few miles above Port Royal, where
two days later he was killed while resisting arrest.

Confederate Troop Dispositions

As December was ushered in and the troop development phase of the Fredericksburg campaign came to an end with the arrival on the field of Jackson's corps from the Shenandoah Valley, Lee's army at first occupied a widely extended, unconnected curving line with its left resting on the south bank of the Rap-

MAJOR GENERAL R. H. ANDERSON, C.S.A.

pahannock opposite Falmouth and its right at Port Royal, twenty miles downstream. Although the official returns of early December showed 91,760 present for duty at Fredericksburg, the cavalry brigades of Wade Hampton and W. P. Jones were on detached missions so it is doubtful if Lee had more than 88,000 combat effectives on the field.

Longstreet's corps was posted along the range of hills west of Fredericksburg and extending in a southerly direction paralleling the Rappahannock, from a point opposite Falmouth almost to Massaponax Creek. The depth of the positions occupied by his troops varied in accordance with the natural strength or weakness of the terrain features along the line of defense. While awaiting the arrival of Jackson's corps, Lee stretched Longstreet's divisions to Hamilton's Crossing where Lee set up his own headquarters for the time being. Ranged in order from left to right of the position were the divisions of R. H. Anderson, Lafayette McLaws—with Robert Ransom in direct support—George E. Pickett, and John B. Hood. The defensive strength of the occupied hills in Longstreet's sector was such that his corps occupied a frontage of more than six miles, with but little depth.

Character of the Battlefield

In front of Longstreet's sector was the upper end of a broken plain which, between the Confederate position and the river, widened out from about 600 yards opposite Falmouth to two miles in the Deep Run area, and then narrowed to a mile at the lower end.

The range of heights below Fredericksburg is broken by ravines and small streams, two of which—Hazel Run and Deep Run—are definite obstacles in the path of a deployed, advancing body of troops—especially if covered by enemy rifle or artillery fire. In December 1862 both streams flowed through ravines that were thirty feet deep and were hidden by woods and dense undergrowth.

Hazel Run in particular was an important tactical feature that was to influence strongly the outcome of the Federal attack against Marye's Hill. Twenty feet in width at the point where it is crossed by the Telegraph Road, it was more of a psychological and physical obstacle in the dead of winter than would have been the case in warm weather, when the effects of a thorough soaking could be accepted by the soldiers with greater equanimity.

The hill slopes of the Confederate position were covered with woods that afforded the occupying troops exceptional advantages of observation. The two hills at the north end, Taylor's and Marye's, are together known as Marye's Heights,

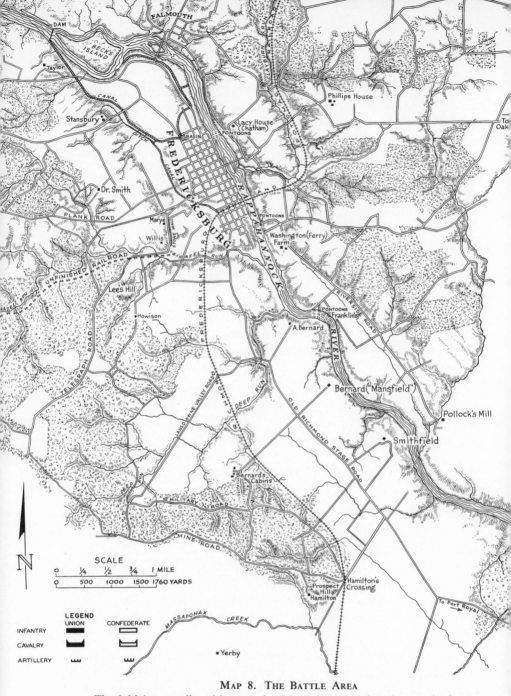

MAP 8. THE BATTLE AREA

The initial troop dispositions, omitted here in order that the terrain features may be portrayed clearly, are shown on Map 9.

which at its lower extremity is cut by Hazel Run. Marye's Hill rises steeply and abruptly from the flat ground below, a mental as well as physical hazard for the boldest attacker. The most prominent features of the whole ridge are known as Stansbury's Hill, Cemetery Hill, Telegraph (Lee's) Hill, and Prospect Hill. All these hills are from forty to fifty feet above the lower level.

The town of Fredericksburg at the time of the battle extended from the river bank perhaps a quarter of a mile in the direction of Marye's Heights. The generally open terrain between the western limits of the town and the strong Confederate defensive position on the heights would appear to offer room for maneuver, were it not for the canal that bisected the area and the wide, neighboring drainage ditch that carried off the waste water from the canal.

In 1862 there was a dam several miles above Fredericksburg, where the canal originated. The canal is still very much in evidence, with a full, rapid flow of water. The diversion of water through the canal, together with the rapids below the dam and a fine collection of big rocks in the river bed, combined to discourage troop crossings of the river or the canal, which by itself was destined to be a serious handicap to the maneuver of the Union divisions.

Three main roads and several minor ones led from the streets of Fredericksburg across the battlefield-to-be. The Plank Road, of later Chancellorsville fame, crossed the ditch over a wooden bridge in front of Marye's Heights, and, ascending the ridge, kept on to Chancellorsville and Orange Court House. The Telegraph Road crossed Hazel Run and, passing around the base of Marye's Hill, headed southward to Richmond. At the foot of Marye's Hill it became a sunken road, with a stone wall on either side, which continued for over 500 yards and was destined to prove the major stumbling block to Federal success.

The old Richmond stage road and the main railroad to Richmond ran south between the river and the foothills to the west. The bridges by which these two crossed Deep Run had been either destroyed or damaged, as had those by which the Plank

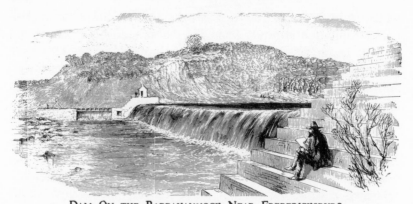

DAM ON THE RAPPAHANNOCK NEAR FREDERICKSBURG
The magazine illustrator who sketched this and other drawings used herein
has included himself in the picture. From the following Brady photo it would
appear that the artist was A. R. Waud. Waud, a staff illustrator of Harpers
Weekly, accompanied the Army of the Potomac in the field.

and Telegraph Roads crossed the ditch obstacle in front of
Marye's Heights. The Confederates apparently had no intention
of making Burnside's task any easier.

Disposition of Jackson's Divisions

Although Lee had definitely decided to fight on the Rappahannock, if and when Burnside should advance, rather than
fall back to the North Anna, he was uncertain where the Union
army would cross. He rather expected the perfectly natural
move of a flank action by a crossing either above or below
Fredericksburg. The latter now seemed more logical, since
Burnside had already passed up the opportunity to cross above
Fredericksburg when his army marched down from Warrenton.

Port Royal, seventeen miles down river in a direct line from
Fredericksburg, and that much closer to Richmond, was very
much on Lee's mind. When Jackson came up in advance of
his column he was directed to spread his troops over a wide
area, with D. H. Hill's Division at Port Royal, Early's (Ewell's)
at Skinker's Neck, twelve miles southeast of Fredericksburg,
A. P. Hill's at Yerby's house, three miles to the right rear of
Longstreet's right flank, and Taliaferro's at Guiney's Station,
four miles further to the south on the line of the Richmond-

Fredericksburg Railroad. Stuart's four cavalry brigades were posted to move wherever they might be useful. D. H. Hill's Division reached Port Royal just in time to encounter and drive back several Federal gunboats steaming up the river. Jackson had no liking for the position at Fredericksburg, insisting that it could easily be outflanked by the use of the fords above the town. He was in favor of the North Anna position, but Lee, while of the same opinion, had yielded to Jefferson Davis and that was the way it had to be despite Jackson's strong objections.

Tactical Considerations

The initial disposition of Jackson's divisions illustrated the mental flexibility that invariably characterized Lee's strategic conceptions. He reasoned that Burnside's logical move, in the

A. R. WAUD, STAFF ARTIST OF HARPERS WEEKLY
During the Civil War most on-the-spot pictorial coverage was provided by sketchers who accompanied the troops. Sometimes they allowed their imagination and artistic license to "color" their drawings, but in general the results provide today's readers with a fair notion of how persons and events appeared. Since it was impossible to take a quick snapshot with a camera, the drawings were sometimes even better than photos for the purpose of portraying action.

face of the strong Confederate defensive position on the heights of Fredericksburg, would be an attempt to turn his, Lee's, flank in the direction of Richmond; so he took precautionary measures to thwart such a design by making a river crossing below Fredericksburg an expensive venture for the Union army. Both sides of course knew that the Rappahannock was navigable for gunboats as far upriver as Fredericksburg, which meant a crossing by pontoons, if at all, would have to be expected at a spot where the river was narrower than at Port Royal.

Burnside had considered doing just what Lee anticipated, although the crossing point that his engineers recommended was at Skinker's Neck, twelve miles south, rather than at Port Royal, five miles further down the river. Lee had posted a division at each place, just in case. The Federals had two balloons aloft and the aerial observers had reported large bivouacs in the Skinker's Neck-Port Royal area, although because of the wooded sections Burnside could know only in a general way where the Confederates were, not how many or their precise location.

Why Burnside, with all the time in the world and plenty of cavalry at his disposal, neglected to observe the fundamental doctrine of thorough ground reconnaissance to determine more precisely the strength and exact location of the widely separated elements of Jackson's corps below Fredericksburg, has never been explained. Particularly since a young engineer lieutenant had succeeded in crossing the river at several points to examine the western bank for possible pontoon placements, and to make sure that artillery could cross successfully; and each time he was able easily to avoid the Confederate pickets. It was this lieutenant who had recommended Skinker's Neck as the best location for placing the pontoons at the lower end.

The widely dispersed divisions of Jackson's corps suggested one of two things: either Lee was so unsure of Burnside's intentions that he wanted to be in position to concentrate Jackson's divisions only after Burnside had committed his army to a definite line of attack; or he purposely scattered the Second

Corps as an open invitation to his opponent to walk into a trap, at which time Lee would withdraw Early and D. H. Hill from their delaying positions on the Rappahannock to the high ground where A. P. Hill and Taliaferro had already been posted. Whatever his motives, Lee was as usual the agile boxer

BRIGADIER GENERAL WILLIAM B. TALIAFERRO, C.S.A.

who depends on quick footwork to take advantage of any opening afforded by his heavier but slower moving opponent.

There was little room for maneuver directly opposite Fredericksburg where Longstreet occupied Marye's Heights and the high ground in prolongation to the south. The lower half of the plain presented a different picture and it was that area to which Lee suspected Burnside would be attracted.

Burnside's Tentative Plan

A few days after the Union army had been fully concentrated near Falmouth, Burnside called his generals together, communicated to them his intention of crossing a maneuvering force in the vicinity of Skinker's Neck, and asked for comment. True to form, Hooker was the only one who took issue with what was presented to them as a decision, stating that it was preposterous to talk about crossing the Rappahannock in the face of Lee's army.

This was the same Hooker who only a short time before had

MAJOR GENERAL JOSEPH HOOKER

urged Burnside to let him take his Center Grand Division across the Rappahannock on an independent drive in the direction of Bowling Green, presumably to the glory of Joe Hooker, whose ambitious soul caused him so to ignore the hierarchy of command that he sent a direct communication to Secretary of War Stanton inquiring whether rations could be made available to his command at Port Royal within three days. Burnside's disapproval of Hooker's request on the ground that the move would be premature was undoubtedly registered without knowledge of Hooker's irregular, if not downright insubordinate letter to Stanton. One wonders how Burnside would have reacted had he been in possession of all the facts. In any event, he ignored the objection, stating that his mind was made up and the proper orders would issue in due course.

A few days after that conference, Major General William F. Smith, commanding the Sixth Corps of Franklin's Left Grand Division, accompanied Burnside on a short ride along Stafford

MAJOR GENERAL WILLIAM F. SMITH

Heights immediately below Fredericksburg, on the Federal side of the river. On that occasion Burnside is reported by Smith to have told him that his earlier plans had been changed and the crossing would be effected much closer to Fredericksburg than Skinker's Neck. Smith was admonished to keep the information strictly to himself. He volunteered the opinion that Burnside would have no difficulty in crossing at the upper point but his troubles would begin after he was across, because of the range of hills about a mile back from the river, presumably occupied by the enemy. Burnside's overconfident reply was that he knew where Lee's forces were and expected to surprise them and occupy the hills before Lee could bring anything serious to bear against him.

Burnside's thinking at that stage seems to have been based on the fact that Lee was widely dispersed and could be outwitted by a rapidly executed surprise crossing that would drive a wedge between his two wings, forcing him to withdraw from Fredericksburg in order to consolidate the wings and remove the threat to Richmond. There were however at least two major flaws in that estimate; first, there could be no surprise in laying pontoons and crossing a large body of troops; second, Lee was a past master of the art of rapidly concentrating widely separated elements of his army at the point of impact at the psychological moment, as at First and Second Bull Run, and Antietam. Burnside should have known this and given the possibility due weight.

The Commanding General of the Army of the Potomac had by this time painted himself into a corner where there was no visible door. The longer he waited the worse his situation became; none of his tentative plans seemed to meet with wholehearted approval from his grand division and corps commanders. The truth of Lincoln's remark that the Fredericksburg move could succeed only if the army moved fast had been confirmed. Now that Lee's army was all present or accounted for, there was a foreboding among Burnside's officers and even many of the enlisted men that the forthcoming attack already had two strikes against it. The third strike would be imposed principally through the incapacity and ineptitude of a confused army commander who just couldn't make up his mind either what to do or how to do it. Confidence in Burnside had reached an understandably low ebb!

BOMBARDMENT OF FREDERICKSBURG

CHAPTER 7

THE CURTAIN RISES SLOWLY

THE LENGTHY PRELUDE to open combat at Fredericksburg, which was extended well over a week after both
armies were fully assembled and facing each other across the
Rappahannock, was reminiscent of the bear and the bees; the
massive Federal army of 120,000 men in the role of the bear
and the relatively smaller Confederate army of 90,000 defending the hive. The former, wanting badly to get at the honey, had
been stung so many times that it was somewhat wary of stirring up the bees, and was taking no chances on disturbing them
without making certain that the first blow of its massive paw
would be a lethal one.

In setting the stage for the Battle of Fredericksburg, Nature
had managed to achieve an intriguing result. The right-angle
bend in the Rappahannock River, coupled with its progressively
narrowing width and increasing depth immediately below Fredericksburg; the string of hills west and south of the town, which
were made to order for a defensive line; the dominance of Staf-

117

SOME OF GENERAL HUNT'S ARTILLERY
Three 4½-inch Parrott guns belonging to Trumbull's battalion, emplaced on the high ground back of the Ferry farm.

ford Heights along the east bank, giving the Federals a terrific artillery advantage—these and other terrain features such as Deep Run, an important barrier to easy maneuvering, the many deep ravines, and the ditch or canal between Marye's Heights and Fredericksburg, six feet deep and thirty feet wide, all played significant roles during the battle. Nor did the thrifty Confederate leaders, accustomed by necessity to extract from all resources, animate and inanimate, every conceivable advantage to match Federal superiority in manpower and equipment, neglect to do so in this campaign. Lee may in retrospect have seemed on occasion to violate the principles of war, but his strategems in the end served but to confirm those principles and to give them new life and meaning.

The Union Army Prepares to Cross the River

Lee was quite aware of the fact that he could not prevent the Union army from crossing the Rappahannock because Stafford Heights, which confronted Fredericksburg from the opposite shore, dominated both the town and the plain below. Conversely the Federal guns could not, without displacing forward, reach Marye's Heights and the ridges to the south where the Confederates planned to make their main defense.

General Hunt, able Chief of Artillery of the Army of the Potomac, had skilfully placed 147 of his 312 guns at appropriate intervals along Stafford Heights, from which they could individually and collectively deliver their fire on the just and unjust alike, in the unfortunate event that any of the former— civilian inhabitants of Fredericksburg—should choose to remain in or return to their homes after Lee had advised them to evacuate.

McLaw's Division of Longstreet's corps had upon its arrival on November 25 been ordered to occupy Fredericksburg with part of the command. Accordingly Barksdale's Mississippi Brigade of 1600 men was assigned the mission of occupying Fredericksburg and picketing the river bank with detachments, under instructions to dig rifle pits and loop-hole the houses along the river from which the men could with relative impunity pick off the engineers of the Union army when they should finally reach the point of laying their pontoon bridges.

One evening during the period of watchful waiting, several Union bands, assembled near their end of the railroad bridge, decided it would be a good idea to keep their instruments in working order by playing a few patriotic airs such as "Hail Columbia" and "The Star Spangled Banner," which they did with great gusto but without eliciting a response from the suspicious Southerners. Finally the bands struck up "Dixie." That broke the ice, figuratively, for there is no record of its having melted the half-inch crust ice that covered the river at the time. There was much cheering and laughter on both sides of the river, but the entertainment proved to an expensive lark for the Federals. General McLaws, whose suspicions were aroused, promptly caused his men to construct even more of the rifle pits from which the Mississippians would shortly create havoc among the bridge builders.

Halleck Withholds Approval

Burnside meanwhile was feverishly burning the midnight oil at his headquarters in the Phillips house, sending off dispatches to Halleck in Washington in a rather pathetic invitation for some encouragement from the General-in-Chief which might assist the army commander in reaching a decision and perhaps,

MAJOR GENERAL LAFAYETTE McLAWS, C.S.A.

collaterally, shift some of the responsibility for the attack plan to higher headquarters.

The telegraph wires carried the following message to Washington on the night of December 9:

HEADQUARTERS ARMY OF THE POTOMAC,
December 9, 1862—11:30 p. m.
GENERAL: All the orders have been issued to the several commanders of grand divisions and heads of departments for an attempt to cross the river on Thursday morning. (Ed. Note: December 11) The plans of the move-

ment are somewhat modified by the movements of the enemy, who have been concentrating in large force opposite the point at which we originally intended to cross. I think now that the enemy will be more surprised by a crossing immediately in our front than in any other part of the river. The commanders of grand divisions coincide with me in this opinion, and I have accordingly ordered the movement, which will enable us to keep the force well concentrated, at the same time covering our communications in the rear. I am convinced that a large force of the enemy is now concentrated in the vicinity of Port Royal, its left resting near Fredericksburg, which we hope to turn. We have an abundance of artillery, and have made very elaborate preparations to protect the crossings. The importance of the movement and the details of the plan seem to be well understood by the grand division commanders, and we hope to succeed.

If the General-in-Chief desires it, I will send a minute statement by telegraph in cipher to-morrow morning. The movement is so important that I feel anxious to be fortified by his approval. Please answer.*

A. E. BURNSIDE,
Major-General, Commanding.

General G. W. CULLUM,
Chief of Staff, Washington.

The next day Halleck made the following pointed reply:†

WAR DEPARTMENT,
Washington, D. C., December 10, 1862.

Major-General BURNSIDE, Falmouth, Va.:

I beg of you not to telegraph details of your plans, nor the times of your intended movements. No secret can be kept which passes through so many hands.

H. W. HALLECK,
General-in-Chief.

Clearly the hopeful general in the field was to receive neither encouragement nor suggestions from topside! Still, a more per-

---

*This dispatch, except the last two words, was also sent to General Halleck.
†Actually the Confederates had planted an agent in the military telegraph office at Aquia Station. Presumably he kept Lee fully informed of the messages passing between Burnside and Washington.

ceptive or less calculating general-in-chief might at such a moment conceivably have taken a quick run down to Burnside's
headquarters at Fredericksburg at least to talk things over.

The Crossing Points Are Finally Determined

Burnside's vacillation as to where his army would cross at
long last came to an end with his decision to effect crossings
simultaneously at three points: at the northern and southern
extremities of Fredericksburg for Sumner's right wing, and just
below the mouth of Deep Run, a mile or so below the town, for
Franklin's left wing. Burnside's message to Halleck December
9 and his decision to cross at and just below Fredericksburg,
rather than at Skinker's Neck, meant that his mind was made
up that Lee's two corps were widely separated, and that Franklin's grand division could be neatly inserted in the opening as
the first step in turning the *left* flank of Jackson's corps. The
precise locations and other tactical instructions were determined
for army headquarters by the Chief Engineer of the army, a
brilliant young lieutenant by the name of Comstock, whose
order to his engineers was a model of brevity and conciseness:

> Two pontoon bridges to be thrown at site of old pon-
> toon bridge, one of them to have approaches for artillery.
> One pontoon bridge at site of old canal-boat bridge;
> approaches for artillery.
> Two pontoon bridges just below mouth of Deep Run, a
> mile below Fredericksburg; one to have artillery approach.*
> Major Spaulding to throw three upper ones; Major Ma-
> gruder to throw the next, and Lieutenant Cross the lowest
> one.
> Bridge equipage, now at White Oak Church, to move
> up and go into park near Phillips' house by dark. At mid-
> night trains to move down within 400 yards of river, and
> to move down and begin unloading at 2 a. m.
> If enemy's fire is kept down, bridges to be thrown as
> soon as boats are unloaded; if too hot, wait till artillery
> silences it.

---

*Actually three bridges were constructed at this point. *Editor.*

FRANKLIN'S GRAND DIVISION PASSING BURNSIDE'S HEADQUARTERS AT THE
PHILLIPS HOUSE

Upper two bridges to be covered by two regiments of
infantry; canal-boat bridge by one regiment; two lower
bridges by two regiments and a 12-pounder battery.

Corduroy at Skinker's Neck to be laid during to-morrow
night; woods to be felled, etc.

As soon as pontoons are on bank of river, all teams to
be taken away.

Lack of Confidence in Burnside

A search of the official records fails to reveal a transcript of
what transpired at Burnside's conference with his major commanders on December 10, following their receipt of his warn-
ing order of late afternoon the preceding day. The preliminary
order, dated 5 A. M. December 9, had merely prepared them
for an early movement to cross the river, directing that they put
their divisions in readiness with cooked rations for three days
and sixty rounds of ammunition to be carried by each soldier,
and report to army headquarters at the Phillips house next day
at noon, when more detailed oral orders would be issued for the
movement of the infantry and cavalry.

Without doubt Burnside at the December 10 conference outlined to his grand division commanders initial missions for their commands, but he was silent or at least vague as to precise blueprints for their subsequent actions after crossing to the Fredericksburg side of the river.

Sumner's Right Grand Division was assigned the north zone, including Fredericksburg; Franklin's Left Grand Division was directed to cross on the two lower bridges and operate in the open plain to the south; Hooker's Center Grand Division was designated as army reserve, to remain on the left bank in readiness to throw its weight wherever the developing situation might require.

Burnside's subsequent orders and written memoranda to his grand division commanders for the most part were postmarked at ungodly hours in the early morning, long before daylight, a time of night when man's vitality is supposed to be at its lowest ebb. It has never been suggested that Burnside did not try, only that he lacked the gray matter that an army commander must have to handle a major task that requires topflight mental capacity, imagination, moral courage, and experience in charting the battle course of a complex army of over 100,000 officers and men. Burnside didn't spare himself, but it is possible that he would have thought his problems through more clearly had he taken the proper amount of sleep, unless indeed he was the sort of character who prefers to work at night and sleep in the daytime.

Be that as it may, Burnside gave his grand division commanders precise instructions as to the actual crossing of the river. Beyond that his orders were indefinite, conditional, and completely devoid of positive, specific attack missions. There seemed to be only a hazy, general picture in his mind which he passed on to them in fragmentary form. At no time was the combat mission of either wing defined specifically so that the corps and division commanders could feel a surge of confidence that the architect at the top had blueprinted the job to be done in such a way that they in turn could embody in their orders a definite task for their divisions, brigades, and regiments.

Generals Sumner, Hooker, and Franklin must have had their earlier misgivings intensified at the December 10 conference, because a new and puzzling Burnside confronted them. All were professional soldiers and had known the army commander socially and officially for a long time. Since his elevation to army command, Burnside's relations with his principal lieu-

BRIGADIER GENERAL ORLANDO B. WILLCOX

tenants had apparently been cordial and understanding. Franklin and Sumner were honorable officers and gentlemen, and, so far as Burnside knew, loyal to his leadership. But there is nothing in the military record of either to suggest that they were exceptionally gifted leaders, or that there was anything like the Damon-Pythias rapport that existed between Lee and Jackson, Lee and Stuart, or even Lee and Longstreet.

All three of his grand division commanders were older men than Burnside, who was only 38 years of age at the time of the Fredericksburg campaign. Sumner, who had entered the Army in 1819, five years before Burnside was born, was now over sixty. Hooker had graduated from West Point in 1837, Franklin in 1843, and Burnside in 1847, the latter in a class of only thirty-eight graduates which included, among others, Union corps commander Orlando B. Willcox and the Confederate division commander, Ambrose P. Hill, who was an important spoke in Lee's wheel at Fredericksburg.

The sizes of the classes at the Military Academy in the years before the Civil War were quite small by today's standards, which meant that those who carried through for four years be-

COLONEL RUSH C. HAWKINS

came intimately acquainted with their own classmates and were also afforded the opportunity to learn the capabilities and characteristics of cadets in the classes above and below their own. The roster of West Pointers who commanded divisions and corps at Fredericksburg, in both armies, reads almost like a roll call of the two forces. With the exception of Sumner, Sickles, Butterfield, and Birney, who did not attend the Military Academy, the great majority of them, Union and Confederate alike, had graduated during the 20-year span between 1837 and 1856. The older graduates were Lee, Humphreys, and Meade, who finished their respective undergraduate careers in 1829,

1831, and 1835, respectively. Indeed, under more appropriate auspices, the field of Fredericksburg might have provided the stage for a good old-fashioned reunion of close friends and acquaintances, for many of the brigade and regimental commanders, as well as those commanding divisions and corps, had been fellow cadets at the Point. (See Appendix I.)

Rumors and gripes are indigenous to armies by their very nature. Without them, commanders have every right to start worrying. The Army of the Potomac was no exception. Time hung heavy on the hands of the men and officers before Fredericksburg, as they watched the Confederates building earthworks on Marye's Heights and moving artillery into position as far as the eye could see, and the morale of the men in the ranks deteriorated as a result.

There were officers in the Union army who were familiar with the Fredericksburg terrain. One of them was brevet Brigadier General Rush C. Hawkins, a brigade commander in Getty's division of Burnside's old corps, the Ninth. Hawkins has testified to the strong opposition that was developing, among the more thoughtful tacticians in Burnside's army, to the general's rumored plan of attack which was being freely discussed around the Federal campfires, with evident lack of enthusiasm for its soundness.

Word of this adverse comment reached Burnside's ear; he summoned all the general officers of Sumner's grand division to a conference at Sumner's headquarters, known as the Lacy house, on the evening of December 9, in the course of which he disclosed in part his plan for the pending battle. After the conference Burnside casually asked Hawkins and Colonel J. H. Taylor, a member of Sumner's staff, what they thought of the plan. Hawkin's reply, to which Taylor agreed, was: "If you make the attack as contemplated it will be the greatest slaughter of the war; there isn't infantry enough in our whole army to carry those heights if they are well defended." Taylor's comment was even more positive: "The carrying out of your plan will be murder, not warfare." Burnside seemed surprised and understandably irritated at the frank criticism of the two officers, who patently pulled no punches in expressing themselves. Possibly their former corps commander, Burnside, had conditioned his junior officers to say what they thought, but one may also venture the opinion that such freedom of expression to an army commander just before a battle strongly implied a serious lack

MAJOR GENERAL DARIUS N. COUCH

of confidence in and respect for the judgment and capacity of their commanding general.

Major General Darius N. Couch, commanding the Second Corps under Sumner, while more restrained in his comments on the conference, was no less postitive in declaring that "there were not two opinions among the subordinate officers as to the rashness of the undertaking." Couch felt pretty sure that Sumner himself did not concur in Burnside's plan, but expressed the opinion that "that noble old hero was so faithful and loyal that he wanted, even against impossibilities, to carry out everything Burnside suggested."

It is a surprising fact that the general lack of confidence failed to impair the Union army's fighting spirit. On the contrary, there is every reason to note, when the chips were finally down and the blood bath proceeded, that the Army of the Potomac put aside its doubts and defeatism and fought as courageously and stubbornly as any army has ever fought. All that it lacked at Fredericksburg, as elsewhere during the early years of the war, was top leadership of a quality that it deserved but never seemed to get.

Burnside's Battle Orders Vague and Indecisive

Assuming that the conference of generals was held at noon December 10 as planned, and that the grand division commanders were given some inkling of what was expected of them after they had crossed the river, Burnside required the rest of that day and most of the following night to piece together the mosaic of his forthcoming attack plans in his own mind sufficiently to enable him to convey the makings of a potential attack order to his worried subordinates. But that was as far as the orders went, as disclosed by a careful reading of the pre-daylight messages of December 11 to Sumner, Hooker, and Franklin, all of which have the characteristics of postscripts to letters. The tim-

THE PHILLIPS HOUSE
Burnside's headquarters.

ing, it must be noted, was almost simultaneous with the hour when the engineers were scheduled to start laying the bridges.

HEADQUARTERS ARMY OF THE POTOMAC,
December 11, 1862—4.20 a. m.
Maj. Gen. E. V. SUMNER,
Commanding Right Grand Division:
In addition to the verbal orders already given you, I will add the following:
Your first corps, after crossing, should be protected by the town and the banks of the river as much as possible until the second corps is well closed up and in the act of crossing; after which you will move the first corps directly to the front, with a view to taking the heights that command the Plank road and the Telegraph road, supporting it by your other corps as soon as you can get it over the river. General Hooker will immediately follow in your support, and will see that your right flank is not troubled.
General Franklin crosses below, as you are aware, thus protecting your left. The extent of your movement to the front beyond the heights will be indicated during the engagement.
Please inform me if you propose to change your headquarters before the head of your column reaches the river, that I may send you guides for the roads. I send one with this. If you desire further instructions, please send word by the orderly.
I have the honor to be, general, very respectfully, your obedient servant,
A. E. BURNSIDE,
Major-General of Volunteers, Commanding.

HEADQUARTERS ARMY OF THE POTOMAC,
December 11, 1862—4.45 a. m.
Maj. Gen. JOSEPH HOOKER,

Commanding Center Grand Division:
General Sumner is ordered, after crossing the river to move immediately to the front, with a view to taking the heights commanding the Plank and Telegraph roads. After crossing, you will hold yourself in readiness to support either his column or General Franklin's which crosses be-

low Deep Run, and will move down the old Richmond road, in the direction of the railroad. Should we be so fortunate as to dislodge the enemy, you will hold your command in readiness to pursue by the two roads.

My headquarters will be at the Phillips house, where, if you will send an aide at 8 o'clock, guides will be furnished you to lead your column. I will be glad to see you at headquarters before the head of your column reaches the river.

I have the honor to be, general, very respectfully, your obedient servant,

A. E. BURNSIDE,
Major-General, Commanding.

HEADQUARTERS ARMY OF THE POTOMAC,
December 11, 1862—5.15 a. m.

Major-General FRANKLIN, Commanding Left Grand Division:

General Sumner will, after crossing the river, move immediately to the front, with a view to taking the heights which command the Plank and Telegraph roads. I have ordered General Hooker to hold himself in readiness, as soon as he has crossed the river, to support either General Sumner's column or your own. After your command has crossed, you will move down the old Richmond road, in the direction of the railroad, being governed by circumstances as to the extent of your movements. An aide will be sent to you during your movements.

My headquarters will be at the Phillips house.

I have the honor to be, general, very truly, your obedient servant,

A. E. BURNSIDE,
Major-General of Volunteers

Observe that Sumner was ordered "after crossing the river, to move immediately to the front, *with a view to taking* the heights commanding the Plank and Telegraph roads."

Hooker was told: "Should we be so fortunate as to dislodge the enemy, you will *hold yourself in readiness* to pursue by the two roads."

And to Franklin: "After your command has crossed, you will *move down the old Richmond Road,* in the direction of the

BUILDING A CORDUROY ROAD

railroad, being governed by circumstances as to the extent of your movements."

These were march orders, nothing more.

The Bridges Are Laid Under Enemy Fire

The engineer troops, thoroughly briefed on their duties, were well organized and efficient, as engineers usually are. Burnside could count on an excellent performance, despite the half-inch of ice that coated the river and made the bridge laying more difficult. The idea was that they would move into position during the night, prepared to start the actual bridging as soon as there was enough daylight.

The throwing of the bridges was scheduled to start simultaneously at the three points selected for the crossings, at daylight December 11; with luck the job could be finished in a couple of hours, at which time the grand divisions would be on their way.

At Skinker's Neck the Federals essayed a bit of deceptive strategy that might have proven effective had the overall program moved along with reasonable speed. But it did not turn out that way. Down there, where Early's Confederate Division

held forth, and in the general vicinity of which Burnside erron-
eously still believed that Jackson's entire corps was massed,
husky and experienced Northern woodsmen were at work
throughout the night cutting down trees by the light of numerous
fires and laying a corduroy road, with a view to persuading
the Confederates across the river that a major crossing at that
point was imminent. It was love's labor lost, of course, because
the success of such strategy depended on quick Federal surprise action at other points while the enemy was still mentally
off balance. Whatever Early's troops may have thought, General
Lee failed to get excited, made no change in his dispositions,
and simply continued his policy of alert, watchful waiting for
more positive evidence of Burnside's intentions.

The preparatory movement into position of the bulky pontoon equipment on the night of Wednesday, December 10,
naturally could not be carried out in complete silence. During
the night the pickets on the Confederate side of the river became
suspicious and reported preparations underway on the opposite
shore. General Lafayette McLaws of Longstreet's corps, in command of the defense of the Fredericksburg sector, convinced
by 4:30 on the morning of December 11 that the long-awaited
crossing was about to start, ordered the two designated Confederate guns to fire the pre-arranged signal. The element of
Federal surprise promptly went up in the smoke from the muzzles of the two guns as the Confederate rank and file seized arms
and leaped to their posts, while the pre-battle tenseness that
every veteran knows descended grimly on the more than 200,000
men facing each other across a few hundred feet of water.

The Shooting Starts

A thick early morning haze covered the river and the valleys
so that visibility was limited to a few yards. Confederate sharpshooters on the edge of town strained their eyes and tensed their
trigger fingers as they watched for the pontoniers to come into
view through the fog. Finally they appeared and the crackle
of musketry rang out, toppling the leading Union engineers into

BARKSDALE'S MISSISSIPPIANS RESISTING THE LAYING OF PONTOON BRIDGES

the water and driving the rest back into the protection of the fog. As the haze thinned out and visibility improved, Barksdale's picked men commenced firing at human targets who were not even armed and hadn't the ghost of a chance at that short range of less than a hundred yards. Repeatedly the nervy engineers rushed to the leading pontoons in an effort to extend the bridges, but each time they were driven back. Cover fire from infantry on their own side of the river was ineffectual since the Confederates were sheltered in cellars or rifle pits and presented only fleeting targets that were difficult for the Union soldiers to hit.

The tense situation on the waterfront at Fredericksburg continued until the morning was half spent. Hunt's Federal artillerymen on Stafford Heights were unable to depress their gun muzzles sufficiently to deliver plunging fire on the annoying Confederate sharpshooters, and Lee's artillery along the heights beyond the town withheld its fire to avoid killing Confederates and damaging the homes of their own people. As a result, the bridge layers suffered mainly from the sharpshooters.

At 10:00 o'clock the Federal artillery opened with a terrific bombardment in the hope of driving out the annoying Mississippi

BUILDING A BRIDGE OVER THE RAPPAHANNOCK
Hall's brigade of Howard's division ferrying across the river to drive the Confederate infantrymen back so the Federal engineers can complete the bridge.

contingent that was so successfully blocking all attempts to get the bridges laid at the three selected crossing points opposite Fredericksburg. Soon houses were burning fiercely and the resulting smoke, added to the still present fog, created a Dante's inferno that made the town a decidedly undesirable place in which to remain. A newspaper correspondent who was present wrote that "the earth shook beneath the terrific explosions of the shells, which went howling over the river, crashing into the houses, battering down walls, splintering doors, ripping up floors. Sixty solid shot and shells a minute were thrown 'till 9,000 were fired." The bombardment failed however to dampen the spirits of Barksdale's indomitable sharpshooters, for as soon as the guns ceased firing, the musketeers popped out of their holes and resumed their deadly work.

Volunteers Cross in Boats

General Hunt, a realist as well as a keen artillerist, let it be known finally that his artillery simply couldn't do the job. He suggested that the only solution seemed to be to call for volunteers to ferry across a couple of regiments in the pontoons by rowing, if the bridges were ever to be completed. The nearest candidates were those infantry outfits which had been attempting from the left bank to cover the bridge layers by firing on the Confederate sharpshooters. At the upper bridge the 7th Michigan, 19th Massachusetts, and 20th Massachusetts accepted the challenge and the two first named regiments made their preparations. At the center bridge it was the 89th New York that volunteered.

The first party to cross, about sixty men from the 7th Michigan, jumped into pontoons and paddled rapidly across the river, with ample intervals between boats to minimize casualties. The plan worked beautifully, with a loss of but one man killed and several wounded. Quickly outflanking the Confederates in a rush, they captured a sizable batch of prisoners and established a bridgehead. The rest of the volunteers rowed quickly to the Fredericksburg side while Hunt's artillery laid down what would be known in World War I as a box barrage—a curtain of artillery fire in a protective arc that enabled the two regiments to get across without further loss and enlarge the bridgehead so the engineers could finish their job. This was accomplished in a short time without further interference from the Confederates. The 20th Massachusetts followed the other regiments in the

BRIGADIER GENERAL WILLIAM BARKSDALE, C.S.A.

boats, through a misunderstanding of orders which contemplated that they would be the first to cross on the finished bridges. Similar results were accomplished by the New York regiment at the lower bridge.

Even then General Barksdale was not ready to yield Fredericksburg. Bitter street fighting continued through the few remaining hours of daylight on Thursday, December 11, as the Federal infantry fanned out from their bridgeheads and proceeded to clear the area of Confederates. It was not until 7:00 P. M., after darkness had fallen, that Barksdale concluded his mission had been accomplished, and his men had done all that could reasonably be expected of them. This is something of an understatement in face of the fact that 1,600 Confederates had stalled the entire Army of the Potomac for a full day and quite possibly ruined the chances for a Union victory which would have been achieved under more able leadership and more effective coordination of effort.

Couch's Second Corps was to be the first across, followed by Willcox's Ninth Corps, on the upper bridges. Because of Barksdale's bulldog tenacity, only O. O. Howard's division and Hawkins' brigade of the Ninth Corps crossed on the 11th, bivouacking for the night in the streets of the town. The other five divisions of Sumner's Right Grand Division marched over on the morning of December 12.

The Crossing Below Fredericksburg

The spirited and successful Confederate delaying tactics at the three upper bridges were not to be duplicated at the three lower bridges at the mouth of Deep Run, where Franklin's Left Grand Division, composed of Reynold's First and Smith's Sixth Corps, three divisions each, were directed to cross. Lee had expected a crossing further south, when he placed Early's Division at Skinker's Neck and D. H. Hill's at Port Royal. To that limited extent Burnside sprang a mild surprise on his opponent, for the lower bridges were thrown with negligible interference from a few Confederate pickets, who were quickly disposed of, and two bridges were completed by 11:00 A. M. December 11. The third bridge was laid that night.

Franklin appears to have been instructed to synchronize his crossing with that of Sumner's at Fredericksburg, a fact which should be closely scrutinized, for thereby hangs a tale. There was nothing, absolutely nothing, to prevent Franklin from quickly passing over a couple of divisions or even his whole force, the mere presence of which on the Fredericksburg side would have caused Barksdale to evacuate Fredericksburg at least a half-day earlier than he actually did. The lower bridges were only a mile or so below the town, and it would have been a simple matter for Franklin to clear the waterfront to the north in short order so that the coordinated development of both grand divisions could proceed concurrently as Burnside had planned.

An interesting parallel to the opportunity which opened to Burnside on this occasion is found in the historic affair of the Remagen Bridge over the Rhine River in World War II. The difference was that General Eisenhower thought fast in 1945 whereas Burnside's mind was turning over slowly in 1862. Such fleeting opportunities occasionally occur in war; in most cases no one ever hears about them unless they are skillfully exploited or miserably bungled. Burnside's failure to take advantage of his opening reflected the agonizingly slow mental processes which he exhibited after he first sat down at his headquarters in the Phillips house. There were plenty of horses available, but Burnside's sole visit to his grand division commanders, after the army had been committed, occurred during the night of December 12-13, some time after the river crossing operations had commenced.

One wonders indeed why several regiments were not rowed over under cover of darkness the preceding night to seize bridge approaches and facilitate the rapid laying of all six bridges at daylight rather than be forced to perform the task the hard way the next afternoon. If Burnside really expected to employ the principle of surprise in his Fredericksburg adventure, he went about it in a strange way, with the unfortunate result that his own grand division commanders, not the enemy, were the ones upon whom most of the surprise was inflicted.

The lower bridges were not used until 4:00 P. M., when the leading brigade of Franklin's Sixth Corps trudged across, followed by several other brigades, only to receive countermanding orders to retrace their steps because the three upper bridges had been delayed. The result was that all the troops retraced their steps except the leading brigade, which remained as a bridgehead to cover the crossing of the entire grand division the next day, December 12.

The ponderous machinery of the Army of the Potomac badly needed oiling, plus some other things which commander Burnside failed to provide simply because it wasn't in him. One of the most important was the ability to make clean cut decisions and issue understandable directives for their execution, leaving some discretion to subordinate commanders so that they would be granted at least a modicum of flexibility in carrying out their assigned missions.

BATTLEFIELD AS SEEN FROM HAMILTON'S CROSSING

CHAPTER 8

CONFEDERATE COUNTERMEASURES

HAMILTON'S CROSSING was one of two key positions at the Battle of Fredericksburg. The other was the stone wall along the sunken road at the foot of Marye's Heights.

The tactical significance of Captain Hamilton's landmark lay in the fact that it was the southern terminal of the seven-mile long range of hills whose northern end rested on the Rappahannock River west of Falmouth. As its name implies, it was contiguous to the road fork by which the Mine Road from the west, close by the nose of the ridge, joined the new military road and another road which led directly from the south, across the railroad to the Fredericksburg-Bowling Green-Richmond Pike that parallels the course of the Rappahannock midway between Hamilton's Crossing and the river. The Richmond, Fredericksburg and Potomac Railroad, traveling the eastern base of the ridge, paralleled the Richmond Road for some distance and then turned directly south at Hamilton's Crossing. Massaponax Creek, a half mile to the south, rounded out the tactical picture at that vital point in the battle area.

Lee Concentrates on His Right Flank

General Lee had promptly selected Hamilton's Crossing for his initial command post when he reached Fredericksburg on

MAJOR GENERAL J. E. B. STUART, C.S.A.

November 21. Entirely satisfied that Longstreet's dispositions along the ridges west of Fredericksburg had provided adequately for the defense of that sector, Lee now concentrated his attention on the more vulnerable, sensitive, maneuverable area to the south, where anything could happen. As previously recounted, he had widely dispersed Jackson's four divisions and Stuart's cavalry brigades in such a way as to throw dust in Burnside's eyes without too greatly impairing his own ability to reconcentrate his army for the pay-off battle. Lee, a skillful exponent of the art of taking calculated risks, had supreme

GENERALS LEE, LONGSTREET, AND JACKSON ON TELEGRAPH HILL
This Odgen painting shows the Confederate commander watching the action,
on December 13, from the hill which now bears his name.

confidence in both Jackson and Stuart. This wasn't the first time
he had taken long chances and gotten away with them, nor
was it the last.

Hamilton's Crossing was a rather exposed spot for the person
of an army commander, one might think; and so it would have
been except that Jeb Stuart's cavalry was covering the flank.
The Federal cavalry, on the other hand, managed to play a
most insignificant part in the Battle of Fredericksburg, being

conspicuous chiefly by its absence or at least inactivity on the Confederate side of the river. The fault lay not with the mounted troops themselves, but with the high-ranking Federal generals who had never taken the trouble to learn how to employ cavalry as a combat arm and who concealed their ignorance by using the mounted regiments in fragmentary detachments on vague reconnaissance missions, as escorts to army and corps commanders, and as individual couriers. The Federal cavalry was destined to be rejuvenated and given appropriate combat missions in 1863, but such was not the case at Fredericksburg.

Calm and confident, Lee bided his time, employing his abundance of military gray matter in an unhurried, continuous evaluation of the situation from the standpoint both of his own forces and those of the enemy, with particular attention to possible plans open to Burnside. Unlike the Federal commander in his new role of army commander, Lee was a strong believer in seeing as much as possible for himself. He spent much time in the saddle visiting his corps and division commanders, examining battery positions, checking the advantageous and disadvantageous features of the terrain over which his men would have to fight. Thus he familiarized himself, personally and in advance, with any tactically favorable factors which might and usually did contribute to his apparently uncanny knack of being able to defeat his adversaries each time.

Early on the morning of December 11, Lee rode to Telegraph Hill, the highest elevation on Longstreet's line, which afforded an ideal observation post which overlooked the Rappahannock and the intervening open terrain south of the town, as well as the southern and western exits of Fredericksburg. It was the logical spot for a forward battle command post, not only because there was no better place from which to keep an eye on unfolding events in the maneuver area, but also because it was practically the center of the line which Lee had determined in his mind to occupy if and when the tactical situation should call for a wholly defensive battle by his army. Since it turned out just that way, Telegraph Hill became the spot where Lee spent most of his time after the battle was joined, and it became known thereafter as Lee's Hill.

Two Historic Plantations

Lee's forward command post afforded an excellent view of Stafford Heights across the Rappahannock, now covered for its full length by the yawning guns of Burnside's artillery. Even without his field glasses Lee couldn't fail to see George Washington's boyhood home. But in all probability his glance rested more often and with greater feeling on Chatham, otherwise known as the Lacy house, where in earlier years Lee was a regular visitor and in the garden of which he courted his bride-to-be, Mary Custis. Chatham, which served as Sumner's headquarters, was a plantation of several hundred acres that had been built about 1750 by William Fitzhugh. Situated on high ground overlooking the river and the town of Fredericksburg, opposite its north end and directly above the highway bridge over the

CHATHAM
Also known as the Lacy house. Used during the battle as Gen. Sumner's
headquarters.

Rappahannock, it served as a convenient Federal observation post during the battle. It was less effective than Lee's Hill, because of its location on the extreme right flank of the Union army. Visitors to the site of the Lacy house today will be disappointed to see, from the main highway, nothing recognizable of the famous old plantation. Nevertheless the original mansion, which has been remodeled in recent years, is still standing— somewhat back from the present highway.

Only a few hundred yards down river from Chatham, on the same Stafford Heights, is the site of Ferry farm. It is situated off the highway in the direction of the river and, like Chatham, looks down on the Rappahannock and across it to the center of present-day Fredericksburg. The original manor house has been superseded by a later model, built on the foundations of the home in which young George spent the better part of his boyhood—but the foundation outlines of the smokehouse and other outbuildings can be seen, together with a still standing, aged two-story frame building that proclaims to the believers and the skeptical alike that here was the first office in which the future President pursued his chosen profession of surveyor.

A cherry tree proudly spreads its branches within a few feet of the very spot where its famous ancestor allegedly bit the dust at the hands of the youthful hatchetman. A trip down the hill to the river bank will bring the curious visitor to the very spot where Washington threw a Spanish silver dollar across the intervening 275 feet of water, probably aiming it at the old ferry wharf which once marked the upper limit of navigation on the Rappahannock.

While on Telegraph Hill, Lee watched and listened to the Federal artillery bombardment of Fredericksburg, remarking bitterly on the destruction of the homes of civilians. He received with evident pleasure the periodic reports from Barksdale on his success in rebuffing the efforts of the Federal engineers to lay their bridges. Federal success in completing the two bridges at Deep Run before noon, and the upper bridges in the late afternoon, seemed to have little effect on Lee's immediate plans for

FEDERAL UNITS CROSSING ON THE EVENING OF THE 11TH

the redisposition of Jackson's four divisions, still at Port Royal, Skinker's Neck, Guiney's Station, and the Yerby house below the Massaponax.

Why didn't Lee react more positively to make Franklin pay a higher price for the privilege of crossing at Deep Run? Mere token resistance was offered by the Confederates at that point; Stuart's cavalry was available and the redoubtable Pelham alone, with his artillery battery, could have made Franklin's move to the south shore an expensive piece of business. There is only one answer that makes sense; Lee *wanted* the Army of the Potomac to come across and put the river at its back so that its attack would be made against a strongly-defended line of hills. Such an assault would be launched from a narrow zone in which it would be difficult for large troop units to maneuver, and would cause the normal development from column to line to become a difficult if not extremely hazardous undertaking. It probably would have pleased Lee had Franklin come across while Sumner and Hooker were still on the other side, although that is mere speculation.

Darkness had fallen on the evening of Thursday, December 11, before the town of Fredericksburg was given up by McLaws' Confederate Division and taken over by Howard's Second Division of Couch's corps and Hawkins' brigade of Getty's division. The marching and countermarching at the Deep Run bridges was over for the night and one Federal brigade (Devens') manned Franklin's bridgehead on the south shore.

Lee Calmly Shifts His Weight

Then and only then did Lee make the first move to pull in any of Jackson's corps. A. P. Hill's Division was ordered up from Yerby's and Taliaferro's from Guiney's Station, with instructions to occupy the ridge immediately behind the railroad, extending Longstreet's line to the south and relieving Hood's Division which had been temporarily overextended to cover the right of the position.

The situation as it was developing began to have all the earmarks of another Antietam, on the occasion of which battle Jackson's corps was engaged in taking over Harpers Ferry as McClellan moved against the other half of Lee's army at Sharpsburg, some fifteen miles away. Here at Fredericksburg it just didn't make sense to Lee that Burnside would seriously consider a concentrated frontal attack with his entire army against the prepared and natural defensive position occupied by Longstreet, and thus forfeit the opportunity to use his preponderance of manpower by executing a turning movement against Lee's vulnerable right.

Lee naturally gave Burnside credit for a reasonable amount of intelligence. He was still unwilling to believe that the Deep Run crossing was intended as anything more than a feint and that the principal mass of maneuver would operate from the direction of the Skinker's Neck-Port Royal area. Therefore he allowed the divisions of Early and D. H. Hill to remain where they were—determined that they would stay until Burnside should lay all his cards on the table.

Heavy fog again covered the area on the morning of December 12, forming a curtain that prevented the Confederates from observing enemy movements on their front. Sporadic Federal shelling of Fredericksburg punctuated the morning calm, but Lee did not reply. He was conserving his ammunition and sticking to his decision not to shell the town, so the explosives came only from the guns of the attackers. During the morning

A. P. Hill and Taliaferro moved into their new positions. When the fog lifted about noon Lee rode over to the right with Jackson on a personal reconnaissance to see what might be going on down by the Richmond Road in Jackson's sector.

Von Borcke, a huge Prussian volunteer who was a member of Stuart's staff, joined the generals and reported that the Federals were massing in front of the Confederate right, that he had personally been close to their advance units and seen them himself. This was important intelligence, but Lee still wanted the more positive confirmation that his own eyes and ears would give him. So off they rode, Lee, Jackson, and von Borcke, in the direction of Deep Run. Approaching the point that von Borcke had recently left, the distinguished entourage dismounted and on foot crept along a ditch to within rifle range of the Federal troops, from which covered approach they were able to observe through their field glasses a panorama of Blue troop movements of such magnitude as to convince Lee that a general advance was underway. As far as the eye could see, regiment after regiment of infantry was moving steadily down to the river and across two of the pontoon bridges, while on the other, artillery and wagon trains were following one another in closed-up formation.

That was enough for Lee and Jackson. It was almost unbelievable, but the evidence before his own eyes was what Lee had been waiting for. It was now apparent that Burnside's pivot would execute a holding attack to keep Longstreet pinned down at Fredericksburg, while the major attack would be made against Lee's vulnerable right flank. In Lee's estimation that was infinitely better than a turning movement at Port Royal, which would inevitably have forced him into the more difficult maneuver of having to disengage in the face of a superior force and fall back on his originally conceived line on the North Anna River, thirty-six miles further south in the direction of Richmond.

As Lee and Jackson retraced their steps and remounted, Jackson was dismissed with instructions to order Early and D. H. Hill to lose no time in rejoining the main body. The two

FRANKLIN'S DIVISION

generals went their separate ways with minds turning over rapidly as they digested this fresh information and mentally weighed the tactical plans that would be formulated promptly to prepare for the passage-at-arms now clearly forecast for the following day.

History Repeats Itself

Thanks to Burnside's slowness in effecting the development of his army and initiating the attack even after the bridgeheads had been safely secured, Lee was given an additional day and two nights to evaluate his opponent's plan and make his own dispositions to meet it. Just as at Antietam, where Lee had succeeded in conćentrating his army at the point of impact at the psychological moment to turn imminent defeat into a stalemate, so at Fredericksburg he waited patiently for Burnside to reveal his intentions. Then he moved with confident alacrity to con-

CROSSING THE RAPPAHANNOCK

solidate his two wings on an almost impregnable defensive position whose Achilles' heel could be pierced only by a general with more ability than the ill-fated Burnside could bring to bear.

D. H. Hill had much the longer march to bring him back to the main position, but both Early and Hill made good time in forced marches, so that shortly after daylight on December 13 the Army of Northern Virginia was snugly posted on the high ground all the way from Longstreet's left on the Rappahannock to Jackson's right at Hamilton's Crossing, with Stuart's two brigades of cavalry and horse artillery hinging the door and covering the flank in the mile-wide space between Hamilton's Crossing and the Rappahannock, at right angles to the main Confederate line and astride the Richmond Road.

As finally placed, Longstreet was covering about five miles of front, while Jackson's frontage was less than two miles. But

Longstreet could defend with very little depth, while Jackson had a more difficult assignment which called for a flexible defense in depth and a readiness to shift his forces on short notice to counter possible penetrations or turning movements by the Union army.

The actual troop density was about nine men per yard of

MAJOR GENERAL GEORGE E. PICKETT, C.S.A.

front in Jackson's sector, three per yard along the two miles of Marye's Heights, and approximately six per yard spread over the remainder of the line, including Stuart's flank position. However, the new military road which the Confederates had constructed along the rear of their position nullified the military significance of such academic calculations, for Lee was able to shift troops readily from one place to another whenever and from whatever direction the threat should come.

Infantry entrenchments and earthworks for artillery positions were traced lightly, but strong fortifications were not constructed. These were built after the first day's fighting was over, when Lee confidently expected the Union army to renew the attack. The trenches with their parapets are even today clearly defined, from the left flank to the right, along the military crest of the ridge in some places and at the foot of the ridge in others, particularly along the line held by McLaws' Division.

Jackson put A. P. Hill's Division in the forward position, in

BRIGADIER GENERAL JUBAL A. EARLY, C.S.A.

two lines, with the front line along the railroad, while the divisions of Taliaferro and Early were placed side by side as a third line. D. H. Hill was posted south of the Mine Road, as corps reserve in a position of readiness, with the possibility that his divison might become the front line if the Federals should succeed in penetrating Stuart's screen and coming in on the rear around Hamilton's Crossing. Jackson's battle command post was on Prospect Hill, behind A. P. Hill's second line and in front of Early's Division, where he was in position to observe the front and exercise close control of his several divisions.

Thus massed on the wooded hills on Lee's right flank, 39,000 men of Jackson's corps waited for the fog to lift on December 13.

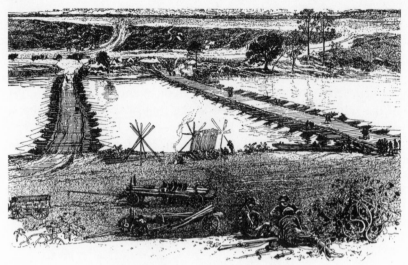

PONTOON BRIDGES AT FRANKLIN'S CROSSING

CHAPTER 9

OVER THE RIVER—AT LAST!

WASHINGTON, December 11, 1862.
Major-General BURNSIDE.

Permit me to suggest the importance of pushing re-enforcements across during the night, so as to be able to resist any attack during the morning. This seems to me of vital importance.

H. W. HALLECK,
General-in-Chief.

The most surprising thing about that message is that it should have been necessary for Halleck to even think of sending it. It failed of its purpose nevertheless. Earlier in the evening of December 11 Burnside had sent two dispatches to Halleck which informed him that *four* bridges had been laid and the fifth was expected to be completed during the night; that one division was across and occupying Fredericksburg, and he "hoped to have the main body over early tomorrow." Though not reported at this time, Burnside had six bridges laid by the morning of December 12.

Something was seriously wrong with Burnside. Either his

154

mental apparatus wasn't functioning or he was grossly incompetent. Probably both. One would expect an untrained junior officer to exercise sounder judgment than to talk, as Burnside had, about springing a surprise on Lee by an expeditious crossing at Deep Run that would catch him with his saddlebags down, and then, after taking all of one day to lay his bridges and cross a token force, to allow the succeeding night to pass without pouring over as many additional divisions as the logistical factors would permit.

Burnside appears to have had inhibitions about river obstacles and may still have been obsessed by the fear that had caused him in mid-November to withhold approval when Sumner first arrived and wanted to cross the river by fording. Such a move was entirely feasible at the time, because the rains had not started, but Burnside was fearful of a situation which might split his army and leave Sumner's 30,000 troops unsupported and at the mercy of the Confederates.

In any case, willingness such as characterized Lee to take a calculated risk wasn't one of the fixations which troubled Burnside. Neither, apparently, was experience in or even a desire to attempt a night operation. Yet a movement across the river under cover of darkness, with a short march to a jump-off position, would have permitted an attack on Jackson before Early and D. H. Hill arrived at the defensive position. It would have been a potential asset that could have chalked up a credit line on the Burnside balance sheet, which up to this time had already recorded quite a number of liabilities, with only the initial and praiseworthy march from Warrenton to Falmouth on the asset side.

We are not told what impression, if any, Halleck's message urging that reinforcements be pushed across the river during the night may have made on Burnside's mind. Presumably he had already decided not to do so, and, since Halleck hadn't shown much interest in his tactical plans, Burnside ignored the suggestion, and went back to sleep. Whatever he may have thought, no change was made in the orders and the night passed uneventfully for the shivering soldiers on both sides of the river.

A Busy Morning for the Union Army

The weather early on the morning of December 12 was a duplicate of that of the day before—a heavy, damp mist which served the Union army well in concealing its movements. The infantry and artillery columns moved up unmolested to the crossings in accordance with the prearranged time and space table.

Burnside was keeping a tight rein on his three grand division commanders, allowing them little discretion. After the battle was over, and he had had time to think back over it, he made it appear in his report that his plan had been to fight a holding action against the heights west of Fredericksburg, with Sumner's right wing, while Franklin with the left wing would envelop the Confederate flank. Even in that report it is not clear whether Burnside meant the right flank of the Confederate ridge position or the left flank of Jackson's corps which he thought was waiting for him down around Port Royal.

Everything might have worked out nicely had Lee been more accommodating and played the game the way Burnside planned it. No doubt the latter consoled himself with the thought that he was controlling his corps and divisions in a masterly, flexible manner to prevent them from getting themselves involved in uncoordinated piecemeal attacks until the master mind should be fully ready to turn them loose. The fact was that it was an *indecisive* mind and an unsure hand that was directing the destinies of the Army of the Potomac. One could feel sorry for Burnside at Fredericksburg if he could dismiss from his mind the holocaust of death that Burnside's fumbling strategy was to visit on so many thousands of Union soldiers on December 13.

The morning of December 12 was a busy one for Federal commanders and staffs. A thrilling sight would have been presented to the Confederates had the fog permitted their observers to watch the Union army as it marched by the tens of thousands over the six swaying pontoon bridges. At the corps and division levels were experienced generals who knew their way around, and under whose watchful eyes the brigades and regiments were directed, via the upper bridges, across the river and forward into the streets of Fredericksburg, and by way of the lower bridges on to the plain below the town.

The Confederates were satisfied to mark time on December 12 as they waited for Jackson's last two divisions to rejoin them, so Burnside's forces were not attacked as the columns poured in unending procession across the six bridges and into the limited area between the hostile defense line and the river.

The Federal march table provided that Couch's Second Corps would be the first to cross at Fredericksburg, followed by Willcox's Ninth Corps, the former to fan out for occupation of the center and northern portion of the town, the latter to extend the line to the south, without any indication as to the position on which his left flank should rest. Next day however Willcox did receive orders to extend to the left and connect with Franklin's right at Deep Run. Hazel Run was designated as the dividing line between the two corps.

FEDERALS OCCUPYING FREDERICKSBURG ON DECEMBER 12

At the lower bridges where Franklin's grand division crossed, Smith's corps led the way, followed by Reynolds' corps. By late afternoon the entire force had completed the passage of the river and formed in a continuous arc composed of four divisions in two successive lines, Smith's right resting astride Deep Run, Reynolds' left on the Rappahannock; one division of each corps,

BRIGADIER GENERAL DAVID BIRNEY

Doubleday's and Newton's, being held in reserve near the river. There they bivouacked for the night, halted in place, without orders from higher up for further movement or action and with nothing to do but wait for Burnside to release another fragment of his fuzzy tactical plan.

Six divisions were thus crowded into and immediately south of Fredericksburg and six more bivouacked below Deep Run, while across the river Hooker had been directed to send two divisions (Birney's and Sickles') of Stoneman's Third Corps, and Willcox to move one of his divisions down to the vicinity of the lower bridges, as potential support for Franklin's grand division.

Including Bayard's cavalry of 3,500 troopers, his own grand division, and the three support divisions from Hooker and Sumner, Franklin now had available on both sides of the river upwards of 54,000 men for the major effort that he was to be called upon to make on the following morning.

Sumner's strength was now down to 27,000 and Hooker

BRIGADIER GENERAL DANIEL E. SICKLES

had 31,000 more, but all three of the major commanders were still in a state of uncertainty as to just what Burnside expected them to do now that most of them were parked within less than a mile of the dug-in Confederates on their comfortable tree-covered ridge.

Federal Artillery Skillfully Handled

General Henry J. Hunt, Chief of Artillery of the Army of the Potomac, was indisputably the ablest artillerist of the Civil War, on either side. In preparation for Burnside's crossing of the Rappahannock, he withdrew temporarily all division artillery except one battery which was retained by each division, and at-

FEDERAL RESERVE ARTILLERY
Battery C, 3d U.S. Artillery (Gibson).

tached the mass to the Artillery Reserve, under his own immediate control. Through this organizational device he was able
to arm Stafford Heights, one hundred and fifty feet above the
water-line, with 147 guns, extending all the way from Falmouth
to Pollock's Mill downriver. As usual, under Hunt's direction,
the Federal artillery was emplaced with great skill, prepared to
consider all conceivable fire missions, including counterbattery
fire, protection for the laying of the bridges, prevention of the
movement of possible Confederate reinforcements into Fredericksburg (had they undertaken it), and providing flank protection for the army. When the divisions crossed the river their
light artillery rejoined them.

Having graduated from West Point in 1839 in the same class
with Henry W. Halleck, Hunt won his initial battle spurs as
a battery commander in the Mexican War, in which he fought
with conspicuous gallantry through every battle of Scott's great
campaign from Vera Cruz to the capital of the Montezumas.
During the four years preceding the outbreak of the Civil War
he served as a member of the Board charged with revising the
system of light artillery tactics, and so well did he perform
that task that the Federal artillery functioned throughout the

war at a high pitch of efficiency, proving itself superior to the
Confederate artillery in a majority of the important battles.
Hunt, who directed the Union artillery in all the early battles
of the war, was elevated to Chief of Artillery of the Army of
the Potomac in September 1862 and held that high position
right through to the end at Appomattox.

All the guns on Stafford Heights were rifled; twenty-two
were 20- pounder Parrotts, seven were 4½-inch siege guns, four-
teen were light 12-pounders, thirty-four were 3-inch rifles and
the remaining eighty-four guns were light rifles. The Parrotts
were not as effective as they were cracked up to be. Hunt was
most critical of their performance in his post-battle report,
when he informed the Ordnance Department that they had
functioned unsatisfactorily because of the imperfection of the
projectiles, which he complained were almost as dangerous to
the Union troops as to the enemy and also because the guns
themselves were unsafe and frequently burst near the muzzle.
He added that they were too heavy for satisfactory use and were
suitable chiefly as batteries of position, since they required

PROVOST DETACHMENT GUARDING LOOT IN FREDERICKSBURG

just as many horses and as many drivers to move them as the heavy 4½-inch siege guns.

Nineteen batteries, a total of 104 guns, crossed the river with Sumner's grand division, although during the battle the greater number of the guns could not be used because they were shielded by the buildings. Only seven batteries with Sumner's divisions were either wholly or partly engaged on December 13.

Seventeen batteries for a total of 86 guns crossed with Franklin, and when Sickles' and Birney's divisions of Hooker's grand division were assigned to reinforce Franklin's wing, five additional batteries of 30 guns crossed the river. The battle on the south flank was more open and in that area practically all the guns were effectively employed.

Campfires at night in close proximity to the enemy were not permitted on this occasion, so about all the soldiers in the town had to occupy their attention was the pleasure of looting the houses, which they proceeded to do on the grand scale until their officers put a stop to it. Huge piles of furniture and other household goods were stacked on the Fredericksburg side of the river when details from the Provost Marshal's Detachment picketed the crossings and halted the spreading vandalism.

Burnside Temporizes as His Generals Mark Time

During the late afternoon of December 12 Gen. Franklin, commanding the Left Grand Division, and his corps commanders Reynolds and Smith, all of whom were on the closest official and personal terms, assembled for a conference at the "Bernard house," Franklin's field headquarters.

This place, which Franklin had selected as the command post from which to direct the operations of his reinforced grand division, was a large plantation originally known as "Old Mansfield." At the time of the battle the proprietor was named Bernard, a large slave owner. Bernard objected violently to the Union occupation of his residence, whereupon he was unceremoniously hustled across the river, at Reynold's order, by a brace of pleased soldiers. The Bernard cabins, incidentally, which housed the plantation's slaves, were some distance further away, at the northern extremity of A. P. Hill's position, and so were not similarly disturbed. The ruins of the plantation can still be seen near the river a half mile north of Smithfield. The latter sounds as though it should have been a village; actually it was merely another plantation which was converted into a Federal hospital after the battle, and is today the Fredericksburg Country Club.

Franklin, Reynolds, and Smith discussed the situation and compared notes. They were in agreement that the only sensible attack plan for their wing would be to form their divisions into two assault columns on either side of the Richmond Road and to turn Lee's flank at whatever cost.

About 5 P. M. Burnside showed up, was taken on a quick gallop along the lines, and then sat down with Franklin for a talk, at which time he was urged to authorize the latter to carry out the aforementioned plan. When Burnside left, the other three generals were under the distinct impression that he had given tacit approval and was returning to his headquarters to compose the orders. They proceeded to work out the details for the attack which they thought they were authorized to launch, and then sat around for hours waiting for the order so that they might issue last-minute instructions to their subordinate commanders and get a few hours of sleep.

But nothing happened, so at 3 A. M. December 13 Reynolds turned in for the night and after a further period of frustrating delay the other generals did likewise. It was not until 7:45 A. M. that the long awaited order was delivered to Franklin by General Hardie of Burnside's staff, who had been dispatched with instructions to stay with Franklin during the battle in order to keep the army commander informed of its progress. The delay in drafting and issuing this order was one of the most serious mistakes made by Burnside.

These are the "attack" orders issued by Burnside over the signature of his Chief-of-Staff, General Parke:

BATTERY D, 2D U.S. ARTILLERY IN POSITION NEAR MANSFIELD

HEADQUARTERS ARMY OF THE POTOMAC,
December 13, 1862—5.55 a.m.

Major-General FRANKLIN,

Commanding Left Grand Division, Army of the Potomac:

General Hardie will carry this dispatch to you, and remain with you during the day. The general commanding directs that you keep your whole command in position for a rapid movement down the old Richmond road, and you will send out at once a division at least to pass below Smithfield to seize, if possible, the height near Captain Hamilton's, on this side of the Massaponax, taking care to keep it well supported and its line of retreat open. He has ordered another column of a division or more to be moved from General Sumner's command up the Plank road to its intersection with the Telegraph road, where they will divide, with a view to seizing the heights on both of these roads. Holding these two heights, with the heights near Captain Hamilton's, will, he hopes, compel the enemy to evacuate the whole ridge between these points. He makes these moves by columns distant from each other, with a view of avoiding the possibility of a collision of our own forces, which might occur in a general movement during a fog. Two of General Hooker's divisions are in your rear, at the bridges, and will remain there as supports.

The Bernard house may be seen dimly in the grove at the upper right.

Copies of instructions given to Generals Sumner and Hooker will be forwarded to you by an orderly very soon. You will keep your whole command in readiness to move at once, as soon as the fog lifts. The watchword, which, if possible, should be given to every company, will be "Scott."

I have the honor to be, general, your obedient servant,

JNO. G. PARKE,
Chief-of-Staff

HEADQUARTERS ARMY OF THE POTOMAC,
December 13, 1862—6 a.m.

Maj. Gen. E. V. SUMNER,
Commanding Right Grand Division, Army of the Potomac:

The general commanding directs that you extend the left of your command to Deep Run, connecting with General Franklin, extending your right as far as your judgment may dictate. He also directs that you push a column of a division or more along the Plank and Telegraph roads, with a view to seizing the heights in the rear of the town. The latter movement should be well covered by skirmishers, and supported so as to keep its line of retreat open. Copy of instructions given to General Franklin will be sent to you very soon. You will please await them at your present headquarters, where he (the general commanding) will meet you. Great care should be taken to prevent a collision of our own forces during the fog. The watchword for the day will be "Scott." The column for a movement up the Telegraph and Plank roads will be got in readiness to move, but will not move till the general commanding communicates with you.

I have the honor to be, general, very respectfully, your obedient servant,

JNO. G. PARKE,
Chief-of-Staff

HEADQUARTERS ARMY OF THE POTOMAC,
December 13, 1862—7 a.m.

Maj. Gen. JOSEPH HOOKER,
Commanding Center (Grand) Division, Army of the Potomac:

The general commanding directs that you place General Butterfield's corps and Whipple's division in position to cross, at a moment's notice, at the three upper bridges, in support of the other troops over the river, and the two remaining divisions of General Stoneman's corps in readiness to cross at the lower ford, in support of General Franklin. The general commanding will meet you at headquarters (Phillips house) very soon. Copies of instructions to General Sumner and General Franklin will be sent to you.

I have the honor to be, general, your obedient servant.

JNO. G. PARKE,
Chief-of-Staff

Burnside's Ex-Post-Facto Explanation

In Burnside's official report on the battle he states that it was after midnight when he returned to his headquarters following visits to the different commands and "before daylight of the 13th" prepared the orders quoted in the preceding paragraphs. Burnside then goes on to say:

It should be mentioned that on the evening of the 12th I ordered General Stoneman, with two divisions of his corps, to a point near the lower bridges, as support for General Franklin.

ESTABLISHING COMMUNICATION

These are not early-day flagpole sitters, but members of the U.S. Military Telegraph Construction Corps erecting a pole line. Telegraphic communications were habitually established between Washington and the army in the field, and between army headquarters and the corps. This was supplemented by semaphor from constructed towers or from existing hills or steeples. From December 11 to 13, 1862, four such signal stations were engaged in observing and reporting operations. The flag station at the Phillips house supplemented Burnside's field telegraph connection with Couch's command post in the Fredericksburg courthouse by means of signalmen in the courthouse steeple. The latter's activity finally attracted the attention of the Confederate batteries, whose shells killed 20 men in a nearby field hospital and brought about a cessation of the signalling.

The forces now under command of General Franklin consisted of about 60,000 men,* as shown by the morning reports, and was composed as follows:

Sixth Corps 24,000
First Corps 18,500
Third Corps (two divisions) 10,000
Ninth Corps (Burns' division) 4,000
Bayard's cavalry 3,500

General Sumner had about 27,000 men, comprising his own grand division, except Burns' division of the Ninth Corps. General Hooker's command was about 26,000

*There is a disparity of about 6,000 men between the strength figures used respectively by Burnside and Franklin.

Burnside includes the 14,000 men of the Third and Ninth Corps, in support position but not assigned to Franklin's command.

strong, two of General Stoneman's divisions having reported to General Franklin.

Positive information had reached me that the enemy had built a new road** in rear of the ridge or crest, from near Hamilton's to the Telegraph road, along which road they communicated from one part of their line to the other. I decided to seize, if possible, a point on this road near Hamilton's which would not divide the enemy's forces by

** Shown on Map 7 as the Military Road. This portion of the road was cut through by Gen. Hood while his division was occupying that part of the line—Ed.

BRIGADIER GENERAL GEORGE STONEMAN
Commander of the Third Corps shown with his staff.

breaking their line, but would place our forces in position to enable us to move in rear of the crest, and either force its evacuation or the capitulation of the forces occupying it.

It was my intention, in case this point had been gained, to push Generals Sumner and Hooker against the left of the crest, and prevent at least the removal of the artillery of the enemy, in case they attempted a retreat. The above orders were prepared in accordance with these views.

It will be seen that General Franklin was directed to seize, if possible, the heights near Captain Hamilton's, and to send at once a column of attack for that purpose, composed of a division at least, in the lead, well supported, and to keep his whole command in readiness to move down the old Richmond road. The object of this order is clear. It was necessary to seize this height in order to enable the remainder of his forces to move down the old Richmond road, with a view of getting in rear of the enemy's line on the crest. He was ordered to seize these heights, if possible, and to do it at once. I sent him a copy of the order to General Sumner, in which it will be seen that I directed General Sumner's column not to move until he received orders from me, while he (General Franklin) was ordered to move at once. The movements were not intended to be simultaneous; in fact, I did not intend to move General Sumner until I learned that Franklin was about to gain the heights near Hamilton's, which I then supposed he was entirely able to do. I sent the order to General Franklin by General James A. Hardie, a member of my staff; it reached him at 7.30 a.m.

Significantly Burnside makes no reference to his discussion earlier in the evening with General Franklin, nor does he explain why he allowed the night of December 12-13 to pass without giving his army any indication whatsoever as to his specific attack plans. It will never be known whether Burnside was tired, took a nap and overslept, or simply couldn't make up his mind. Certainly the written orders and his own report, studied together, indicate a man on the horns of a dilemma, finally dredging up a general idea since he had to issue some kind of attack orders.

The traditional "fog of war" which normally hinders the

tactical vision of the commander of a large body of troops in contact with the enemy was on this occasion thickened by a Burnside-induced fog that blew in on an unhappy Franklin in the form of the belated order which Hardie delivered in person after taking time out for a hearty breakfast. It will be noted that Franklin's message, postmarked 5.55 A.M., the hour it was presumably signed by Burnside's Chief-of-Staff, was handed to Franklin at his headquarters, the Bernard house, one hour and fifty minutes later, although the distance between the respective headquarters was a mere two and a half miles by road, a matter of fifteen minutes at an easy hand gallop.

The Army Orders Are Still Indecisive

The orders to General Sumner in Fredericksburg involved for the time being merely an extension of the current deployment of his divisions in preparation for an assault by a single division, and that only when Burnside should give the signal. Hooker's order told him only that he was to place his divisions near the bridges on the east side of the river, prepared to support the forthcoming attack by the two grand divisions already across. The wording of this order was so phrased as to keep the troops under Hooker's immediate direction, which meant control by Burnside.

It was the order to Franklin, who was to make the major attack with more than half of the army at his disposal, that caused the greatest consternation in the minds of Franklin, Reynolds, and Smith, because it was entirely different from their own conception, which they had been confident Burnside had accepted the evening before. Obviously Burnside was sending a boy to do a man's job when he ordered one division from each wing to initiate a pseudo-coordinated attack under conditions of poor visibility, at a time when everybody else was convinced that their only hope lay in a powerful flanking assault against Lee's right, the sole weak spot along his entire position.

The phrase "if possible," the use of the verb "seize" rather than "carry" or "capture and hold at all costs," the timid caution to "keep the line of retreat open," and the reference to possible collision with friendly troops in the fog—these were Milquetoast terms that could hardly be expected to put confidence and the offensive spirit into the minds and hearts of able corps and division commanders, and an aggregation of stout fighting men who had already, and for quite some time, been convinced that they were being led down a blind alley by a blindfolded leader.

Franklin's own plan was indeed the one that made sense, and by all the rules of warfare it should have succeeded handsomely. If Burnside had been less enamored of his own brainchild, which unfortunately was an anemic cripple even in the embryo, he would have approved Franklin's plan, issued by 9 P.M. a simple army attack order effective at daylight December 13, and gone to bed, with justifiable confidence that the next day Lee and not he, Burnside, would have to do the worrying.

With their hands thus untied, Sumner, Franklin, and Hooker could have coordinated their attack orders at an hour's conference, crossed two of Hooker's divisions at the lower bridges to replace Smith's corps as bridgehead security, (as Franklin had vainly urged Burnside to do), moved their assault divisions to the jump-off positions before daylight, and thus have faced at daylight a hopeful set of circumstances that would in all likelihood have resulted in a battle with the odds heavily weighted in favor of the Union army.

Instead of which, Burnside shackled his subordinate commanders to a role of virtual rubber stamps, delayed interminably the use of the stamp, and when he did finally apply it to the ink pad, the resulting impression was so difficult to read that the Union cause would have been better served had Burnside in his youth never learned to read or write.

MEADE'S MEN CHARGING ACROSS THE RAILROAD

CHAPTER 10

FEDERAL FAILURE ON SOUTH FLANK

To ACHIEVE more than a superficial understanding of the Battle of Fredericksburg requires time and patience on the part of the reader, whether he be a serious student of military tactics or merely one who is casually interested in Civil War campaigns and battles. The characteristics of the Fredericksburg battlefield, both natural and man-made, were such as to offer a surprisingly large number of tactical opportunities for the alert commander, from corps down to squad and even to the individual soldier. Maps 8 and 9 should prove helpful to an understanding of the battle itself.

Lee's Keen Appreciation of Terrain

The advantage of terrain lay with the defending Confederates, not only because nature had provided a range of wooded hills and complementary stream obstacles that cut across the plain over which the Union army was ordered to attack, but also because General Lee had a keen sense of terrain appreciation and an incomparable team of corps commanders in Longstreet and Jackson. These two distinguished generals had fought many a successful battle under every conceivable combination of circumstances, were completely en rapport with their army com-

172

mander, and were old hands at the game of making the most of what they had in materiel and manpower, in the character of the terrain, and the errors of their opponents.

Lee's ability to appraise the favorable and unfavorable aspects of the ground features and to dispose his forces to take full advantage thereof was never better exemplified than in his defensive strategy at Fredericksburg. By far the greater extent of his seven-mile-long position was occupied on the left by Longstreet's five-division corps of about 41,000 men, a line thinly held because Lee and Longstreet were both confident that the Federals could not successfully storm the heights or achieve a penetration on that front. For that reason, coupled with the fact that the ground was frozen hard and digging was difficult, little effort was made on Longstreet's section of the line to throw up infantry entrenchments or to emplace the guns in depressed pits except in very exposed locations.

In Jackson's sector the situation required a different type of defensive treatment. There, in the two mile stretch between Deep Run and Hamilton's Crossing, Lee massed Jackson's entire Second Corps of 39,000 men, exclusive of Stuart's cavalry and artillery, disposed in depth to make the best possible use of cover, elevation, ravines, and streams. The heights were covered with a dense growth of timber, which was heavier than on Marye's Heights and the other hills to the north. While some attention was paid to building breastworks, in the time Burnside thoughtfully allowed him, Lee gave first priority to the important task of cutting roads through the woods in rear of the position, for lateral communication and to facilitate rapid movement of regiments or brigades in order to be prepared to meet the enemy with superior numbers at threatened points.

Jackson's theoretically vulnerable right flank may not actually have been so easy to turn as the map might indicate, because the valley of the Massaponax Creek, which cut the line of hills at Hamilton's Crossing, had some marshy characteristics. Also, the creek itself, running east and west about a half mile below Prospect Hill, the nose of the ridge where Jackson established his battle command post on the extreme right, was a positive obstacle not easily surmounted by enemy troops under battle conditions. In those days troops attacked in parade-ground formation, and, when a line was broken, confusion and loss of control resulted.

The canny Lee shrewdly anticipated and prepared for every

MAJOR GENERAL J. B. HOOD, C.S.A.

possible tactical maneuver that Burnside might conceive, personally directing the posting of many of the 306 artillery guns which were skillfully sited along the seven-mile position, while on the right flank, where a turning movement seemed to be the most logical move for the Union army, Jackson's corps and Stuart's cavalry were ready and willing.

The Union army, on the other hand, found itself in a most unenviable position, awkwardly straddling an unfordable river with only a handful of tenuous lifelines against a possible disaster that might necessitate a hazardous withdrawal. Six narrow, shaky threads that were the bridges were capable of being

HAY'S BRIGADE, EARLY'S DIVISION, NEAR HAMILTON'S CROSSING

destroyed by Confederate artillery fire if Lee should change his mind and decide that the loss of property along the eastern fringe of Fredericksburg was not too high a price to pay for a Federal debacle.

An army of over 100,000 men even moving in close order requires plenty of space in which to maneuver for effective work. It takes a lot of marching and deployment and the intelligent transmission and understanding of a succession of orders down through the chain of command to prepare such a large body of troops for a coordinated assault, if the attack is to attain any measure of success.

It may be unkind to say it, but in retrospect it appears that Lee had not two, but three corps commanders to help him, and the name of the third was Burnside. Burnside's bungling had finally put the Army of the Potomac in a position where nothing but sheer guts and the stout hearts of a mighty host of fighting men would serve to extricate them. He had managed to maneuver them into a serious pocket, a relatively shallow oval-shaped area, with a narrow open end at the south between

Hamilton's Crossing and the Rappahannock; except that it wasn't a real opening for the reason that Stuart's cavalry and Pelham's artillery were blocking a possible end run on that flank. At the backs of the Union army was the Rappahannock River and directly to their front rose a formidable row of hills bristling for seven miles with gray-clad soldiers who were figuratively licking their chops as they waited, poised, for the "blue bellies" to "come and get it."

The preliminaries were now out of the way and the gladiators were on the battlefield, over 200,000 of them, facing one another and ready to spring. Some 90,000 confident Confederates, knowing exactly what they intended to do and determined to add one more to their string of victories, were pitted at close quarters against 120,000 Federals, with 26,000 more in reserve a few miles away and about 50,000 others protecting the upper Potomac and the defenses of Washington.

Historians have always experienced great difficulty in reconciling Confederate strength figures as given by the various generals in their own written accounts, frequently long after the event, with the strength reports in the *Official Records of the Rebellion*. This may be partly explained by the fact that straggling was even more a matter of concern to the Confederate high command than to the Federal. Among the Southern sol-

---

MAP 9. THE SITUATION JUST BEFORE DAWN ON DECEMBER 13, 1862
Federal divisions selected to make the attack have crossed the river and are bivouacked in the positions shown. The Confederates, having watched or heard them cross, are aware that an attack is pending, but are uncertain as to where the main effort, if any, will be made. But by now Lee is satisfied that there will be no wide turning movement to the south, in the Port Royal area, and he is moving Jackson's two flank divisions up to the vicinity of Hamiltons Crossing, where they will arrive about daybreak. The positions of Hunt's reserve artillery east of the river are indicated though the names of the batteries are not shown. Similarly the Confederate battery positions are shown by symbols which do not necessarily indicate the number of guns in each emplacement. It will be noted that a sixth pontoon bridge is now in place, making three at Franklin's crossing site. This bridge was built late on the 11th. There were few displacements of artillery during the battle, except for the release of some of the organic batteries accompanying the attacking Federal divisions. Therefore, for simplicity, artillery positions will not be generally repeated on succeeding maps.

MAP 9.

diers it was not so much a matter of malingering as it was a privilege which many enjoyed, with considerable impunity in the early part of the war, of taking French leave between campaigns to fall out and visit with friends and acquaintances in home territory. There they could find food and shelter which was an improvement over the army ration and the open fields and woods. Consequently the custom became widespread, although most of the AWOL's were in the habit of rejoining their outfits whenever a battle appeared imminent.

Straggling has of course always been a serious headache in every army composed of a preponderance of untrained recruits who have not been physically hardened in campaign and have yet to learn how to take proper care of themselves. Even under a strict disciplinarian it always presents a problem that can be eradicated only by time and intensive training and marching. It must be concluded, therefore, that the official returns for the Confederates as a rule exceeded, by varying amounts and depending on other circumstances, the number of combat effectives under arms and present in person for any particular engagement. In this book the *Official Records* are used for strength figures wherever possible, without making allowance for stragglers, men on sick call, or engaged in administrative duties.

Franklin Gets Unexpected Orders

Once again the valley was covered with an early morning fog on Saturday, December 13, a day that was soon to terminate the career of many a good man. A high wind and bitterly cold night had caused such discomfort to the thousands of men resting on their arms on that congested battlefield-to-be that the chance to get into blood-warming action, even if it should hasten death or dismemberment, was preferable to freezing to death from numbing inaction.

Burnside was at least correct in expecting that there would be a fog, as on previous mornings, but that it would be dissipated in a couple of hours, as indeed it was. Meanwhile, as of 7:45 A.M., Franklin had his orders. A few minutes later corps

commanders Reynolds and Smith were given the bad news, and
the Left Grand Division began to stir.

Since Burnside had refused to release any of Hooker's divisions on the eastern shore, which would have freed Smith's
Sixth Corps for use as Franklin might see fit, without worrying
about bridgehead security, Franklin assigned the attack mis-

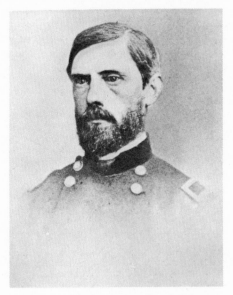

MAJOR GENERAL JOHN F. REYNOLDS

sion to Reynolds and his First Corps. Reynolds in turn selected
Meade's division, with Gibbon's in support, to spearhead the
advance "to seize if possible the heights near Captain Hamilton's, on this side of the Massaponax, taking care to keep it
well supported and its line of retreat open."

Scarcely an inspiring attack order, to say the least! Meade was
an excellent division commander, who had one of the best outfits in the army, although the smallest at Franklin's disposal,
with a strength of only about 4,500 men. It is assumed that he
and Reynolds kept the wording of Burnside's order to themselves; they must have if they expected the men of Meade's

regiments to put their hearts into the effort. Imagine telling a bunch of two-fisted soldiers to *try* and grab those hills up there by the crossroads *if possible,* with a promise to hold a path open for retreat!

Gibbon's division, slightly larger than Meade's, was directed to support Meade on the right, while Doubleday, commander of Reynold's remaining division, was held in reserve. By 8:30

MAP 10. ACTIONS ON THE SOUTH FLANK UP TO ABOUT NOON, DECEMBER 13
Meade moved out from his position near Smithfield at 8:30 A.M., his delay being due to the late arrival of orders from Burnside. He moved across the fields in column of brigades, parallel to the river for about 600 yards, then turned sharp right and headed for the sunken road which ran toward Bowling Green. Gibbon followed, deploying on his right. Doubleday followed Gibbon, continuing parallel to the river. When the two leading divisions reached the main road they came under enfilading fire from two guns commanded by Pelham. Meade advanced toward the Confederate position two or three hundred yards, then halted in the formation shown on this sketch. An artillery duel ensued for about two hours, as a result of which Pelham's advanced guns were withdrawn. General Hardie, of Burnside's staff, remained at the south flank in observation, his messages to Burnside giving a succinct description of events:

9 A.M.
General Meade just moved out. Doubleday supports him. Meade's skirmishers, however, engaged at once with enemy skirmishers. Battery opening on Meade, probably from position on old Richmond Road.
9:40 A.M.
Two batteries playing on Reynold's advance, in rear of his first line, cause him to desist the advance. They are on the Bowling Green Road, near the river. They must be silenced before he can advance. Heavy firing in our front.

11 A.M.
Meade advanced half a mile, and holds on. Infantry of enemy in wood in front of extreme left; also in front of Howe. No loss, so far, of great importance. Later.—Reynolds has been forced to develop his whole line. An attack of some force of enemy's troops on our left seems probable. Stoneman has been directed to cross one division to support our left.

12 Noon
Birney's division is now getting into position. That done, Reynolds will order Meade to advance. Batteries over the river are to shell the enemy's position in the wood in front of Reynold's left. He thinks the effect will be to promote Meade's advance. A column of the enemy's infantry is passing along the crest of the hills from right to left, as we look at it.

The last sentence of Hardie's message refers to the movement of D. H. Hill's division to a position on the flank as a countermove to a possible advance around the Confederate flank by Doubleday (see Map 11). It soon became evident that the Federals had no such intention, so Hill was moved back to his reserve position. No other shifts of Confederate forces, other than of some of Pelham's guns, were made by Jackson at this time.

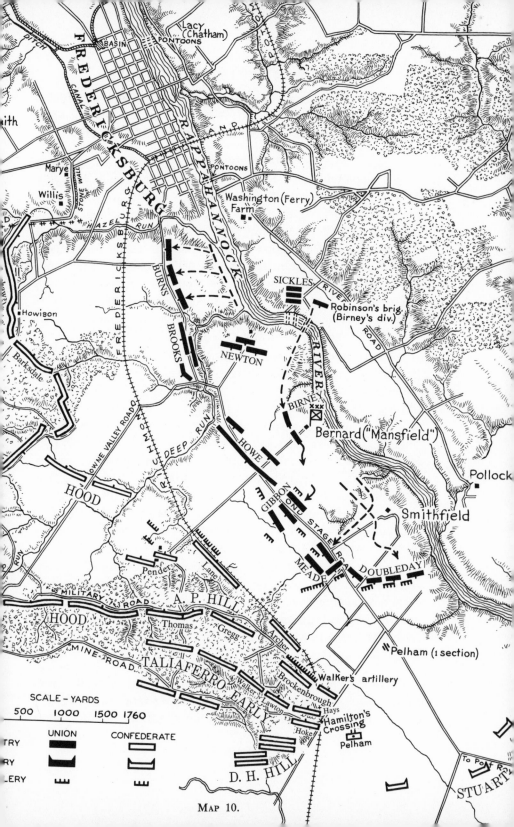

MAP 10.

A.M. Meade was ready to move out, a creditable piece of work considering the fact that only forty-five minutes had elapsed since Hardie reached Franklin with the unexpected order.

A Breath-Taking Military Pageant

The deployment of Reynold's corps began while the plain between the river and the Confederate heights as well as the town of Fredericksburg was covered by the dense fog of early morning. Aided by the low visibility, the forward movement of Meade's and Gibbon's divisions made excellent progress against only sporadic enemy gunfire which had no targets upon which to sight. The Confederates were aware that something interesting was afoot, for they could hear the sharp bark of commands all along the front even though they could see nothing through the heavy curtain of fog.

About 10 o'clock the brilliant rays of the sun struggled through the mists, which were quickly dissipated to reveal to the startled but admiring eyes of thousands of watchers on the hill a panorama that must have been breath-taking in its scope and grandeur. Like a suddenly rising curtain at the opening of a play, there was displayed Franklin's huge force of over 50,000 men, rank on rank, foot, horse, and artillery pieces, with the bright sun reflecting from thousands upon thousands of flashing bayonets, and with officers dashing up and down on galloping horses. The Left Grand Division covered the plain and presented a martial pageant that would never be forgotten by those who had the fortune to occupy front-row seats.

While it may sound like an anachronism to twentieth century veterans, adjutants were observed moving to the front of their regiments and reading battle orders, after which the successive lines of Federal troops, standards flying, moved out to battle as though on parade. The show was on!

Meade's Division Spearheads the Attack

Paced by bursting shells from scores of heavy field pieces which swept the plain before the advancing regiments, Meade's all-Pennsylvania division moved to the attack in line of brigade

GROUP OF DIVISION COMMANDERS
Left to right: Gibbon, French, Meade, Hunt, Humphreys, Sedgwick. Hunt
was army artillery commander. Sedgwick, a corps commander, was not at
Fredericksburg.

columns, two brigades in line abreast, with the third in column
echeloned to the left rear and the artillery advancing between
the two leading brigades. They crossed the Smithfield ravine
and turned sharply to the right across the Richmond Road.
From Deep Run to the far end of Meade's line this road was
sunken, in places six feet deep. The road offered protection,
but also was an obstacle to forward movement, consequently
there was a delay at this point while the men tore down the
hedge fences flanking the road and bridged the drainage ditches
on either side to provide a passage for the artillery. While this
work was in progress the division was badly hurt by converging
artillery fire from Jackson's batteries on the crest above Hamilton's Crossing and from Pelham's guns on the left. Reynold's
field guns promptly rushed forward to the rise of ground between the Richmond Road and the railroad and replied briskly
to the Confederate artillery fire, dividing their attention between
Jackson's guns on the heights and Stuart's on the flank.

After crossing the Richmond Road at a point approximately

a mile south of the Deep Run or Lansdowne Valley Road, Meade's advancing columns paralleled that road which cut through the line of hills occupied by the line of Confederates. Following Reynolds' instructions, their immediate objective was a point of woods which jutted out like a salient into the open end of the plain. That particular section of woods, as it turned out, offered a more gradual ascent for the attackers than did other portions of Jackson's line. It was Reynolds' plan that Meade's division would gain the crest and then turn left along it towards Jackson's right flank at Hamilton's Crossing, where the bulk of the enemy artillery appeared to be massed. Gibbon's division advanced on Meade's right, echeloned to the rear, brigades in successive lines. Gibbon's had suffered equally with Meade's from the Confederate shelling, especially from batteries near Bernard's cabins. At the same time, Reynolds directed Doubleday's division to change front to the left facing

---

MAP 11. THE ATTACK OF REYNOLDS' CORPS.
ACTIONS ON THE SOUTH FLANK UP TO ABOUT 1:30 P.M.
General Hardie's messages continue:

12:05 P.M.
General Meade's line is advancing in the direction you prescribed this morning.

1 P.M.
Enemy opened a battery on Reynolds, enfilading Meade. Reynolds has opened all his batteries on it. Reynolds hotly engaged at this moment.

1:15 P.M.
Heavy engagement of infantry where battery is. Meade is assaulting hill.

1:25 P.M.
Meade is in wood in his front. Seems to be able to hold on. Reynolds will push Gibbon in if necessary. The battery and wood referred to must be near Hamilton's house. The infantry fighting is prolonged and quite heavy. Things look well enough. Men in fine spirits.

1:40 P.M.
Meade having carried a portion of the enemy's position in the wood, we have 300 prisoners. Enemy's batteries on our extreme left retired. Tough work. Men fight well. Gibbon has advanced on Meade's right. Men fight well. Driving the enemy. Meade has suffered severely; Doubleday, to Meade's left, not engaged.

As described in the text, Meade's initial rush penetrated A. P. Hill's center, turned the flanks of and partially broke up Lane's, Archer's, and Gregg's brigades, and gained the new military road. Gibbon advanced only to the railroad. His men, seeing that no one on their right was advancing, and not being told that they were not to be supported by a general advance, were wavering and drifting to the rear. A. P. Hill has requested help from Early, and it is on the way, as the sketch shows.

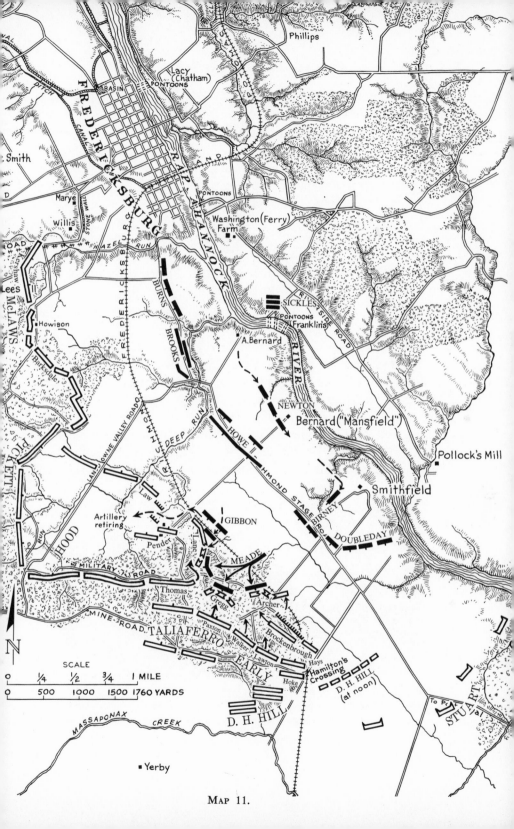

MAP 11.

BRIGADIER GENERAL MAXCY GREGG, C.S.A.
Killed on December 13 when his line was attacked by the Federals under Meade.

Stuart's cavalry on the flank, in order to take the weight off Meade's advancing left flank and to prevent a surprise attack from that quarter. Meade also took similar precautions by facing his reserve brigade to the left.

The Federals hugged the ground as the artillery duel raged for well over an hour. The redoubtable Pelham, commanding Stuart's artillery on the extreme Confederate right, stood well out in front of the cavalry with two venturesome guns exposed,

CONFEDERATE LINE IN THE WOODS

far to the front in the triangle formed by the junction of the
Mine Road with the Richmond Road. Nimbly shifting his guns
each time the Federals found his range, the young officer kept
many times his own number of Federal guns engaged until
Stuart, fearing to lose the brave but rash artilleryman, issued

BRIGADIER GENERAL C. F. JACKSON
One of Meade's brigade commanders; killed during the fighting in the woods.

peremptory orders that he give up the unequal gun fight and
retire to a safer position.

As Meade and Gibbon advanced, none of the Confederates
on the crest or forward slope of the wooded ridge were visible.
The attacking Federals were allowed to approach the railroad,
within 800 yards of the crest of the ridge, before running into
trouble. At that stage all the Confederate batteries opened
with a crash, with such effect that Meade's men were stopped
in their tracks, wavered, and pulled back. It began to appear
that the Federals had been stopped almost before they started,
because several hours now passed before they pulled themselves

together for a second attempt. About one o'clock the Federal batteries laid down a strong and well directed concentration of fire on the woods that were Meade's initial objective and the Confederate guns on either side of it. Under the protection of this fire Meade and Gibbon resumed their advance, crossed the railroad, and drove the Confederates back into the woods and up the hill.

Along the one and one-half mile front held by A. P. Hill's Confederate Division, the left of Archer's Brigade was separated from the right of Lane's Brigade by 500 yards of swampy woods which the Confederates had failed to reconnoiter carefully or which they negligently assumed could not be crossed by the enemy, overlooking the fact that the ground was frozen sufficiently to make it possible. In rear of the swamp Hill had placed Gregg's Brigade, as a part of the second defensive line, but the open space between Lane and Archer proved too wide for mutually supporting fire.

The swampy woods, which Jackson's generals thought would be a deterrent, proved to be nothing if the sort; Meade's brigades surged through the woods, taking between them several hundred prisoners, smashing Gregg's Brigade and mortally

---

MAP 12. THE CONFEDERATE COUNTERATTACK. SITUATION ABOUT 2:30 P.M.

Hardie's next two messages are not so cheerful:

2:15 P.M.

Gibbon and Meade driven back from the wood; Newton has gone forward. Jackson's corps, of the enemy, attacks on the left. General Gibbon slightly wounded. General Bayard mortally wounded. Things do not look so well on Reynold's front; still, we will have new troops in soon.

2:25 P.M.

Dispatch received. Franklin will do his best. New troops gone in. Will report soon.

Early's prompt and vigorous counterattack struck Meade at a time when his brigades had become attenuated and had lost cohesion in the woods. The Federals were driven down the hill, out into the open, and back half way to the road. Gibbon's division became involved in the rout. The Confederates were stopped by several batteries of light artillery posted on the rise from which Meade had launched his assault, and by Birney's division, just arrived. Newton has arrived in support and Sickles, also sent for, is approaching. Doubleday is held in check by the threat of Stuart's cavalry. Meade's and Gibbon's broken units are streaming back through Birney's lines, to be re-formed on the ground where they had bivouacked the previous night.

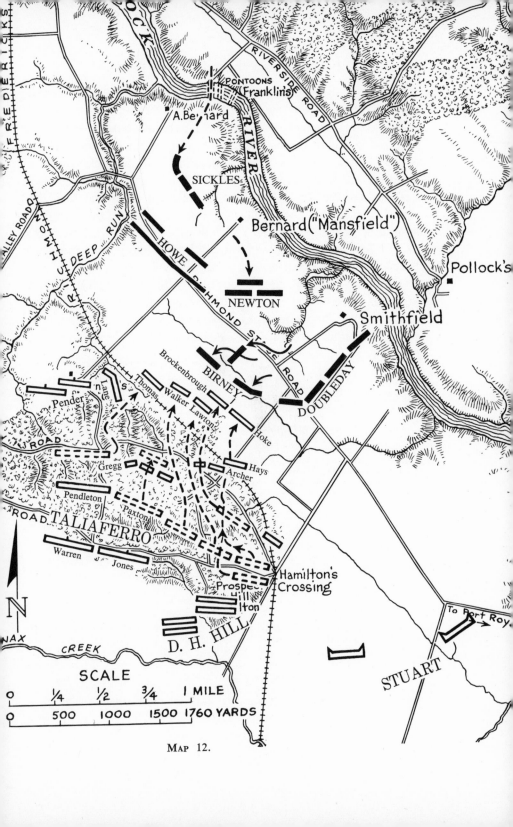

Map 12.

wounding its commander. Gibbon, on Meade's right, advanced only to the Confederate front line. In the dense thicket the divisions lost contact and opened a gap, whereupon the Confederate brigades promptly rallied, counterattacked, and drove Meade's men back in great confusion. Although Taliaferro's Division was in direct support of Gregg's Brigade, it was Early's that rushed over from the right to meet the crisis and turn the tables on Meade. Lane's Brigade put the damper on Gibbon's assault which had reached the railroad but not much further, except for small groups and individual soldiers who followed Meade's example and advanced into the woods.

Enthusiastic rebel cheers, coupled with rapid footwork and vigorous musket fire, followed the retreating Federals down the hill and over the railroad. Gibbon was wounded and forced to retire. Brigadier General C. F. Jackson, one of Meade's brigade

---

MAP 13. ACTIONS ON THE SOUTH FLANK FROM ABOUT 3 P.M. TO DARK

Hardie's last three messages fail to disguise the fact that the attack of Franklin's grand division has failed:

3 P.M.

Reynolds seems to be holding his own. Things look better, somewhat.

3:40 P.M.

Gibbon's and Meade's divisions are badly used up, and I fear another advance on the enemy on our left cannot be made this afternoon. Doubleday's division will replace Meade's as soon as it can be collected, and, if it be done in time, of course another attack will be made. The enemy are in force in the wood on our left, toward Hamilton's, and are threatening the safety of that portion of our line. They seem to have detached a portion of their force to our front, where Howe and Brooks are now engaged. Brooks has some prisoners, and is down the railroad. Just as soon as the left is safe, our forces here will be prepared for a front attack; but it may be too late this afternoon. Indeed, we are engaged in front, anyhow. Notwithstanding the unpleasant items I relate, the morale of the troops generally is good.

4:30 P.M.

The enemy is still in force on our left and front. An attack on our batteries in front has been repulsed. A new attack has opened on our left; but the left is safe, although it is too late to advance.

Howe and Brooks were "engaged" to a very minor extent indeed, this consisting of the short run down Deep Creek by Torbert's brigade, the capture of some 15 prisoners, with Law's Brigade of Hood's Division chasing Torbert back almost to the road and punishing him severely. With the arrival of Birney, Newton, and Sickles, Early felt it prudent to stop his counterattack. He withdrew his line to the railroad. Law's adventure is indicated on the sketch. There is also shown the general disposition of all units on the south flank at the end of the day's fighting.

Phillips

To Whi
Oak Chu.

Lacy (Chatham)
PONTOONS

FREDERICKSBURG

BASIN

Marye

RAPPAHANNOCK

PONTOONS

Washington
Farm

Howison

RIVERSIDE ROAD

PONTOONS
Franklin's

A.Bernard

BROOKS

RIVER

Bernard("Mansfield")

Pollock's Mill

Torbell

MEADE

GIBBON

NEWTON

Smithfield

HOOD

Law

SICKLES

BIRNEY

DOUBLEDAY

Pender

nard
Cabi

Thomas Walker Lawton

Gregg Paxton Archer Hoke Hays

MILITARY ROAD

MINE ROAD

TALIAFERRO

Brockenbrough

N

Hamilton's
Crossing

SCALE

¼   ½   ¾   1 MILE

500   1000   1500   1760 YARDS

Prospect
Hill
lton

MASSAPONAX   CREEK

D. H. HILL

To Ft Royal

STUART

Yerby

MAP 13.

commanders, was killed. Reynolds, Meade, and officers of lesser rank did their best to halt the backward drift of the broken regiments, but the troops of both divisions had had all they wanted and there was no stopping them in their sullen withdrawal, particularly those of Meade's division, through the hastily formed line which Birney's division of the Third Corps brought up in support. Birney had fortuitously arrived on the scene at the critical moment; he struck the Confederate right flank and in turn drove the counterattackers back into the woods with a loss of more than 500 killed and wounded. His own casualties were heavy, but his brigades fought magnificently as the retreating elements of Meade and Gibbon streamed through their lines to the rear. Had it not been for Birney, there is no telling what might have happened.

At two o'clock Reynolds' corps, strengthened by Birney's and then by Sickles' division, both of Stoneman's Third Corps, which had finally been summoned from the east shore, still held the railway line. But they were unable to make progress against Jackson's strong defense. Later in the afternoon the entire line was withdrawn to re-form in the shelter of the Richmond Road from whence the attack had been launched in the morning.

The Federal Attack Lacked Power and Depth

Franklin's failure to make better use of Smith's corps was as much a reflection on his generalship as on Burnside's. Granted that the latter's directive was vague and inconclusive, a more energetic wing commander, having committed two divisions to the attack against the Confederate heights, would and should have utilized Smith's 25,000-man corps, the largest in the Union army, to better advantage. As it was, that corps remained virtually static deployed along the Richmond Road from Deep Run on the right, two divisions in the line and one in support. When Meade and Gibbon were repulsed, Newton's support division was shifted to the left to back up Birney, but remained in column of brigades in a position of readiness on both sides of the road and never did get into action. This was equally true of Doubleday, who had deployed and advanced a short distance toward the flank, but who played a virtually inactive role throughout the battle.

About the only actual fighting in which Smith's corps engaged was a lively succession of artillery duels with the Confederates in the Deep Run area, and a spirited advance and

COLONEL ALFRED TORBERT
Commanding a brigade under Howe. Later a cavalry commander.

bayonet charge by a portion of Colonel Torbert's brigade of Brook's division, which in the middle of the afternoon attempted to drive the Confederates from a railroad cut in the Deep Run (Lansdowne) Valley where the railroad crossed a deep ravine. Torbert's troops succeeded in driving back a regiment of Pender's Brigade of A. P. Hill's Division, and capturing several dozen of the enemy. Torbert in turn was counterattacked and forced to retire by Law's Brigade of Hood's Division. Lansdowne Valley was a well-known landmark at the time of the battle and since it was approximately the dividing line between the two Confederate corps, and appeared to be a natural avenue of attack along the upper reaches of Deep Run, the sortie might have had important results had it been launched with sufficient strength and depth.

What should have been a major and decisive turning movement by Franklin's 54,000-man force, against not much more than half that number of Confederates on Lee's right flank, thus turned out to be a relatively inconclusive although very sanguinary engagement in which a majority of the forces available to each of the opposing commanders was not fully engaged. The reported casualties significantly tell the story (see Appendix II); Meade's division lost 1,853 officers and men; Gibbon's losses were 1,267; Birney's were 950; Doubleday and Sickles suffered, respectively, only 218 and 100 casualties, mainly from Confederate artillery fire; while the other four divisions lost a mere 473 men altogether, for a grand total of 4,861 casualties among the troops under Franklin's command. The opposing Confederates lost approximately 3,400, mostly in the divisions of A. P. Hill and Jubal Early.

As the afternoon waned, Stonewall Jackson made preparations for a counterattack which he judged it would be safer to launch under cover of darkness, just in case it might be necessary for his divisions to retire to their secure haven on the heights after making the attack. The plan called for his artillery to precede the infantry, but nothing came of it because, in Jackson's own report: "The first gun had hardly moved forward from the wood one hundred yards when the enemy's artillery reopened, and so completely swept our front as to satisfy me that the proposed movement should be abandoned."

Whose Fault—Burnside's or Franklin's?

While it can fairly be said that Burnside's attack order to Franklin was much too indefinite and restrictive for the required effort, the army commander did have an out in that he had directed an attack by *at least one division*. At the same time, however, and somewhat conflictingly, Franklin was told to hold his entire command in readiness for a rapid movement down

the Richmond Road. It was clearly Burnside's expectation that
the spearhead division (Meade's) would gain the heights and
Lee would then hasten to withdraw his troops to the south, at
which moment Burnside wanted the bulk of Franklin's grand
division to be ready to move after him in a rapid pursuit.

In the heat and excitement of battle, what a general thinks

BRIGADIER GENERAL E. M. LAW, C.S.A.

and does is sometimes quite different from what he subsequently
testifies to explain his motivations and actions. In the early part
of 1863, in the lull between the Battles of Fredericksburg and
Chancellorsville, a Congressional Committee on the conduct
of the war received testimony from both Burnside and Franklin,
among others, on the controversial order to the latter. Burnside's ex-post-facto explanation was that he had been informed
by a "colored gentleman" from Fredericksburg that the Confederates had built a military access road in rear of the heights,
to avoid long detours, that Burnside wanted possession of that
road, and his instructions to Franklin contemplated that the

latter would capture it, separate Lee's two wings, throw confusion into Lee's ranks, and then Burnside would push the
frontal attack on the right of the Union army. If that were
actually the case, it is difficult to understand why Burnside did
not so stipulate in his order to Franklin, who in turn testified
that he interpreted the order which he received at 7:45 that

BRIGADIER GENERAL JAMES LANE, C.S.A.

morning to call for "an armed observation to ascertain where
the enemy was." Franklin testified further: "I put in all the
troops that I thought it proper and prudent to put in. I fought
the whole strength of my command, as far as I could, and at
the same time keep my connection with the river open." In view
of the historic facts, that was the overstatement of the year.

Franklin clearly interpreted the order too literally. Had he
been mentally more flexible, he would with complete justification
have thrown Smith's corps of three divisions into a strong holding attack against the high ground to *their* immediate front,

which in turn would have served to keep a portion of the Confederate line so busy that they could not with impunity have come to the aid of A. P. Hill's Division, which manned the Confederate first and second lines and which, as the battle progressed, was with help able to neutralize the efforts of the divisions of Meade and Gibbon.

BRIGADIER GENERAL ABNER DOUBLEDAY

Nor did Franklin attempt to explain his surprising reluctance to promptly summon the divisions of Birney, Sickles, and Burns, which had been assembled and were waiting near the river for the express purpose of supporting his attack. It is true that he did call in Birney, belatedly and barely in the nick of time, to block the Confederate pursuit of the divisions of Meade and Gibbon, in their headlong retreat. But the other two divisions were merely placed on the field in a defensive position along the Richmond Road without achieving any constructive result.

When the score was finally added up, it was clear that Franklin, who Burnside believed would make the major attack, had badly misinterpreted the army commander's intentions and employed offensively only three of the nine divisions, one-third of his strength. By that failure, which Burnside must share, he lost the opportunity to turn Jackson's flank in advance of the frontal assault by Sumner's divisions in Fredericksburg.

The Congressional Committee reached the following conclusions: "The testimony of all the witnesses before your committee proves most conclusively that had the attack been made upon the left with all the force which General Franklin could have used for that purpose, the plan of General Burnside would have been completely successful, and our Army would have achieved a most brilliant victory."

In the opinion of the committee, at least, Franklin more than Burnside was to blame for the failure.

But now that all available evidence is on hand and has been carefully weighed, it appears that the foregoing conclusion of the Congressional Committee is of doubtful worth. The plan of Burnside *might* have succeeded (1) if the attack had been launched early, before D. H. Hill and Early were in position; (2) if the Federal cavalry been used to screen the left flank, neutralizing Pelham and Stuart; (3) if the assault had been made as an envelopment, striking west at Hamilton's Crossing; and (4) if Doubleday, Newton, Birney, and Sickles had been thrown into the assault as well as Meade and Gibbon. All this would have been possible had the attacking force been moved under cover of darkness and fog, shortly after midnight of the 12th, and been in the jump-off position at or before daybreak.

COBB'S AND KERSHAW'S TROOPS BEHIND THE STONE WALL

CHAPTER 11

SLAUGHTER AT THE STONE WALL

LONGSTREET'S CORPS, having moved in and oc-
cupied the ridge bastion west of Fredericksburg shortly after the
Army of the Potomac had reached the vicinity of Falmouth,
had, through Burnside's inability to make up his mind on his
next move, been granted over three full weeks in which to improve and strengthen its already naturally strong defensive
position.

The selection of artillery gun positions, which received Lee's
careful personal attention, was made with meticulous care. There
can be little doubt that all five of the divisions of Longstreet's
First Corps were not only thoroughly briefed on the individual
and collective combat roles they would be called upon to play,
but were in all probability put through terrain exercises, by way
of rehearsal, that would serve to counter every conceivable tactical maneuver open to the Federal forces once they had bridged
the river.

Significant Terrain Features

Without repeating the detailed description of the ground features in and west of the town of Fredericksburg itself (see pages 107 and 109), the reader is at this point invited to focus attention on the Plank Road, the Telegraph Road, the vital canal ditch, Hazel Run, Marye's Hill, and the stone wall that ran along the sunken road (part of the Telegraph Road) at the foot of Marye's Hill. All are clearly shown on Map 8.

It will be remembered that Burnside's order to Sumner early on the morning of December 13 had directed him to extend his left to Deep Run, but gave him the discretion of extending his right "as far as your judgment may dictate." Sumner was told also to "push a column of a division or more along the Plank and Telegraph Roads, with a view to seizing the heights in the rear of the town." The latter movement was to be readied but not started until Burnside should give the word.

As in the order to Franklin, Sumner was told to support the attack column "so as to keep its line of retreat open"; further evidence, if by now any were needed, of the type of morale-shattering psychology which the bemused Burnside was employing.

One of the injunctions laid on Sumner in the order may have contained greater significance than meets the eye. He was told to remain at his headquarters, the Lacy house, on Stafford Heights opposite the north end of Fredericksburg, until the army commander could confer with him. Strangely enough, Sumner remained there the entire time that his grand division was engaged in the bloody fighting and during its aftermath. The presumption must be that he was acting under instructions from Burnside. General Couch, commander of the Second Corps, expressed the thought that, Sumner having shown himself in earlier battles to be a hard fighter, Burnside may have considered him rash and impetuous, and was unwilling to risk the chance that Sumner would go all out in his efforts to dislodge the enemy. There is also the fact that Sumner's attack was not to be initiated until Franklin had broken Lee's line on the right, which Burnside expected to occur early in the action, or at least that was the explanation in his post-battle report. Even granting Burnside credit for what may have seemed to him a sound reason for keeping Sumner close to his own headquarters, the fact remains that the grand division commander remained separated by the river from his troops and their battle. This was a bitter pill for the gallant old Sumner to swallow.

It would appear from a study of the map, without the confirmation of the monotonously bloody series of repulses to be given to the repeated frontal attacks of the right grand division, that the natural approach corridor for the Federals to reach the Confederate ridge would be the gap which Hazel Run cuts through the hill range at the south end of Marye's Hill. It will be noted that the Telegraph Road runs around the nose of Marye's Hill, makes a couple of sharp turns and then crosses the bed of an unfinished railroad which extends in a north-easterly direction from Hazel Run almost to Fredericksburg and stops just short of a connection with the Richmond, Fredericksburg and Potomac Railroad. Presumably this unfinished railroad would provide some cover to advancing troops, even though the Confederates must have thoroughly reconnoitered the area. Since McLaws' and Pickett's Divisions, which held the line south of Hazel Run, were extended considerably,

GROUND BETWEEN FREDERICKSBURG AND MARYE'S HEIGHTS
The road on the right is the Telegraph Road. The ditch or swale in the foreground is where the Federals deployed for their advance.

the possibility exists that it was planned that way as a king-size trap into which Lee may have hoped "those people" might curiously stick their heads. It is conceivable, however, that Burnside would have had a fighting chance to penetrate Longstreet's line at that point, while there was little hope for the success of an effort to butt his head against a stone wall, which was what he tried.

Couch's Corps Leads Off

General Couch and his Second Corps were selected by Sumner to make the attack against the heights. The written order, received at 8:15 A. M., directed that he extend his right to prevent the possibility of a Confederate occupation of the upper end of the town, and then alert two divisions, one to be prepared to advance in three lines "in the direction of the

---

MAP 14. ACTIONS ON THE NORTH FLANK, ABOUT 11 A.M. TO NOON

Federals: French's division formed up about midmorning in the streets where his brigades had spent the night. Three regiments detailed as skirmishers moved at 11 A.M. toward the front, marching in two columns—the right via Hanover Street and the left on a street parallel to the railroad. They trotted from the western exits of the town, across the bridges over the sluice, turned left and right, respectively, faced into line and advanced. They were met by heavy artillery fire from Marye's and Willis' Hills, but continued to dash forward. The skirmishers were followed by the brigades in the order 1st, 3d, and 2d, at intervals of about 150 yards. Then came Hancock's division in the same formation. Meanwhile Howard had formed his brigades on the right of Plank Road, having been told that he would attack on the right of French and Hancock. But these orders were countermanded and his men were held in column in the streets, ready to advance. Sturgis' division also formed up in the streets, preparing to move out in column along the railroad. Whipple's division moved down from its bivouac north of the Lacy House, crossed over the upper bridge, and commenced taking over picket duty in the northwest portion of the city from Howard. Getty's men remained crouched at the lower end of the town near the river.

Confederates: Longstreet's defense was largely entrusted to McLaws, supported by Ransom. Cobb's brigade was behind the stone wall at the foot of the heights, with the 24th North Carolina Volunteers of Ransom's Division occupying that portion of the front between Plank Road and the extension of Hanover Street. The remainder of Ransom's Division was held back of the artillery on the heights; but when the Federals appeared, Cooke's brigade was rushed forward to the crest, from where they reinforced the small-arms fire of the troops behind the wall. At least initially, the greatest damage to the advancing Federals was caused by the Confederate artillery firing from Marye's and Willis' Hills.

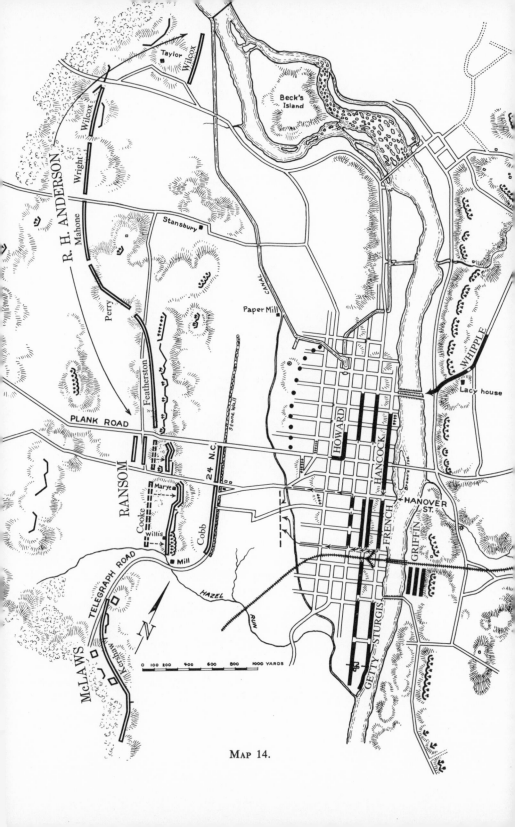

Map 14.

Plank and Telegraph Roads for the purpose of seizing the heights in rear of the town," the other to be held in readiness to support the movement of the leading division.

Couch at once designated French's division for the advance, with Hancock to follow, each division in brigade columns of battalions with 200 yards distance between brigades. By 11

BRIGADIER GENERAL WINFIELD S. HANCOCK

o'clock, Burnside had evidently despaired of the early success which he had anticipated on Franklin's front, for at that hour Couch received from Sumner the order to advance, transmitted over a field telegraph line which the Federal signalmen had run from the Lacy house, Sumner's headquarters on the opposite side of the Rappahannock, to the Fredericksburg courthouse building in which Couch had set up his command post.

Under modern battle conditions a unit the size of a division normally moves into its jump-off position by regiments or battalions in columns of fours, twos, single file, or in squad or platoon columns, depending on the nature of the available cover and the configuration of the ground over which the development takes place. When within enemy machine gun and rifle fire the modern deployment into skirmish formation is effected to present a minimum of bunched targets, while the friendly artillery lays down a stationary or rolling barrage ahead of the troops to keep down the enemy fire.

It didn't happen that way at Fredericksburg, for the reason that Hunt's guns on Stafford Heights for the most part were unable to reach the Confederate position, and the debouchment from the streets of the town presented a difficult problem in itself. At 12:00 noon French's brigades moved out from the shelter of the town by the two streets which led into the Plank and Telegraph Roads. As they emerged from the cover afforded by the buildings they found themselves descending a gradual slope on an open plain with Marye's Heights at the far end and about 800 yards distant from the town's western edge. This plain, obstructed in spots by an occasional house and garden, was bisected at right angles to the direction of the Federal advance by the canal drainage ditch, which could be conveniently crossed only at the bridges. Beyond the ditch the ground rose slightly toward the Confederate ridge and provided cover of a sort, behind which the troops could deploy before charging the heights. The entire plain was exposed to converging artillery and musketry fire, and the advancing Federals suffered many casualties while in column before they could be hurried over the two bridges to the slight cover on the far side.

The Grim Reaper Has a Field Day

The Confederate guns on Lee's Hill commanded the valley of Hazel Run and were effectively sited to cover the plain which the Union forces had to cross to reach Marye's Heights. The attacking Federals came under the fire of these guns and others from the heights on Lee's left as soon as they moved out from the cover of the town buildings. Most of their early losses were caused by Lee's artillery. Two Confederate siege guns in particular were much in evidence during the early stages of the

battle; these were the "thirty-pound" Parrott rifles, weighing
4,200 pounds and throwing a 29-pound projectile, which had
recently been transferred from the defenses of Richmond for
use at Fredericksburg. Enfilading Couch's left flank in the attacks on Marye's Heights, these heavy guns created havoc in
the Federal lines from their positions on Lee's Hill until both
blew up in the faces of the Confederates, one on the thirty-ninth
discharge, the other after fifty-four rounds had been fired. The
first to go was firing within a few feet of where Lee, Longstreet,
and Pendleton, Lee's Chief of Artillery, were standing when it
burst at the muzzle. But by a miracle no one was touched by the
flying fragments.

As soon as the advancing lines came within musket range a
sheet of flame greeted them from behind the four-foot stone
wall at the foot of Marye's Hill, where Cobb's Georgia Brigade
of McLaws' Confederate Division and a North Carolina regiment of Ransom's Division were posted. The withering fire cut the
attackers down by the hundred. But the grim advance continued,
ignoring casualties, until the leading wave was within sixty
yards of the wall. At that point flesh and blood could take

MAP 15. THE SITUATION ON THE NORTH FLANK FROM ABOUT NOON TO 1 P.M.
Federals: This sketch shows the charge of French's and Hancock's divisions
against Marye's Heights. The picture may be likened to successive waves
of a surf dashing against a shore, breaking up, receding, leaving a thin line
on the sand to mark their farthest reach. Each Federal brigade suffered
heavily from artillery fire as it came in sight at the edge of the town, then
encountered long, tearing sheets of musketry volleys as the men neared the
stone wall. The leading guides planted their guidons within 100 yards or
so of the stone wall, but the lines for the most part melted away. Couch
says that the plain seemed to be alive with men, some lying down, others
running about, while a steady stream of wounded was returning to the town.
Whipple, who crossed the river about noon, has used one brigade to take
over picket duty on the right from Howard. His 2d Brigade (Carroll) has
moved down to the left behind Sturgis. Howard, having received orders
to support Hancock, is moving two brigades to the left toward Hanover Street.

Confederates: Two of Cooke's regiments ran down the slope into the sunken
road with Cobb's men. Ransom has brought the remainder of his own brigade
to the crest just south of Plank Road. Cooke is wounded. Cobb suffers a
cut artery in the leg and bleeds to death quickly despite surgical aid. McLaws
orders Kershaw to bring up his entire brigade and to assume overall command
in place of Cobb.

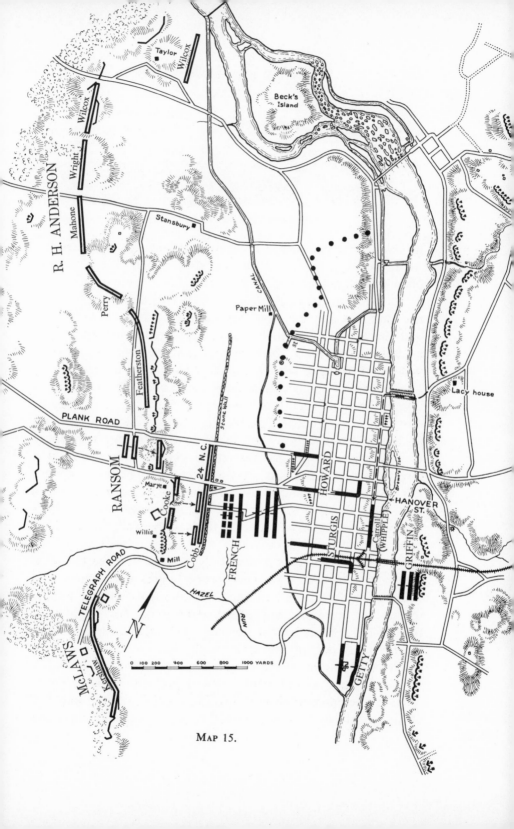

MAP 15.

THE ATTACK AGAINST MARYE'S HEIGHTS

no more. In truth, even if the spirit had been willing, there just weren't enough soldiers remaining to cover the last stretch of open ground before closing in hand-to-hand combat.

The Second and Third Brigades of French's division followed the First, but they too were stopped in succession at sixty yards and the survivors faded back to the rear, leaving three regimental flags to mark their furthest advance. French's division was out of the fight, leaving a third of its men on the ground.

The turn of Hancock's division came next. The safe attraction of the stone wall, breast-high for the average man standing upright, was such that Confederate reinforcements had in the meantime crowded into the sunken road until they were firing in four ranks as fast as men could change places, and at a resultant cycle of fire that was more than four times the normal rate. As a result, Hancock's reception was worse than French's and although his brigades passed the high water mark of their predecessors and got within forty yards of the wall, they couldn't quite reach it.

By this time the plain was literally covered with the blue-clad dead and wounded. With these prone figures were others who could go no further but still had the intestinal fortitude to stay where they were and inflict such damage as they might with rifle fire to collect partial payment from the securely posted Confederates behind the stone wall, from which the hail of death kept spouting at every head that was raised.

Two Union divisions within an hour had with supreme battle courage offered themselves as a fruitless sacrifice to the stupidity of an incompetent army commander whose capacity for compounding his initial lack of tactical judgment seemed limitless. Having made the decision to spearhead with a single division a frontal attack over open ground against what was obviously an almost impregnable position, the stubborn Burnside could think of nothing better than to keep pouring other divisions with endless monotony into the same funnel regardless of losses. Casualties in the divisions of French and Hancock alone amounted to 3,200 men and officers killed, wounded, and missing. Before the day was over, 6,300 Federal soldiers would become casualties at the base of Marye's Heights out of more than 10,000 for the battle as a whole.

The Stone Wall as a Magnet

Corps Commander Couch, observing such portions of the battle as could be glimpsed through the haze and clouds of smoke which shrouded the field, from the cupola of the courthouse with General Howard at his side, concluded that it was

HAZARD'S BATTERY

Only seven batteries accompanied the troops on the north flank across the river. One of these was Hazard's, which galloped into position between Howard's lines and Humphreys', within about 400 yards of the Confederates. Hazard fired rapidly at the Confederates on Marye's Heights until Humphreys asked him to stop so that the infantry could advance through. Hazard's losses were heavy. Though most of the horses were down, the men preserved an old artillery tradition by dragging away the guns by hand. Gen. Howard, who watched the action, said, "Captain Hazard's conduct was equal to anything I ever saw on the field of battle."

time to vary the monotony by adopting a new tack. Howard's division was the only one remaining to him, so to Howard he gave instructions to move his division off to the right where he might find it easier going with the possibility of flanking that devilish stone wall. Apparently the idea didn't occur to either Couch or Howard to send a few officer scouts and skirmishers ahead to test the ground and determine in advance that the plan was feasible.

Howard moved promptly to carry out the order, but his regiments, after crossing the ditch as the others had done, and then slanting off by the right flank, ran smack into a marshy lowland caused by seepage from the drainage ditch. Forced to the left by this obstacle, Howard's troops found themselves heading for the same stone wall that seemed like a magnet to draw the successive waves of Federal attackers inevitably into its field of influence.

Now all three of Couch's divisions were immobilized in a small area from which they could move neither forward nor back without stopping a Confederate bullet or shell. Howard's 900-odd casualties brought the Federal total in Sumner's zone to more than 4,000. But the orders kept coming over from the remote army commander to continue the attack, as though by

---

MAP 16. THE SITUATION ON THE NORTH FLANK FROM ABOUT 1 P.M. TO 2:30 P.M.

Federals: The remnants of French's and Hancock's divisions are scattered in front of the stone wall. Survivors who have drifted to the rear are being rallied in the small ravine along the ditch. Sturgis is following Hancock, Ferrero's brigade in the lead. Nagle's brigade starts to deploy on the left, then sidles to the right oblique and follows Ferrero. Howard, deployed on the right with two brigades, is advancing; his third brigade is held in reserve on the right of the Plank Road. Griffin's division, coming in as part of the Fifth Corps reinforcing the Ninth Corps, has crossed the bridge and is moving forward on the left; Carroll's brigade of Whipple's division, ordered to support Sturgis, has joined Griffin instead and is moving forward with him. Sykes has moved down to the upper bridge. Humphreys is still in bivouac.

Confederates: Kershaw has moved two of his regiments to the top of Marye's Heights thence down into the sunken road to reinforce Cobb's regiments. Three additional regiments are following to the top of the hill. Ransom has brought his regiments forward to the crest and one of them is in the sunken road reinforcing the 24th North Carolina.

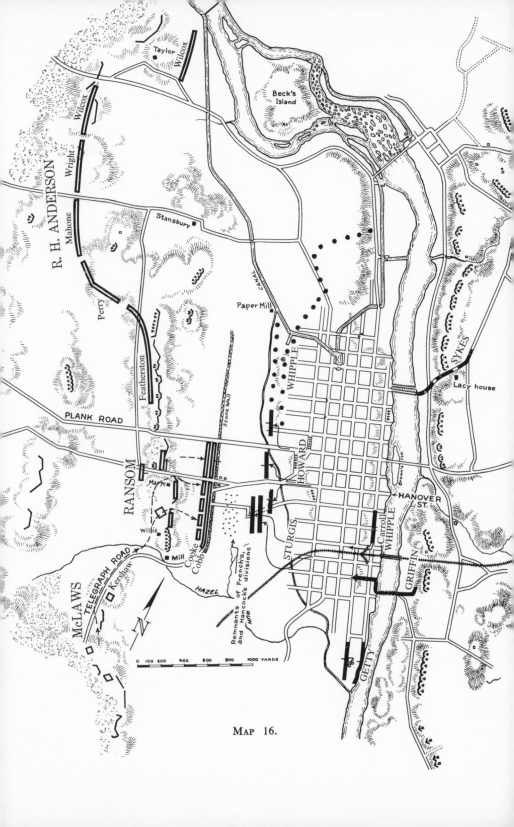

MAP 16.

sheer repetition or a miracle of some sort he could pluck a victory from what had by now become crystal clear to the lowliest private—that the Army of the Potomac was taking another terrible licking in trying to achieve the impossible.

Dead horses, dead comrades, rocks, fragments of demolished fences, all were used as parapets by individual soldiers as partial shields against the point-blank musketry fire which continuously battered them from behind the stone wall.

The official report of Confederate General McLaws, in command of that part of the line which included Marye's Heights,

---

MAP 17. THE SITUATION ON THE NORTH FLANK FROM ABOUT 2:30 P.M. TO DARK

Federals: Howard's two leading brigades have reached a line near the stone wall. His third brigade has been moved to the left of the Plank Road in the shelter of the ravine. Humphreys crossed the river shortly after 2:30 P.M. and formed a battle line in the ravine, to the right and left of Hanover Street. At dusk he advanced in a bayonet charge, which was repulsed. Meantime Griffin, with Carroll's brigade self-attached, has advanced astride the railroad for a short distance then straight toward the stone wall. His brigades attacked successively, Barnes at about 4 P.M., Sweitzer and Carroll a half hour later. Both lines being repulsed, the third brigade of Griffin's division was thrown into the cauldron, but it too accomplished nothing. Sykes moved to the upper bridge at 2 P.M., crossed at 4 P.M., moved out Hanover and George Streets and formed battle line with two brigades in the ravine. His third brigade remained in the town and did not participate in the action. At 5 P.M. Getty advanced on the left in a column of brigades. His leading brigade almost reached the stone wall before being thrown back, mostly by enfilade fire from its left. The supporting brigade remained behind the railroad embankment. By dark the Federal situation generally was that the foremost elements still lay on the ground in front of the stone wall, the units broken and intermixed. Another irregular line was in the ravine, and still more wounded and stragglers were back in the streets.

Confederates: Kershaw's three remaining regiments are placed in position near Marye's house. A battalion is moved forward to the gap in the unfinished railway embankment on the right of Willis' Hill in order to thwart any possible Federal advance up Hazel Run. At about 4:30 P.M. the battalion of Washington Artillery, being out of ammunition, is replaced by a part of Colonel Alexander's battalion. Ransom, fearful that his left flank would not be supported by Featherston, asked for reinforcements. Kemper's brigade of Pickett's division was sent to him at about 4:30, and two of these regiments at dark were placed in the sunken road to relieve the 24th North Carolina. Other readjustments of units were made after dark. The Confederates had repulsed the Union attack so easily and with so little loss to themselves, that Lee could scarcely believe that there would not be a renewal of the attack the next day. But the battle was over.

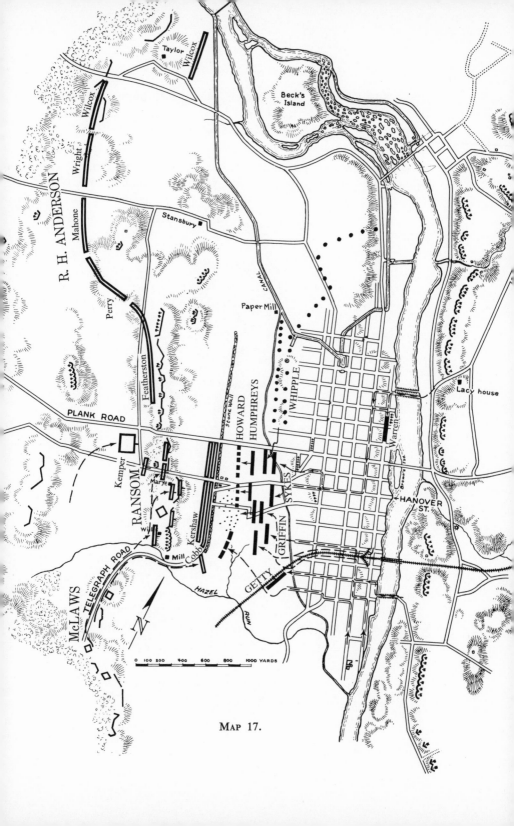

MAP 17.

stated that "the body of one man, believed to be an officer, was found within about thirty yards of the stone wall, and other single bodies were scattered at increased distances until the main mass of the dead lay thickly strewn over the ground at something over one hundred yards off, and extending to the ravine, commencing at the point where our men would allow

BRIGADIER GENERAL CHARLES GRIFFIN

the enemy's column to approach before opening fire, and beyond which no organized body of men was able to pass."

Meantime, about noon, Willcox (Ninth Corps) had ordered Sturgis to support Couch's attack. Sturgis moved forward in two columns along the railroad, his brigades echeloned to the left rear of Hancock. The leading brigade deployed, came under enfilade attack from the guns on Lee's Hill firing down the railroad cut; it was stopped behind Hancock's shattered units. The second brigade was ordered to deploy on the left but it too suffered from the enfilade fire, obliqued to the right, and, like the first, took cover behind the slight rise in the middle of the plain.

Several Federal batteries dramatically galloped across the bridge over the ditch and made a heroic effort to counter the Confederate fire. General Couch himself rode the length of his line, courting death the whole distance and bringing considerable comfort to his men, who understandably were more enheartened to see their corps commander take the same chances for punishment as themselves.

Whipple's division of Stoneman's Third Corps (Birney and Sickles having been released to Franklin), had been sent across the river to free Howard's division on the right to join in the direct attack, and Griffin's division of Butterfield's Fifth Corps was sent in to support Sturgis, while the divisions of Humphreys and Sykes, of the Fifth Corps, were ordered across to support Couch.

In desperation and somewhat wildly Burnside now ordered Franklin to charge the enemy on his front with his whole force in an effort to take some of the weight off the bogged-down divisions on the right; at the same time he ordered Hooker to renew the attack on the stone wall, with two of his remaining reserve divisions of the Fifth Corps. While these divisions were crossing the river, Hooker himself went on ahead to look the situation over and confer with Couch and Hancock. What he saw decided him to try to dissuade Burnside from sacrificing any more men. By the time he had ridden back to the Phillips house, made his plea, been flatly turned down and returned to the front, it was after 4:00 o'clock. The early December twilight was beginning to reduce visibility with its promise of blessed relief to the endangered Federals lying in the open before the stone wall.

Burnside's order to Franklin to charge with his whole force was the subject of considerable subsequent controversy between the respective headquarters of the two generals. The former took the position that Franklin had disregarded the order, while the latter maintained that it was received too late to be of any use. In any event Franklin did *not* make a general advance, which may or may not prove that the general who is under fire on the actual ground is in better position to appraise the possibilities for success or failure.

Nevertheless, two more divisions—Gettys' and Humphreys— were thrown against the stone wall. Willcox had held Getty's division as a reserve and to guard the left of the town. But at 4 P. M. he decided to advance this division, hoping thereby

BRIGADIER GENERAL A. W. WHIPPLE

to relieve the pressure on the right. Getty got under way at 5 o'clock, just about dusk, advanced to the right oblique in column of brigades toward the point where the railroad curves off to the left. His second brigade stopped at the railroad embankment, but the leading brigade continued on, through enfilade fire from Lee's Hill, across a small tributary of Hazel Run, until it reached a line within less than a hundred yards of the left portion of the stone wall. Here it was stopped by fire from the front and the left. The survivors lay down, then were withdrawn, first to the shelter of the railroad embankment, then into the town.

Casualties Nearly Equal Pickett's at Gettysburg

While Hooker was on his way to talk with Burnside, Hancock's men had mistaken a troop movement on the Confederate heights, involving the replacement of the Washington Artillery by Alexander's battalion, for a retirement. Hancock reported this to corps commander Couch who in turn told Humphreys: "Now is the time for you to go in!" Humphreys was quick to act. Apparently under the impression that the Confederates were withdrawing and his assault would not involve the fire fight which had halted the earlier attacks, or because he may have figured that an attack with cold steel might succeed where all previous attempts had failed, he directed his troops to fix bayonets without waiting to load their muskets. He promptly led forward the two brigades, composed of Pennsylvania boys who were experiencing serious action for the first time.

Humphreys' division succeeded in getting closer to the stone wall than any other. But that was all, because the alleged Confederate withdrawal was a false alarm; the fresh artillery battalion of six batteries took position in time to open on Humphreys' men. Furthermore the riflemen behind the stone wall were present in even greater numbers than before. The result was a casualty list of over 1,000 for Humphreys. This brought the score for the stone-wall Confederates to approximately 6,300 Federals killed, wounded, and missing, almost as many men as Lee was to lose in Pickett's charge at Gettysburg six months later.

An interesting story is told about Humphreys, who established a reputation for gallantry, sound judgment, a keen sense of justice and magnanimity which, coupled with his own magnetic personality and skill in handling men, was surpassed by no other Union officer during the Civil War. He entered West Point in the class of 1831 before he had reached the age of 17. Those in power at Washington distrusted him because of his intimacy with Jefferson Davis before the war. That however did not prevent his assignment to duty with the Army of the Potomac, and the lack of trust quickly disappeared as a result of the brilliant soldierly qualities which he displayed from the beginning. After the war he was appointed Chief of Engineers, a position which he held for thirteen years, and in which he exhibited administrative ability of a high order.

Humpheys' assault, which terminated in semidarkness, was

BRIGADIER GENERAL GEORGE SYKES

the last of six massive but unsupported Federal attacks on the fortified heights. It marked the end of the day's fighting. Hooker ordered the men to fall back from their advance position with this rather morose and sardonic thought, which he later em· bodied in his official report: "Finding that I had lost as many men as my orders required me to lose, I suspended the attack."

The order from Hooker for the troops in front of Marye's Heights to retire from their advance position on the open plain was something akin to Falstaff's boast that "he could call up vasty spirits from the deep," and the retort of his companion— "Yes, but will they come?" Withdrawal under Confederate fire was a ticklish business even in the twilight. It wasn't until night had fully come that it was practicable to effect the relief of the able-bodied survivors, who were greatly relieved at being able to again move about freely in the comparative safety and comfort of the streets of Fredericksburg.

Under cover of darkness, then, some semblance of order was introduced among the badly mixed up and exhausted thousands of still living Federals, both walking-wounded and unhurt, who remained in the open plain before Marye's Heights. Accuracy of fire was of course out of the question, so the Confederates used their ammunition sparingly, but with sufficient regularity to prevent their enemy from carrying out salvage operations with any degree of effectiveness. Some units were relieved and replaced by those which were still fairly intact, and it became possible to do something for the wounded.

Sykes' Division Takes Over

Sykes' division of the Fifth Corps, the only one in Sumner's or Hooker's grand divisions that had not been in action during

THE SUNKEN ROAD IN 1884

Looking north. Most of the stone wall had been used to build a gatehouse for the National Cemetery, nearby. A fragment of the wall is still to be seen in front of the house. Just beyond the wall is the end of the extension of Hanover Street.

FREDERICKSBURG FROM THE FOOT OF WILLIS HILL
The right of the stone wall is seen in the middle foreground. The Federal
columns debouched from the town by the streets emerging from the part of
town showing between the two steeples.

the battle of December 13, was sent forward late in the day
to relieve a portion of Couch's corps which had been so badly
mauled in the succession of frontal attacks on the stone wall.
The division reached the western edge of the town while there
was still enough daylight for them to see. The field in their
front was full of soldiers, living and dead. The sun, about to
set, showed red through columns of smoke and haze.

The battle was over. In a short time the shooting and the
tumult of battle sounds died away except for desultory artillery
fire. As the men watched and waited for further orders in the
gathering darkness, shells from the Confederate battery positions etched bright lines with their burning fuses as they streaked
across the black sky.

There Sykes' men remained under arms, catching what sleep
they could, until they were roused shortly before midnight,
when they formed into line and marched away from the town
towards Marye's Heights. Moving quietly, with whispered commands, they were then formed in two lines and bivouacked for
the few remaining hours of the night within a stone's throw of

the stone wall, finding considerable difficulty in locating places on the ground where they could lie down because of the shattered forms of those who had already died or who were so badly wounded that they could neither be moved nor expect to see the sun rise on the morrow.

The Battle as Seen From the Confederate Side

The crest of the ridge along which the Confederate guns had been posted with such care and foresight, and below which ran the sunken road lined fore and aft by the stone wall, afforded an incomparable vantage point from which to observe the drama about to be enacted on the stage below.

A small group of Confederate artillery officers, lounging comfortably in the yard of the Marye House in the sector assigned to the Washington Artillery, were smoking their pipes late on the morning of December 13 as, in company with the rest of Longstreet's corps, they waited expectantly for the Federals in Fredericksburg to reveal their intentions.

The fog had cleared and from their lofty position some fifty

WASHINGTON ARTILLERY FIRING FROM MARYE'S HILL

feet above the open plain they were able to see everything on two feet or four that moved in the open fields betwen the ridge and the town a half mile to the east.

It was close to noon when a courier came up to the artillery commander, saluted, and handed him a dispatch from General Longstreet to be read before he carried it down to General Cobb of McLaws' Division whose brigade was charged with the

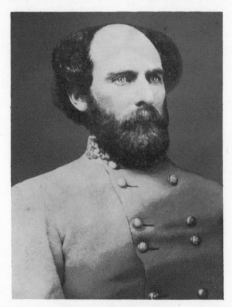

BRIGADIER GENERAL ROBERT RANSOM, C.S.A.

infantry defense of Marye's Hill. Hardly had the messenger started down the hill when rifle fire broke out from the direction of Fredericksburg. As the artillerymen watched, a Federal column emerged jogging in double time from one of the streets of the town, arms at the right shoulder, crossed the bridge over the canal ditch, and disappeared from sight behind a rise in the ground. The Confederate skirmishers fell back, firing as they ran, to the cover of the sunken road.

The fight was on.

Having deployed, the Federals reappeared over their own

low crest. They advanced in columns of brigades, bayonets flashing in the sunlight in a way that one of the Confederates reported "made their line look like a huge serpent of blue and steel." The Washington Artillery, opening with shell and solid shot, tore great gaps in the compact Federal lines, which flowed over and through the garden and farm fences as though they

BRIGADIER GENERAL THOMAS COBB, C.S.A.
Killed at the stone wall.

didn't exist. Now the attackers were close enough for enemy canister to get in its deadly work. The blue mass slowed perceptibly, but still came on, until Cobb's infantry, sighting over the stone wall, loosed a terrific hail of bullets at close range. The Federals faltered, seemingly dazed, then broke and sought cover behind the bank to their immediate rear. Almost at once a second line of blue appeared from behind the crest and came gallantly forward. This line was thinned out rapidly, but reached a point a little closer to the stone wall. Soon those who were still standing broke ranks and commenced drifting to the rear, singly or in small groups.

At this stage an additional Confederate brigade was moved into the sunken road to reinforce Cobb. About 2:00 o'clock the third Federal attack was launched, with the same spirit and an even stronger determination, apparently, to carry the position. This attack crested even closer to the stone wall than the second; but the murderous fire from the sunken road and the plunging artillery fire from the heights was too much for them.

The Confederates by this time were beginning to be a little worried lest succeeding assaults, of which there seemed to be no end, might by sheer weight of numbers smother the defenders in spite of their protective shield and deadly fire. To make certain that wouldn't happen, three more regiments were ordered up from Ransom's Division, which was serving as a backstop for McLaws' front line. Casualties were increasing in the Confederate ranks. General Cobb had been mortally, and

THE MILL ON HAZEL RUN
This is the point at which Kershaw's brigade filed across Hazel Run and marched up the west side of Willis Hill to their positions on Marye's Heights.

General Cooke seriously wounded. The Federal sharpshooters had gotten the range and the number of dead and wounded on the hill and even behind the stone wall began to mount.

Still the Federal attacks continued, but always with the same final result. Confederate artillery ammunition was running low, the frozen ground had thawed and turned to mud and slush, and the artillery had to call on the infantry to help man the guns. At 5:30 in the afternoon the last of the Federal attacks was launched and repulsed. The Confederate defenders breathed heavy sighs of relief, understandably indeed in view of the long period of fighting and strain they had undergone for five solid hours. For unbelievable as it may sound, only 6,000 muskets and no more than 20 guns had borne the defense of Marye's Heights against the driving weight of seven Federal divisions whose aggregate battle strength exceeded 40,000 men, a ratio of almost 7 to 1.

During the early afternoon it appeared to General Longstreet that the pressure had mounted to such an extent that a reinforcement of the line which had borne the brunt of the Federal attacks was advisable. The inactivity in front of Pickett's Division, on the far side of Hazel Run and in front of Lee's Hill, seemed likely to continue. So Lee shifted one of Pickett's brigades over to Anderson's front on the left flank of his sector to serve the dual purpose of assisting the defenders at the foot of Marye's Hill if needed, and to be prepared to meet a night attack with the bayonet. He regarded this as a possibility in view of the dogged and completely effective resistance being offered by his troops to the repeated but fruitless frontal attacks across the plain.

BURIAL PARTY AFTER THE BATTLE

CHAPTER 12

THE DEPRESSING AFTERMATH OF BATTLE

THE NIGHT OF December 13 was bitterly cold, which caused extreme suffering for the wounded who could not be evacuated. Many died of their wounds and exposure and, wrote General Couch, "as fast as men died they stiffened in the wintery air and on the front line were rolled forward for protection to the living. Frozen men were placed for dumb sentries."

On the morning of December 14 a macabre sight met the eye. Where the night before the plain had been covered with hundreds of blue-clad dead bodies, the field at daylight was dotted with white figures; thinly-clad Confederate soldiers having decided apparently that the corpses would never miss their clothing and that their own needs should take precedence.

The attitude of mind of the men of Burnside's army can be easily imagined. They knew they had been unsuccessful, were

226

depressed by their huge losses, and aside from the normal re-action after the strain of battle, the men in the ranks had joined their high-ranking officers in having completely lost confidence in the army commander.

How Not to Fight a Battle

Sykes' division on the front line found themselves in a most unenviable position when the sun broke through the fog on Sunday morning, December 14. The men were chilled to the bone from having lain for hours on the cold, damp ground. Protected from the view of the nearby Confederates by the early fog, some of them found temporary solace in the warming effect of a pipeful of tobacco and all were able to stretch their aching joints and improve their circulation by limited movements within their assigned positions as they peered through the misty veil at the wreckage on the battlefield.

With the passing minutes the fog grew thinner. Soon the sur-prised infantrymen spotted through the haze, about eighty yards away, the stonewall which had proven the nemesis of Couch's divisions the day before. Behind the wall were men in gray uniforms walking carelessly about, cooking breakfast, cleaning muskets, and performing the usual chores which occupy soldiers when not in actual combat. The first startled impression of the Federals was that they were prisoners of Lee's army, so close did yesterday's victors appear and so isolated from the rest of the Union army did Sykes' men feel themselves to be.

The Confederates saw their enemy at the same time. As the whistle of bullets shocked the Federals into reality, they hit the dirt as one man and there they lay, two lines of blue in their shallow depression, trying to figure out what they should do and what the Confederates *would* do. The fields behind them were flat and obviously subject to converging fire that would make retreat even more dangerous than to remain where they were. The black muzzles of the enemy guns frowned directly down at them from the heights and from them there would be no shelter once the guns opened up. So long as the men kept

DEAD AND WOUNDED OF THE 8TH OHIO IN FRONT OF THE STONE WALL

the prone position, musket balls couldn't reach them, but any movement, even to shift position on the ground in order to gain slight relief from cramped muscles, drew fire from watchful sharpshooters behind the wall.

Apparently the Southerners were enjoying the situation. They whiled away the time in target practice on such stray chickens, loose horses, broken artillery caissons, and live pigs as were to be seen. Their accuracy was such at the short range that the men of Sykes' division almost with one accord reached the conclusion that to lie low and make as few movements as possible was the only sensible guarantee of continued existence.

Men who left the line to get water or for other necessary purposes, before the lines were pinned to the earth, were either killed or wounded on the return journey, almost to a man. But after several hours of this nerve-wracking experience, the limit of patience was reached by a few tobacco-loving souls who had run out of their supply, and had friends in other companies who they felt sure could fill the need. Occasionally one of these bold spirits would suddenly leap to his feet, sprint in a crouching position to another part of the line and throw himself flat on the ground. As moving targets they were not always hit, and the one who was able to run the gauntlet in both directions safely was heartily applauded and congratulated by his comrades as though he had accomplished a feat worthy of a Medal of Honor.

All day long the men of the division sweated it out, the more philosophical ones in fitful catnaps, until finally, but almost hesitatingly as it seemed to the impatient Federals, the red ball that was the sun stood poised on the western horizon. Strained faces turned towards it as to a savior in their eagerness for the short December twilight to arrive and free them from their long and painful bondage.

As the sun disappeared the Federal line sprang to its collective feet. In a moment the Confederates opened fire, but it was then too late for aimed shots. The Federals returned the fire, more to relieve their frustrated feelings than in the expectation of hitting anything, and that was it. A messenger from Fredericksburg brought the welcome recall orders, the troops formed up, and 85 percent of those who had come out from the town just 24 hours earlier formed ranks and marched back to comparative peace, leaving 15 percent of their number as casualties for removal by litter bearers.

Burnside is Dissuaded From Another Suicidal Assault

About 9 o'clock on the night of the battle, Colonel Rush C. Hawkins, commanding a brigade in Getty's division of the Ninth Corps, sat in on a conference of generals in Fredericksburg which included corps commanders Willcox and Butterfield, division commanders Humphreys, Getty, and Meade, and several others. All seemed to expect that the attack would be renewed the following day, but Hawkins has written that he protested emphatically against even considering another attack. He was evidently successful in persuading the others to adopt his views, and was delegated to represent them in attempting similarly to convince Burnside. Hawkins reached the Phillips house to find the army commander absent, but the three grand division commanders, Sumner, Hooker, and Franklin were there, so Hawkins explained his mission to them and they in turn urged him to await Burnside's return, which occurred about 1 o'clock in morning. But let Hawkins take over at this point:

> As he (Burnside) came through the door he said: "Well, it's all arranged; we attack at early dawn, the Ninth Corps in the center, which I shall lead in person"; and then seeing me he said: "Hawkins, your brigade shall lead with the 9th New York on the right of the line, and we'll make up for the bad work of today."
>
> When he had ceased there was perfect silence, and he was evidently astonished that no one approved. With hesitation and great delicacy General Sumner then stated the object of my visit, and suggested that General Burnside should examine the rough drawing then upon the table, and listen to some reasons why the attack contemplated ought not to be made. After I had explained the enemy's positions, called attention to several pertinent circumstances, and made something of an argument, General Burnside asked General Sumner what he thought, and he replied that the troops had undergone such great fatigue and privation, and met with such a disaster, that it would not be prudent to

MOVING THE WOUNDED FROM FREDERICKSBURG TOWARD THE RAILHEAD

make another attack so soon. General Hooker, who was lying full length upon a bed in one corner of the room, upon being appealed to by General Burnside, sat up and said in the most frank and decided manner that the attack ought not to be renewed that morning. Then a general consultation took place, in which all who were present joined, the result of which was a verbal order, transmitted through me, countermanding the arrangements for a second attack.

Evidently Burnside had been convinced, the second day's attack was canceled, and on the morning of the 14th the soldiers were put to work digging trenches along the western edge of the town. The army was very much on the alert against an expected counterattack by the Confederates, even though the order to stand by but not renew the attack had not yet filtered down through the chain of command.

Sunday noon Burnside called another council of war to ascertain the views of his grand division commanders about falling back but retaining Fredericksburg. Hooker was positive in his opinon that it would be a mistake to retreat, while others felt that if the fight was to be renewed, it would be foolish to yield Fredericksburg and then have to re-take it. The consensus of opinion was that Fredericksburg should be held and the council was dismissed with instructions to Hooker and Couch to arrange for a better defense of the town.

So the Army of the Potomac sat it out in the streets of Fredericksburg and on the plain to the south all day Sunday the 14th, and Monday the 15th, as Burnside paced the floor of the Phillips house, wondering what to do.

The Army of Northern Virginia also remained quiet on their secure ridge, as Lee pondered the situation and awaited further evidence of Federal offensive operations, which all the Confederate generals except Hood were sure would be attempted. Lee had advised Richmond by telegram at the end of the first day's fight that he expected a renewal of the attack on the 14th, expressing the belief that the disastrous frontal assaults would be discarded in favor of a more likely turning movement, which he had credited Burnside with the intelligence to undertake in the first place. In preparation for such an eventuality, Lee issued orders which resulted in a reshuffle of his divisions with a view to holding his defense position with reduced strength, while assembling a large reserve that he could use for maneuver, counterattack, or any other measure which might require quick and flexible troop employment.

When the sun dissipated the fog on the second morning, the Confederates could see that the Federals were still occupying the ditch in front of Marye's Heights, but had also barricaded the streets leading west from the town, which in itself implied defensive preparations. On Jackson's end of the line the enemy could with equal facility be observed resting on their arms, row after row of them, but giving no indication whatsoever of an intention to resume the offensive. Thus the second day passed with only an occasional exchange between skirmishers and a few desultory shells from Federal batteries. General Lee was puzzled and scarcely able to believe what his eyes told him.

On the afternoon of the 15th, Burnside sent a flag of truce to

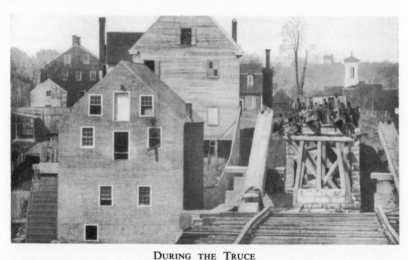

DURING THE TRUCE

A remarkable Brady photo taken during the burial truce. Shows a group of Confederates staring at the photographer from the end of the partially repaired railroad bridge.

BURYING THE DEAD IN FRONT OF MARYE'S HEIGHTS

suggest time out for burial of the dead and relief for such of the wounded as still managed to survive. Lee consented and the burial parties and medical corpsmen from Fredericksburg commenced their gruesome task, encountering here and there an avaricious Confederate soldier evidently hoping it was not too late to salvage a pair of good boots or other useful bit of clothing or equipment from the fallen Federals.

That night it rained. All who could naturally sought what shelter was available. The next morning the usual haze covered the fields and buildings and there was no sign of the men of the Army of the Potomac. Like the Arabs, they had folded their theoretical tents and silently stolen away. Burnside had concluded there wasn't much point in just passing the time in ineffectual idleness on a field where he had been so soundly defeated. He had ordered a night withdrawal which, needless to say, was accomplished with alacrity and with commendable efficiency by his army. The Confederates, not having been informed of his plan, were for their part able to derive little satisfaction from their lack of alertness in allowing such a huge force to

THE WITHDRAWAL
Troops crossing to Falmouth on the night of Monday, December 15.

sneak away and with impunity take up its bridges under their very noses.

The successfully executed withdrawal helped slightly to restore the shattered equanimity of the Union army and, conversely, caused a natural chagrin on the part of Lee and his generals. The gratification of the latter over their decisive victory with inferior numbers, and with casualties of only 5,588 against Burnside's 12,660, was tempered by disappointment that they had not been able to exploit the victory.

The strategic fruits were of no real value to the Confederate cause, and nothing much had been accomplished except another setback for the Union, which was better able to replace its manpower losses and equipment, and would soon recover its breath and try again.

Lee's feelings were reflected in his very brief initial report on the Fredericksburg action which disposed of the action on Longstreet's front in a few words:

> Soon after his repulse on our right, he (the enemy) commenced a series of attacks on our left with a view to obtain-

ing possession of the heights immediately overlooking the town. These repeated attacks were repulsed in gallant style by the Washington Artillery, and a portion of McLaws' Division, which occupied these heights. The last assault was made after dark, when Colonel Alexander's battalion had relieved the Washington Artillery and ended the contest of the day.

In the last analysis, and in retrospect, it was the townspeople of Fredericksburg who suffered most grievously, other than the 2,000-odd soldiers of both armies who had lost their lives. The buildings had been thoroughly shelled by Hunt's artillery, and in the latter stages by Longstreet's, many had been burned, and all were thoroughly ransacked by a Federal army which by now had apparently given up all pretense to the chivalrous attitude with which the war had started out. War was indeed assuming a grim aspect.

The Federal Cavalry at Fredericksburg

The lack of imagination which characterized the employment of the Federal cavalry by Burnside, Sumner, Hooker, and Frank-

PART OF FREDERICKSBURG AFTER THE BATTLE

lin alike, no one of whom appeared to have given more than passing thought to the thousands of horsemen available to the army and assigned respectively to the three grand divisions, is strikingly illustrated in a paragraph from the post-battle report of Brigadier General Pleasonton, who commanded the cavalry division attached to Sumner's Grand Division:

> On December 11, agreeably to the orders of the Major General Commanding the right grand division, this division, consisting of the First Brigade, under Brig. Gen. J. F. Farnsworth; the Second Brigade under Colonel D. McM. Gregg, 8th Pennsylvania Cavalry; and Pennington's battery, Second United States Artillery, massed in columns of squadrons in rear of the ridge commanding the approaches to the upper bridges. This position was held by the command until the army had recrossed the Rappahannock.

In other words, Sumner's cavalry for five days had done little but feed and, it is hoped, groom their horses and themselves on the north side of the river, waiting for a mission that nobody ever thought to give them. The rest of Pleasonton's brief report merely mentions the zones picketed by several cavalry regiments and refers to a reconnaissance made by two squadrons of the 8th Illinois Cavalry which crossed the river at one of the fords above Fredericksburg but "found the enemy's pickets strongly posted at the bridge over the canal." This bridge was presumably the one close by the river opposite Falmouth, and there the two squadrons remained "in observation" until the Army recrossed; an unsanguinary if not supremely bold accomplishment.

The brigade assigned to Franklin's Left Grand Division was not quite so sedentary, but still contributed little of value to the campaign. This outfit, commanded by Bayard, crossed the bridges with the rest of Franklin's force, following Smith's Sixth Corps, and according to Franklin's official report, "proceeded to the front to make a reconnaissance." That apparently was all, except for the regretful statement that their commander, the promising young Brig. Gen. George D. Bayard, was killed by a piece of shell while at Franklin's headquarters at the Bernard house, where he was standing by for orders on the chance that Franklin might think of some worthwhile task for his 3,500 troopers to undertake.

Bayard was highly regarded both as cavalryman and man by all who knew him. His death occurred within a few feet of

BRIGADIER GENERAL GEORGE D. BAYARD

Franklin, as their group was about to go in to lunch. A friend of Bayard's, an artillery captain, narrowly escaped death from the same shell fragments that killed Bayard, his sword belt being cut in two without injury to himself.

Least active of all the cavalry units during the battle was the brigade under Brig. Gen. William W. Averell, attached to General Hooker's Center Grand Division. On December 10 Averell received an order from Hooker to move to a position immediately in rear of Butterfield's corps, directly opposite Fredericksburg, and there the brigade remained December 11-15 without further orders.

It could be, of course, that Burnside had figured Franklin's 55,000 men were going to slice between the separated wings of Lee's army and turn his flank at Hamilton's Crossing, and it may possibly have been a part of his plan, most of which he kept to himself, to hold his cavalry in reserve for the pursuit which he visualized as following on Lee's retreating heels.

Burnside had earlier neglected to employ his cavalry on advance reconnaissance to secure positive ground information of the strength and disposition of the Confederates reported by his balloon to be in the vicinity of Port Royal and Skinker's Neck. Therefore it may have been expecting too much of him to send a couple of brigades, or even more, to cross at the upper fords and operate in Lee's rear for the purpose of creating at the very least a diversion that would assist the major attack on either flank of the battle line.

It is little wonder that the foot soldiers of the Army of the Potomac were in the habit of inquiring, "whoever saw a dead cavalryman?" The trouble lay not with the troopers themselves— they possessed the same soldierly, or unsoldierly, as the case may be, qualities as their compatriots of the other arms—but rather with the high command, which used cavalry chiefly for reconnaissance, escort duty, and mounted messengers, despite the combat example set for them by Stuart and other Southern cavalry leaders.

It was Joe Hooker who elevated the cavalry to the more honorable and certainly far more effective combat role which marked their activities just prior to Gettysburg and thereafter. It is probable that Hooker, as a result of the waste of manpower which marked the relative idleness of the Federal cavalry during the Battle of Fredericksburg, thought deeply about the matter; for as soon as he succeeded Burnside as army commander, the reorganization of the cavalry became one of his first major undertakings.

THE MUD MARCH

CHAPTER 13

BURNSIDE'S LAST EFFORT

BURNSIDE'S telegraphic report to Halleck, dated December 17, 1862, recounted the major features of the Battle of Fredericksburg, assumed full responsibility for its failure, and commended in terms of high praise "the extreme gallantry, courage and endurance shown by officers and men," which he said were never excelled. "The fact that I decided to move from Warrenton on to this line rather against the opinion of the President, Secretary, and yourself, and that you have left the whole management in my hands, without giving me orders, makes me the more responsible," added Burnside humbly, yet with a rather keen sense of psychology, for it brought a letter to the Army of the Potomac from President Lincoln which referred to Burnside's report of the battle, praised the courage of the army, and applied consoling salve with the statement: "Although you were not successful, the attempt was not an error, nor the failure other than accident."

FRANKLIN'S GRAND DIVISION RECROSSING THE RAPPAHANNOCK

No such letter arrived from the taciturn and consistently dis-approving Halleck. But the President's acceptance of the defeat without recriminations or jerking Burnside out of the driver's seat must have bucked him up considerably, for he immediately started making plans for another offensive.

Lincoln Applies a Checkrein

On December 26, the day after Christmas, Burnside ordered the entire army to stock up with three days' cooked rations and sufficient additional rations on the wagons and on the hoof, plus forage for the animals, to carry the army for an additional ten days. The requisite amount of ammunition for the campaign was ordered loaded and the army directed to be ready to move on twelve hours' notice.

Although the army commander knew what he intended to do, he was afraid that word would leak to the Confederates, so he confided his plans only to those officers who were required to make initial reconnaissances in order to carry out their part of the project. Burnside's plan was to cross the Rappahannock on pontoons at Banks Ford and U. S. Ford, en route to an attack from the west against the Confederate heights above Fredericks-burg.

In the hope of deceiving Lee, a special cavalry expedition of 2,500 troopers, 1,000 of them picked men, was organized and started out before Christmas under command of Brig. Gen. William W. Averell. Averell's instructions were to proceed to Kelly's Ford, some 18 miles above Fredericksburg, cross the Rapidan, fan out in several directions, including Warrenton and Culpeper, cut the railroad at Louisa Court House, blow up the locks of the James River canal, destroy bridges, and finally assemble at Suffolk, where steamers would be waiting to return the cavalry to Aquia Creek. Thus the cavalry would have circumnavigated the Army of Northern Virginia and possibly given Lee a few bad moments.

The detailed orders for the grand divisions had all been composed and were about to be issued for the movement when this message was received from the President:

> I have good reasons for saying that you must not make a general movement without first letting me know of it.

BRIGADIER GENERAL W. W. AVERELL AND STAFF

Burnside immediately countermanded the orders, halted Averell's cavalry, and dashed off to Washington, where he was informed by Lincoln that several of his general officers (Lincoln did not divulge their names) had told the President that the army was not in shape to move, and that was the reason for his telegram. It may be assumed that Burnside, now convinced that it was the part of wisdom to take the President into his confidence even if Halleck were not willing to share with him the responsibility of making major tactical decisions, outlined his plan for the new adventure and was given permission to go ahead as soon as the army had been granted a few weeks for rest and refitting.

There was much more to the conference than that, however, because while Burnside was not overly burdened with brains, he wasn't altogether stupid and quite properly expressed his indignation that a couple of his generals had come to Washington behind his back to tell tales out of school. He wanted to know who they were, so he could prefer charges for insubordination and disloyalty. When the information was denied him he suggested to the President that perhaps the country would be better off if he should resign, adding that his generals lacked confidence in him and as a matter of fact were practically unanimous in opposition to any further offensive operations at Fredericksburg. The lonely general must have appeared to the President somewhat like the fictional little boy in the Fourth of July parade whose doting mother noted that "everybody's out of step but Johnnie."

The "disloyal" brigadiers, John Newton, a division commander, and John Cochrane, one of Newton's brigade commanders, both of W. F. Smith's Sixth Corps of Franklin's Left Grand Division, were neither court-martialed nor even reprimanded, because Burnside failed to learn who they were at that time. They had informed both Smith and Franklin in advance of their purpose in going to Washington, when they were granted leaves of absence. Later developments reveal that in due course Burnside did learn their identity.

PLEASONTON'S CAVALRY PICKETS OPERATING ON THE FLANK OF THE ARMY

Newton and Cochrane, whose trip to Washington to tip the President off to the fact that the situation in the army had deteriorated and needed looking into, failed to do more than muddy the waters. The long-suffering Lincoln considered them suspect and took the occasion to smooth down the ruffled Burnside temporarily, while Halleck, for once agreeing with Burnside that the plotters deserved to be dismissed from the Service, pontificated with a few meaningless platitudes and after several days' delay sent the army commander back to his headquarters on the Rappahannock with the assurance that the Administration approved another advance but that Burnside would have to decide the where and how.

The Mud March

The cavalry of the Army of the Potomac, consolidated under Pleasonton's command, had for some time after the Battle of Fredericksburg been energetically reconnoitering the north bank of the Rappahannock for miles above and below Fredericksburg, reporting what their scouting parties could see of the Confederates here and there on the other side, with particular attention to the fords above Fredericksburg.

The ill-fated army commander now made ready to undertake the last of four attempts to gain the upper hand over his able opponent from Virginia, before finally accepting what was already quite evident to both armies, that he was over his depth in his current role.

His orders to the three grand division commanders, dated January 20, 1863, called for a march along the north side of the Rappahannock, crossings by boats for the leading division of each wing, and throwing of the bridges under the direction of Engineer General Woodbury. These preliminaries were to be followed by the crossing of the entire army and subsequent development leading to a turning movement against the familiar Confederate heights west of Fredericksburg, this time in reverse, however, and at the northern end.

The grand divisions of Hooker and Franklin were directed to cross at points just above and below Banks Ford, about a mile apart from each other and eight miles west of Fredericksburg. This modified plan eliminated the crossing at the U. S. Ford, where the Confederates were reported to be in strength sufficient to block the attempt, in favor of the more concentrated one near Banks Ford. The troops were to be in position at the designated crossing points at 7:30 A.M. on the morning of January 21, ready to expedite the passage as soon as the bridges should be laid. Sumner's grand division was directed to follow the other two when Burnside should give the word. After crossing, the leading grand divisions were to develop in the direction of Fredericksburg, Hooker on the right, Franklin on the left, and initially to seize the high ground and the roads leading to Fredericksburg south of the Rappahannock to and including the Plank Road. To assure adequate artillery protection for the river crossing, and after a careful reconnaissance, Burnside's Chief of Artillery, General Hunt, planned a strong line of batteries along the north bank, aggregating a total of 184 guns (37 more than he had posted on Stafford Heights for the attack of December 13), all the way from Falmouth to a point several miles beyond Banks Ford.

Predicated upon a successful crossing and development, Burnside duplicated his earlier underestimate of Lee's capabilities by indicating his opinion that a vigorous flank attack around the north end of Marye's Heights would cause Lee to evacuate the position. In his mind's eye the hopeful Burnside pictured the army as sweeping eastward between the Rappahannock and the Plank Road, with Franklin making the main effort on the left, Sumner in close support, and Hooker advancing steadily on the right. Between them Franklin and Sumner would outflank Lee's right (formerly his left), take Taylor's Hill and extend to the Plank Road as Hooker swung down the Mine Road which angled off to Hamilton's Crossing. What Hooker was to accomplish by the latter tangential maneuver was not indicated.

It was an ambitious and complicated plan which didn't stand a ghost of a chance of succeeding, even if the corps and division commanders had been cooperative. Burnside's wordy orders to Franklin and Hooker spelled out tactical details that depended progressively on the precise execution of a complicated series of movements by a vast number of units. They would have been difficult of fulfillment without the opposition of an already victorious Confederate army.

Fortunately for the Army of the Potomac, Old Man Weather providentially intervened just at the right moment to save it from still another humiliating battle experience. Rain started to fall on the evening of the 20th, the night Burnside's army was moving towards its new positions preparatory to again crossing the river. Several corps and division commanders, disinclined to allow Hunt to take their artillery away from them at will, delayed the movement of their organic artillery batteries, as the roads quickly became quagmires which upset all march schedules. And the rains continued to descend for two days while the long-suffering Federals struggled manfully but hopelessly to carry out the march orders of their army commander.

General Lee was taking Burnside's ambitious new campaign with his customary calm, having been kept adequately informed of the Federal preparations through cavalry scouts, spies, and

A Hopeless Task, Franklin's Troops During th

TEMPTED FLANKING OPERATION IN JANUARY

his own acute powers of deduction. His report of the latest abortive efforts of his opponent showed that by January 19 he was aware of Burnside's intentions. This was one day before the latter had even issued the march orders to his grand division commanders.

HEADQUARTERS,
Fredericksburg, January 29, 1863.

SIR: On the 19th instant, being satisfied that General Burnside was massing the larger portion of his army in the vicinity of Hartwood Church; that his artillery and pontoon trains were moving in the same direction, and that General Slocum's command was advancing from the vicinity of Fairfax toward the Rappahannock, our positions at Banks' and United States Mine Fords were strengthened and re-enforced, these being the points apparently threatened.

The movements of the enemy on the 20th confirmed the belief that an effort would be made to turn our left flank, and that Franklin's and Hooker's corps were the troops selected for that purpose. About dark that evening the rain, which had been threatening during the day, commenced to fall, and continued all night and the two following days. Whether the storm or other causes frustrated the designs of the enemy I do not know; but no attempt as yet has been made to cross the Rappahannock, and some of the enemy's forces have apparently resumed their former positions.

A second storm commenced before day on the 27th, and continued till this morning. The ground is covered with at least 6 inches of snow, and the probabilities are that the roads will be impracticable for some time.

I have the honor to be, with great respect, your obedient servant,

R. E. LEE,
General.

Hon. JAMES A. SEDDON,
Secretary of War, Richmond.

Bruce Catton, in his description of that last march of the Army of the Potomac under Burnside's command, has dramatized the water-logged, frustrated misery of 100,000 men and animals, thrashing about on a slow-motion treadmill in a sea of gooey mud and clay, in a fascinating account of the famous "mud march."*

As the long columns plodded forward at a pace that became ever slower as the rains persisted and the roads became slippery mud holes, tempers flared, march schedules lost all meaning, caissons and wagons became hopelessly bogged, units were inter- mingled, and prostrate animals smothered in the apparently bottomless pits of Virginia clay. The weak gave up the struggle, dropped out along the road, and some died there, while the sub- sequent sick rolls recorded a large number of cases of pneumonia and other pulmonary diseases.

By the time the second day was half spent, Burnside, con- vinced that the prospects were hopeless, called the whole thing off. The pontoons never had reached their destination, hundreds of soldiers had disgustedly taken things into their own hands and deserted, stragglers were all over the countryside. The Con- federates on the other side of the river were greatly enjoying themselves jeering at the Federals within range of their voices. The problem of the Union army was no longer one of crossing the river to do battle, but just how they were going to reverse their steps, recover some semblance of military order, and be able to function at all, let alone stage an aggressive battle.

The return to their former camps near Falmouth of the dis- gruntled, bedraggled, disheartened soldiers of the Army of the Potomac was in sad contrast to the outgoing march, two days earlier, with regimental colors flying and bands playing in a revival of the martial spirit which was no doubt induced by order, but which by the same token was a necessary and useful device so soon after the Fredericksburg defeat.

It would be a long time before that army would again be ready to do battle. Had Lee's strategic plans permitted, he might have taken advantage of the condition of the Union army to undertake a crossing of his own at the upper fords, to add injury to insult at a time when Burnside's army was in the depths of physical and mental despair. Stuart's cavalry and horse artillery

*Glory Road, pages 98-107. Doubleday & Co., Garden City, 1952.

alone might have managed to strike terror into the Federal camp, but they too had to wait for the roads to improve before they could do any effective maneuvering. On the other hand, Burnside seemed to be so unsuccessful on his own, without help from the Confederates, that Lee may have reached the conclusion that he could accomplish more by standing pat for the time being.

PHILLIPS HOUSE BURNING

CHAPTER 14

THE DISINTEGRATION OF A GENERAL

AMBROSE E. BURNSIDE, Commanding General of
the Army of the Potomac for less than three months in the
winter of 1862, was a friendly man with a relatively low boiling
point, but a weak character who tried his best to execute a task
that was far beyond his capacity. He failed repeatedly, and in
the process developed a complex that superiors and subordinates
alike had failed to support his earnest efforts. The resulting
explosion affords an interesting study in psychology.

It is almost possible to see the slow burn which plagued Burnside from the very beginning, when on November 7 he succeeded
McClellan in command and immediately encountered from
General-in-Chief Halleck stubborn opposition to his proposal to
modify the current army strategy in favor of a march on Richmond by way of Fredericksburg, rather than an attempt to flush
Lee out of Culpeper.

Having been permitted to win that first skirmish against the
better judgment of both Lincoln and Halleck, Burnside scored
an additional point by a commendably efficient and rapid march

to Falmouth, at which place his troubles began when the pontoon bridges failed to show up as expected.

In retrospect it would appear that the early burst of energy had depleted his meager supply, that he had quickly run out of momentum, and that there was little intellectual reserve upon which to draw. In Burnside's view it was all Halleck's fault. It took the general a full month and more to recover his equilibrium while Lee's Army of Northern Virginia improved the time by digging themselves in, further to confuse a mind that seemed to lack the power of concentration either to decide what to do or, having decided, how to do it.

The Battle of Fredericksburg was finally fought, but reflected no credit on the commanding general of the Union army, either in conception or execution. It was Burnside's battle from start to finish, and although he blamed chiefly Franklin and his grand division for the failure, the responsibility was his and his alone. Stricken with remorse at the huge loss of life in front of Marye's

FRUSTRATION

This photo of Burnside and his staff, taken after the battle, shows a grim and unhappy group. The battle had been lost, the headquarters burned, and many subordinates were thought to be disloyal. Little wonder that Burnside looks a bit wild! The man with the clerical vest and French cap is the Prince de Joinville, a son of the King of France.

Heights, Burnside's strange idea of compensatory action was to plan a renewal of the attack the next day, which he would lead in person at the head of his old Ninth Corps, quite possibly in the hope that he would die gloriously in a self-sacrificing charge. Although he was persuaded by Hooker and other generals to abandon the idea on the premise that a renewal of the attack would merely increase the loss of life without tactical success, it was apparent that the army's directing mind, if not temporarily unhinged, was spinning out of control.

Some of the causes of Burnside's mental deterioration may be traced back to Antietam. A penetrating analysis of Burnside's unexplained delay in sending his troops into action at Antietam, despite McClellan's repeated messages to attack, appears in an article by Judge Martin Schenck, World War II veteran and graduate of the Command and General Staff College, Fort Leavenworth, entitled *Burnside's Bridge*.* Schenck maintains that Burnside knew that his unwillingness to expose his men in the dangerous crossing at the bridge, in the face of enemy fire, was a major factor in depriving the Union army of a clear-cut victory, and he had made up his mind not to repeat the error. In the attack on Marye's Heights just three months later Schenck sees Burnside sending division after division "in futile wave after futile wave with practically no cover or concealment against Confederates comfortably and securely intrenched at the base of the hill in a sunken road, flanked by a stone wall which afforded a perfect breastwork." The author concludes with the interesting comment that "it is in the field of psychology—or perhaps psychiatry—that the explanation can be found for basing the almost wanton recklessness at Fredericksburg upon the failure arising from too much caution at Sharpsburg."

The next item on the Burnside agenda after the Battle of Fredericksburg was the inauguration of a renewed offensive against Lee by way of the upper fords over the Rappahannock. This package, all tied up in its originator's mind, quickly came

*Civil War History, Vol. 2, No. 4, State University of Iowa, December 1956.

MANSFIELD IN RUINS
Franklin's and Reynolds' headquarters during the battle.

unraveled when Lincoln put on the brakes and Burnside learned that his generals not only did not agree with him, but felt strongly enough about it to take the matter directly to the President. The offensive was delayed and the universal lack of confidence in their commander, by officers and men alike, must have burned deeply in Burnside's mind and soul, but he weathered that squall as well and kept right on trying.

Finally getting off the ground, but just barely, the famous "mud march" proved the last straw. Even the elements were against him! There was nothing left. Nobody had a good word for Burnside, every man's hand seemed turned against him, and stronger men than he might well have broken under like circumstances.

Burnside's written report to Halleck recounted the major events of the latest fiasco in two paragraphs. Once again the delay in getting the pontoons into position, caused by the heavy rains, was given the major credit for the failure, which would otherwise—he thought—have been a success. Nor could Burnside resist the impulse to bring Halleck into the picture for *his* implied share of the latest blame, as will be noted in the latter part of the report:

GENERAL: I have the honor to inclose copies of the principal orders given, which will explain the operations of this army since the late movement was inaugurated. The detailed orders to the chiefs of my different staff departments are not essential to a general understanding of the events.

In accordance with these orders, the pontoons, troops, and artillery were all started for their proper positions at the designated hours on the 20th instant, but the severe storm that set in at 8 o'clock that night prevented their arrival at the appointed times. The pontoons and artillery were very much behind hand, the roads being so fearfully bad that it was almost impossible to move them. We, however, used every exertion during the day and night of the 21st, up to the morning of the 22d, to get them into proper positions. It was quite apparent during the forenoon of the 21st that the enemy had discovered our movement, and had commenced their preparations to meet us. Could we have had the pontoons there, ready to have crossed early on the 21st, as was hoped, there is scarcely a doubt but that the crossing could have been effected, and the objects of the movement attained; but the detention was unavoidable; the elements were against us. During the day and night of the 21st I had the positions of the enemy reconnoitered as thoroughly as was possible under the circumstances, and on the receipt of the final report of my chief engineer, at 4 a.m. on the 22d, I determined to abandon the attempt to cross the river at that point, but, at the same time, determined not to move the troops from their positions until I had had a consultation with the General-in-Chief as to the future movements, knowing that, whatever they may be, the influence upon movements of other armies, of which I knew so little, would be very great, either for good or evil. I accordingly ordered the commands to remain in their present positions, and telegraphed the General-in-Chief that I was very anxious to see him, asking him if he would come down, or if I should visit him for an hour. His reply made it necessary for me to voluntarily leave my command, in order to see him, which I could not do, even for so short a time. I have, therefore, in accordance with the best judgment I can form, ordered the troops into their original positions, which, I hope, will be satisfactory. The reasons for this are entirely of a local nature, and will be given more fully hereafter.

I have the honor to be, very respectfully, your obedient servant.

A. E. BURNSIDE,
Major-General, Commanding Army of the Potomac.

The Battle of the Generals

It was not until November 1863, ten months later, that General Halleck filed his official report on the Fredericksburg campaign with Secretary of War Stanton. Even more surprising, it was not until November 13, 1865, two and one-half years after Fredericksburg, that Burnside wrote his official report to the War Department, and then only after repeated urgings and, without doubt, in an effort to set the record straight from his

RUINS ON WILLIS HILL

standpoint. Burnside summed up the reasons for his failures in the following extract from his official report:

> Many difficulties had presented themselves to me in the exercise of the command of this army. I was the first officer to take charge of it after its first commander had been relieved. I had not been identified with it in the Peninsular campaign, and was unacquainted with a large portion of its officers. The season was very far advanced, which rendered all military movements precarious. The army had not been paid for several months, which caused great dissatisfaction among the soldiers and their friends at home, and increased the number of desertions to a fearful extent, and, in short, there was much gloom and despondency throughout the entire command. When to this is added the fact that there was a lack of confidence on the part of many of the officers in my ability to handle the army, it does not seem so strange that success did not attend my efforts.
>
> I made four distinct attempts, between November 9, 1862, and January 25, 1863. The first failed for want of pontoons; the second was the battle of Fredericksburg; the third was stopped by the President, and the fourth was defeated by the elements and other causes. After the last attempt to move I was, on January 25, 1863, relieved of the command of the Army of the Potomac.
>
> I am not disposed to complain of my lack of success in the exercise of the command; and, in view of the glorious results which have since attended the movements of this gallant army, I am quite willing to believe that my removal was for the best.

After Fredericksburg Burnside remained in the Army, reverted to the rank of corps commander and operated in east Tennessee, where the disharmony between Halleck and himself, which was so noticeable during the Fredericksburg campaign, continued unabated. In connection with the operations in Tennessee, General Halleck went so far as to charge Burnside with direct disobedience of orders and, by implication, placed the responsibility for General Rosecrans' failure in that State on Burnside's alleged lack of cooperation.

BURNSIDE READING A NEWSPAPER
Probably considering the journalistic war he was fighting with Halleck.

With all the smoke that swirled about the heads of the two generals, in their attitude and relationship to one another, there must have been considerable fire. Fuel was added to the flames in the course of the 1863 investigation by the Joint Committee of Congress on the Conduct of the War. The printed report of that committee, whose chairman summoned all the important key figures for testimony, is an absorbing document, which, in its conclusions, "thought best to submit the oral and written testimony without specific criticism of military plans, movements, or individuals, leaving each reader to form his own conclusions from the testimony, and such opinions of competent military men as it may contain."

The battle between Halleck and Burnside raged in the newspapers during the winter of 1863-64, its revival at that time having been inspired by Halleck's report of November 15, 1863, which stated flatly that Burnside's initial plan, the one that Halleck insisted was approved by the President, was in fact to cross the Rappahannock at the upper fords and seize the Fredericksburg heights from a position south and west of the river, while only a small force was to be moved down the north side of the river to protect the reopening of the railroad and the rebuilding of the bridges.

Burnside testified that such was not the case and that Halleck knew perfectly well that he planned to cross the entire army on pontoon bridges at Fredericksburg. He insisted in oral testimony that his march to Falmouth had been carefully explained to Halleck in person, but the fly in Burnside's ointment was that in his written telegram of November 9, 1862 to Halleck, he simply stated that he planned to "make a rapid move of the whole force to Fredericksburg, with a view to a movement upon Richmond from that point." Nothing whatever was said about how he proposed to reach Fredericksburg.

"A Plague on Both Your Houses"

On the written record, it seems that both Halleck and Burnside were partially right, but since each seemed determined to misunderstand the other, and there was no one between them to pour oil on the troubled waters, their relationship grew steadily worse. Neither can be said to have earned a clean bill of health, if we may judge from the record. Halleck's report to Stanton tells only part of the story; it clearly lay within his power as General-in-Chief to clarify the situation at any time. But he would not so much as lift a finger either to advise the willing Burnside or even to fulfill his own responsibilities to his

FEDERAL TROOPS RETURNING TO BASE CAMPS NEAR FALMOUTH

generals in the field. It is quite probable that Burnside, when he first took command of the army, had not definitely made up his mind whether to cross above or below Fredericksburg, but it is inconceivable that the alternative routes were not discussed between the two men prior to the march. A careful reading of the record suggests strongly that the growing distrust toward one another and the entire absence of the normal collaboration which should have been exercised, led to states of mind from which it became perfectly natural for each to throw the blame on the other.

Halleck's chief stock in trade seems to have been the knack of dodging the responsibilities of his position. This trait was again exemplified when Burnside visited Washington in an attempt to secure Lincoln's concurrence in the publication of General Orders No. 8. On that occasion, while Burnside cooled his heels awaiting a decision, Lincoln discussed the problem with Stanton and Halleck, but was unable to get much help from the latter. So noncommittal was Halleck on that occasion that Lincoln wrote a letter urging him to exercise his authority as General-in-Chief and help the President with constructive advice as to what to do in the matter of Burnside and his "disloyal" generals. Halleck was so offended, or pretended to be, at the tone of the letter, which he considered too harsh, that the patient Lincoln withdrew the letter as he was to withdraw others on other historic occasions when his temperamental generals had their feelings hurt by the penetrating character of the President's comments. On this occasion Halleck submitted his resignation, but withdrew it in turn when the President sidetracked the "offending" letter.

Burnside Loses Another Battle

After the abortive "mud march" was concluded, and within twenty-four hours of the army's dejected return to their camps near Falmouth, Burnside seemed to go to pieces. The combination of frustrating events had finally gotten under his skin, and he determined to strike out in all directions against his imagined detractors and disloyal subordinates. He thereupon composed General Orders No. 8, the purpose of which was to accomplish a thorough housecleaning in the Army of the Potomac, with a view to eliminating grand division commanders Hooker and Franklin, corps commander Smith, and a couple of division and brigade commanders, including the two tale-bearers who had gone to Lincoln to complain of Burnside's incapacity.

It is to be noted that the name of General Sumner, who commanded the right wing more or less in absentia during the Battle of Fredericksburg, was missing from Burnside's list of scapegoats. Sumner was a loyal old soul, a nonpolitical, non-scheming officer of the old school and so Burnside, having nothing against him, naturally excluded him from the sweeping denunciations which, with the exception of Hooker and two generals of Burnside's old Ninth Corps, were directed at Franklin and a select group of generals in his Sixth Corps, including the corps commander. General Sumner's death occurred just two months later, in March 1863, and it is fair to wonder if there was any connection with the Fredericksburg campaign and its aftermath.

This was the order which marks the final disintegration of General Burnside:

HDQRS. ARMY OF THE POTOMAC

January 23,1863.

GENERAL ORDERS,)
No. 8   )

I.   General Joseph Hooker, major-general of volunteers and brigadier general U.S. Army, having been guilty of unjust and unnecessary criticisms of the actions of his superior officers, and of the authorities, and having, by the general tone of his conversation, endeavored to create distrust in the minds of officers who have associated with him, and having, by omissions and otherwise, made reports and statements which were calculated to create incorrect impressions, and for habitually speaking in disparaging terms of other officers, is hereby dismissed the service of the United States as a man unfit to hold an important commission during a crisis like the present, when so much patience, charity, confidence, consideration, and patriotism are due from every soldier in the field. This order is issued subject to the approval of the President of the United States.

II.   Brig. Gen. W. T. H. Brooks, commanding First Division, Sixth Army Corps, for complaining of the policy of the Government, and for using language tending to demoralize his command, is, subject to the approval of the President, dismissed from the military service of the United States.

III.   Brig. Gen. John Newton, commanding Third Division, Sixth Army Corps, and Brig. Gen. John Cochrane, commanding First Brigade, Third Division, Sixth Army Corps, for going to the President of the United States with criticisms upon the plans of their commanding officer, are, subject to the approval of the President, dismissed from the military service of the United States.

IV.   It being evident that the following named officers can be of no further service to this army, they are hereby relieved from duty, and will report, in person, without delay, to the Adjutant-General, U.S. Army: Maj. Gen. W. B. Franklin, commanding left grand division; Maj. Gen. W. F. Smith, commanding Sixth Corps; Brig. Gen. Samuel

D. Sturgis, commanding Second Division, Ninth Corps; Brig. Gen. Edward Ferrero, commanding Second Brigade, Second Division, Ninth Army Corps; Brig. Gen. John Cochrane, commanding First Brigade, Third Division, Sixth Corps; Lieut. Col. J. H. Taylor, assistant adjutant-general, right grand division.

By command of Maj. Gen. A. E. Burnside:

LEWIS RICHMOND,

Assistant Adjutant General

After the war, General Smith, the Sixth Corps commander, made a written record of the fact that he had had several conversations with Burnside after the Battle of Fredericksburg, in one of which he quotes Burnside as having said: "I made a mistake in my order to Franklin; I should have directed him to carry the hill at Hamilton's at all hazards." Smith also quoted Burnside as having told him at one time that he had it in mind to relieve Sumner from command, place Hooker in arrest, and put Franklin in command of the army. In appraising these comments, it must be recognized that they were written after the war, and it would be natural for one of the generals who had been listed for removal in G. O. 8, to have something less than friendly feelings for Burnside. But it also suggests Burnside's mercurial character. The conclusion is that Burnside talked too much at some times and too little at others. Franklin's reaction to Burnside can best be summed up by his quoted remark that "the man had lost his mind."

Whatever else may be thought of G. O. 8, it was exceedingly presumptuous. Burnside lacked the authority to dismiss officers at will, without first ordering them before boards of inquiry or general courts-martial. The insertion of the phrase "subject to the approval of the President," in several paragraphs of the order, was made at the suggestion of Burnside's staff, who likewise advised that publication be delayed until it could be presented to the President in person for approval. Burnside accepted the recommendations and accordingly journeyed to Washington where he laid the order before the President. In requesting that he sanction its publication, the President was told that it was essential if Burnside was to maintain proper authority and discipline over the army, and that his resignation was the only alternative. Lincoln declined to approve the order without consulting a number of his advisors, whereupon Burnside, insisting that delay would result in disapproval, requested that his resignation be accepted at once. The President no doubt informed Burnside that he would do it in his own way, and the general was requested to return that night to receive the President's decision.

When Burnside again called upon Lincoln the President informed him that he would not approve General Orders No. 8, and had decided instead to relieve him from command of the Army of the Potomac and to appoint General Hooker in his place. The brief but historic order of the War Department likewise disposed of Generals Sumner and Franklin, in the following language:

War Department,
Adjt. General's Office,
Washington, D. C. January 25, 1863

GENERAL ORDERS)
    No. 20   )

I.   The President of the United States has directed:

    1st.   That Maj. Gen. A. E. Burnside, at his own request, be relieved from the command of the Army of the Potomac.

    2nd.   That Maj. Gen. E. V. Sumner, at his own request, be relieved from duty in the Army of the Potomac.

    3d.   That Maj. Gen. W. B. Franklin be relieved from duty in the Army of the Potomac.

    4th.   That Maj. Gen. J. Hooker be assigned to the command of the Army of the Potomac.

II.   The officers relieved as above will report in person to the Adjutant General of the Army.

    By order of the Secretary of War:

E. D. TOWNSEND,
Assistant Adjutant General.

FUTILITY
Dead soldier sitting on a litter. Sketched by a magazine artist one or two
days after the battle.

CHAPTER 15

AN APPRAISAL OF FREDERICKSBURG

THE BATTLE OF Fredericksburg illustrates the truth that great battles are rarely fought in conformity with specific blueprints that pinpoint the precise character, time, or place of predetermined action by the commander of either of the opposing armies. There are too many imponderables, many of which are evaluated in the strategic planning, but only the ablest of generals have demonstrated capacity to weigh all the factors of a given situation and act swiftly and surely to convert potential liabilities into assets.

Fredericksburg was a major engagement in which Burnside, inexperienced in handling a large army, and a slow thinker to boot, was pitted against the incomparable Lee, experienced in army command, with a string of victories to his credit, and universally admitted to be the best field general in either army.

The Confederates had recently been turned back at Antietam and forced to return to Virginia. The North was clamoring for action when Burnside took over McClellan's job for the purpose of assuming the offensive. The portents were favorable for the Army of the Potomac and it was up to Burnside to press the initiative and bring Lee to battle.

Burnside had available for the Battle of Fredericksburg close to 150,000 combat troops, if Sigel's and Slocum's respective corps, constituting the army reserve, be included. The result was that the Army of the Potomac outnumbered the Army of Northern Virginia about five to three. Burnside might almost be said to have suffered from an embarrassment of riches—material if not mental—for early in December Slocum's Twelfth Corps had been moved from Harpers Ferry to Fairfax Court House and Sigel's Eleventh Corps was being held at Dumfries, less than a day's march from Fredericksburg. On December 11 Burnside had ordered both corps to Fredericksburg. But at no time does it seem to have occurred to him that

266

those surplus troops, more than 26,000 men, constituted a powerful striking force that with a little imagination and initiative could have been employed, in company with the idle cavalry, to cause Lee considerable embarrassment had they been dispatched against the Confederate rear by an independent crossing either above or below the town.

Neither Burnside nor Lee had specifically planned to fight at Fredericksburg when the campaign first got underway. The former was mistakenly aiming for Richmond rather than Lee's army, and Fredericksburg was to be merely the first stop, on the premise that by taking that route he could more easily cover Washington and collaterally improve his line of communication and supply.

Lee on the other hand, content to act on the defensive and merely delay the enemy until winter should halt active operations, preferred to block Burnside's advance further south on the line of the North Anna River, which in his judgment would both protect Richmond and allow him greater maneuverability for the counteroffensive he was confident of being able to launch successfully once he had brought Burnside to a halt. As the situation developed, Lee revised his strategy and decided to meet Burnside at Fredericksburg, but not until the latter by his protracted delay on the Rappahannock had made such a decision the logical one for Lee to make.

For a few days only, after the Army of the Potomac had reached Falmouth and Longstreet's corps had been sent from Culpeper to hold Burnside there, the two wings of Lee's army were one hundred and fifty miles apart, a situation which presented to an enterprising opponent a rare opportunity to defeat each wing in separate actions. Unfortunately for the North it was an opportunity that Burnside was incapable of exploiting.

In justice to Burnside, who as army commander must bear the major responsibility for the Union failure at Fredericksburg, it is a fact that he not only did not want the assignment, but was frank and no doubt sincere in stating his belief that he lacked the qualifications for the job. To that extent he agreed with the appraisal of most of his fellow generals, who, like himself, were graduates of West Point, which fact did not of course automatically confer the qualities essential to successful high command. It was also true that there would inevitably be dissatisfaction with, or at least skepticism, on the part of the army, towards any successor of the popular McClellan, until he should prove himself on the field of battle.

If that were not enough, the unfortunate Burnside immediately ran afoul of General-in-Chief Halleck and President Lincoln, neither of whom approved of the new general's insistence on modifying McClellan's plan of campaign, which the latter had finally been prodded into initiating, but which was being unfolded with such ponderously slow motion that the Administration in desperation removed him and installed Burnside in his place.

It is an historic understatement to say that Halleck's support of Burnside's operations left something to be desired, but it is questionable whether Burnside would have achieved a victory even if the pontoons had been on hand when his army reached Fredericksburg. His conduct of the battle itself, once joined, showed indecision and even downright tactical incompetence, with not a single flash of the inspired leadership that an army must have to gain success.

Even at this late date, with all the records that are available to the researcher seeking light on the conduct of the battle, it is impossible to determine what actually constituted Burnside's battle plan, if indeed a comprehensive one existed. We know what he said after the battle (see page 168); but his written orders to his grand division commanders were vague and inconclusive, made no provision for teamwork or coordination of effort, and failed to assign concise missions.

Burnside protagonists may contend that neither his superiors in Washington nor his three principal subordinates on the field, Sumner, Hooker, and Franklin, gave him their undivided, loyal support and cooperation during the campaign, and without it he was greatly handicapped. The charge might be sustainable in the case of Halleck and Hooker although a stronger character than Burnside could have taken Washington in his stride and suppressed Hooker with a few well-chosen words. Sumner and Franklin, although dubious about Burnside's qualifications, appear to have given him the benefit of the doubt until proven guilty of sheer incompetence by his own actions and orders, and even then they kept their views pretty much to themselves. There is no evidence of insubordination or nonconformance from any one of the three grand division commanders before or during the battle, although Hooker was on the ragged edge on several occasions. That was not out of character for that gentleman, whose own good opinion of Joe Hooker probably exceeded that of any of his fellow officers.

It has been said that Burnside was a figurehead at Fredericksburg and that Washington pulled the strings. Such a belief may have been based on his frequent but unsuccessful attempts to secure Halleck's approval of his plans, but it certainly was not true. If there were figureheads, they were the grand division commanders, the very generals who under Burnside's own reorganization plan were selected with a view to establishing greater operational efficiency through a reduction in the number of corps commanders with whom the army commander would have to deal. On paper the idea looked good, but Burnside, while preserving the form, nullified the substance of the revamped organizational structure by virtually collecting all the corps and divisional reins into his own hands and reducing the grand division commanders almost to the role of rubber stamps.

Reduced to its simplest terms, although Burnside exercised fully all the functions of an army commander, he lacked certain essential qualities of leadership and executive ability which, had he possessed them, might have brought success rather than failure. Without them, his successive performances gave off an increasingly hollow tone until he himself must have begun to wonder which side was up.

There are nine fundamental principles of war that have

proven sound and valid over the centuries. Burnside violated at least seven of them at Fredericksburg. He seized the initiative at the start of the campaign but quickly lost it to Lee through his failure to *maneuver* when he reached Falmouth or subsequently. He talked glibly about the element of *surprise* but failed miserably to exploit it. *Simplicity* was completely missing both from his battle plan and the orders for its execution, while the *objective* which was Burnside's basis for the campaign was completely lost in the shuffle. Furthermore, he failed to apply the principle of *mass* (combat power) when he neglected to bring his two reserve corps into action and permitted his cavalry to remain immobile.

The principle of *economy of force* was applied only in reverse in the six successive, unsupported, expensive frontal attacks against Marye's Heights. *Cooperation* between the several elements of the army was missing solely because Burnside took no visible steps to coordinate the actions of the two separate wings under Sumner and Franklin. The *offensive* and *security* were in fact the only principles of war that were applied, and in their application it can hardly be said that Burnside employed them to the glory and honor of Northern armies.

Whatever credit may be gleaned from the wreckage of Northern hopes on the Rappahannock during the winter of 1862-63 belongs to the fighting men of the Union army, who went into action under a terrific handicap of inept leadership at the army and grand division levels. They deserved a better fate. The valiant effort by the divisions under Meade and Gibbon should have been given all-out support by Franklin to exploit their initial penetration of Jackson's line, while the troops who shattered themselves against the stone wall before Fredericksburg were as sound and courageous as any who ever wore the uniform of the American soldier.

The Battle of Fredericksburg was a severe defeat for the Union army, in contradistinction to the preceding major engagement at Antietam, which although a tactical stalemate was a strategic victory for the North in having turned Lee back to

Virginia and provided Lincoln with the opportunity to issue his historic Emancipation Proclamation. The apparently inexhaustible resources of the industrialized Northern states were barely dented at Fredericksburg and the battle losses in proportion to total strength were easily absorbed. That was not true of Lee's army, for each great battle that it fought took one more huge bite out of any available manpower and material resources of the Confederacy.

Attrition was slowly but surely whittling Lee down to the point where the bottom of the barrel would finally be reached, and that was about the only consolation the North could derive from Fredericksburg. It could not however be described as a decisive Southern victory, for the simple reason that the word decisive in the military lexicon implies either the destruction of the opposing force or its removal from the scene as an operational unit. Far from achieving that result, the Army of the Potomac was not seriously damaged as a fighting entity—what it lacked most was capable leadership in the top echelons.

The quality of Lee's leadership in this battle was well up to the high standard that had come to be expected of that superior general. He was a strong proponent of the offensive, whenever possible, but this time he fought strictly on the defensive, principally because the natural features of the ground were made to order for the purpose, but also perhaps because Longstreet's corps had preceded him to Fredericksburg and occupied such a strong position that it would have been folly to modify his dispositions.

Longstreet believed implicitly in the defensive, both strategically and tactically, for the Confederate Army, and Lee had confidence in the judgment of his stalwart subordinate, whose firm and frequently expressed conviction was that the South did not have to beat the North to win the war; all that was necessary was to keep the North from beating the South. Longstreet's defensive psychology, which Lee shared for this one battle at least, presupposed a continuation of the ineffectual leadership which had so far characterized the Federal high command, and which in his opinion would in time so discourage the people of the North that the Peace Party would gain the ascendancy.

The inferior quality of Burnside's leadership cannot detract from Lee's effective performance on this occasion. His evaluation of the enemy's capabilities under Burnside, coupled with the calm, unhurried manner in which he prepared to meet his opponent, commands our admiration. A Union victory was clearly a possibility. which Lee was prepared to face but which did not seem to disturb him. Unbounded confidence in his corps and division commanders and a willingness to give them plenty of rope within the scope of his own overall plan, was a hallmark of the Confederate leader, and it was only on rare occasions that his lieutenants failed him.

At the end of the first day's battle only four of Lee's divisions had been engaged. Except for the sanguinary fighting in front of Marye's Heights, and the temporary Meade-Gibbon penetration on the southern end of the battlefield, there had been no fighting of any consequence, and large numbers of troops on both sides had scarcely fired a shot. The Confederates were certain that the action on December 13, bloody as it was, was only the first act of the play. Lee had no idea how badly he had hurt Burnside and naturally expected a renewal of the attack on the 14th, particularly since a Union prisoner had been captured with a message on his person which showed Burnside to have ordered the attack to be resumed next day (later rescinded). The Confederates consequently busied themselves in strengthening their fortifications on the heights and apparently gave no thought to the possibility of going over to the offensive. Lee had not even provided a general reserve nor made plans for a counterattack, a clear indication that it had not even occurred to him that Burnside would give up so easily.

It must have been a strange sight, that of two armies with an aggregate strength of almost two hundred thousand men, virtually locked in each other's arms within an area of not more than twenty square miles, for two days and two nights after a bitter battle, and without either side making a pass at the other. But that is precisely what happened on Sunday and Monday, December 14 and 15, with Burnside debating his next move and Lee waiting to see what Burnside would do.

When the Confederates on Tuesday morning discovered that the Union army had recrossed the Rappahannock during the night without their knowledge, Burnside had scored his only surprise of the battle, and Lee wasn't too happy about it. Although it is problematic what success the Confederates might have achieved, in the face of Hunt's powerful batteries on Stafford Heights, if Lee had launched a general counteroffensive on either of the two days of inactivity before the Federals evacuated, he clearly missed a golden opportunity for violent harassment of his retreating enemy while the Union army was quietly recrossing the river under cover of the darkness.

APPENDIX I

Roster of graduates of the U. S. Military Academy, West Point, who served in the Fredericksburg campaign as army, corps, and division commanders, or as Chief of Branch.

Name	Rank	Class
Robert E. Lee	General, CSA	1829
William N. Pendleton	Brig.Gen. CSA	1830
Andrew A. Humphreys	Brig.Gen. USA	1831
George G. Meade	Maj.Gen. USA	1835
Daniel P. Woodbury	Brig.Gen. USA	1836
Jubal A. Early	Brig.Gen. CSA	1837
William H. French	Brig.Gen. USA	1837
Joseph Hooker	Maj.Gen. USA	1837
Henry J. Hunt	Brig.Gen. USA	1839
George W. Getty	Brig.Gen. USA	1840
William T. H. Brooks	Brig.Gen. USA	1841
Albion P. Howe	Brig.Gen. USA	1841
John F. Reynolds	Maj.Gen. USA	1841
Amiel W. Whipple	Brig.Gen. USA	1841
Richard H. Anderson	Maj.Gen. CSA	1842
Abner Doubleday	Brig.Gen. USA	1842
Daniel H. Hill	Maj.Gen. CSA	1842
James Longstreet	Lieut.Gen. CSA	1842
Lafayette McLaws	Maj.Gen. CSA	1842
John Newton	Brig.Gen. USA	1842
George Sykes	Brig.Gen. USA	1842
William B. Franklin	Maj.Gen. USA	1843
Winfield S. Hancock	Brig.Gen. USA	1844
Alfred Pleasonton	Brig.Gen. USA	1844
William F. Smith	Maj.Gen. USA	1845
Darius N. Couch	Maj.Gen. USA	1846
Thos. J. (Stonewall) Jackson	Lieut.Gen. CSA	1846
George E. Pickett	Maj.Gen. CSA	1846
George Stoneman	Brig.Gen. USA	1846
Samuel D. Sturgis	Brig.Gen. USA	1846
William W. Burns	Brig.Gen. USA	1847
Ambrose E. Burnside	Maj.Gen. USA	1847

Name	*Rank*	*Class*
John Gibbon	Brig.Gen. USA	1847
Charles Griffin	Brig.Gen. USA	1847
Ambrose P. Hill	Maj.Gen. CSA	1847
Orlando B. Willcox	Brig.Gen. USA	1847
Robert Ransom Jr.	Brig.Gen. CSA	1850
John B. Hood	Maj.Gen. CSA	1853
Oliver O. Howard	Brig.Gen. USA	1854
J.E.B. Stuart	Maj.Gen. CSA	1854

APPENDIX II

SUMMARY OF STRENGTH AND CASUALTIES AT FREDERICKSBURG*

ARMY OF THE POTOMAC

	Strength	Killed	Wounded	Captured or Missing	Total
Sumner	31,659	523	4,271	640	5,434
Hooker	40,396	352	2,501	502	3,355
Franklin	46,897	401	2,764	625	3,790
Engineers	1,329	8	49	2	59
Artillery Reserve	1,121	0	15	0	15
Grand total	121,402	1,284	9,600	1,769	12,653

ARMY OF NORTHERN VIRGINIA

	Strength	Killed	Wounded	Captured or Missing	Total
Jackson	38,931	334	2,531	531	3,396
Longstreet	41,294	257	1,496	122	1,875
Stuart	10,701	3	29	0	32
Corps and Reserve Artillery	793	14	60	0	74
Grand total	91,719	608	4,116	653	5,377

* Casualty figures taken from *Battles and Leaders of the Civil War*, Vol. III. Century Co., 1888. Strength figures are a recapitulation from sources cited on following table. The Federal cavalry attached to each of the three grand divisions are presumably included in the totals as shown.

STRENGTH OF THE ARMIES AT THE BATTLE OF FREDERICKSBURG
ARMY OF THE POTOMAC

	(1)	(2)
Right Grand Division		
(Sumner)		
Couch's Second Corps	. . . . . .	15,383
Willcox's Ninth Corps	. . . . . .	13,578
Subtotal	31,659	28,961
Center Grand Division		
(Hooker)		
Stoneman's Third Corps	. . . . . .	19,805
Butterfield's Fifth Corps	. . . . . .	18,041
Subtotal	40,396	37,846
Left Grand Division		
(Franklin)		
Reynold's First Corps	. . . . . .	18,230
Smith's Sixth Corps	. . . . . .	25,215
Subtotal	46,897	43,445
Engineer Corps	1,329	. . . . . .
Provost Guard	1,096	. . . . . .
Miscellaneous	632	. . . . . .
Reserve Artillery	. . . . . .	1,121
Bayard's Cavalry, about	. . . . . .	3,500
Total	122,009	114,873
Reserve Corps		
Sigel's Eleventh Corps	15,562	15,562
Slocum's Twelfth Corps	12,162	11,162
Grand total	149,733	141,597

(1) Official Records: Trimonthly return of the Army of the Potomac (present for duty), for December 10, 1862.
(2) From the Papers of the Military Historical Society of Massachusetts, Vol. III. "Fredericksburg," by Lt. Col. William Allan, C.S.A., Chief Ordnance Officer, Second Corps (Jackson's), Army of Northern Virginia.

ARMY OF NORTHERN VIRGINIA

	(3)	(4)
Longstreet's Corps		
Anderson's Division	9,373	......
Hood's Division	8,569	......
McLaws' Division	9,285	......
Pickett's Division	9,001	......
Ransom's Division	4,394	......
Artillery	672	......
Total, corps	41,294	34,944
Jackson's Corps		
Ewell's (Early's) Division	9,209	......
A. P. Hill's Division	12,978	......
D. H. Hill's Division	10,164	......
Jackson's (Taliaferro's) Division	6,067	......
Artillery	513	......
Total, corps	38,931	33,705
Stuart's Cavalry	10,701	4,500
Reserve Artillery	793	718
Grand total	91,719	73,867

(3) Official Records: Abstract from field return of Lee's Department of Northern Virginia, headquarters at Fredericksburg, December 10, 1862.
(4) Allan, *op. cit.*
Note: In general, Confederate divisions were approximately twice the size of Federal divisions.

BREAKDOWN OF CASUALTY REPORTS BY CORPS AND DIVISIONS

ARMY OF THE POTOMAC
Major General Ambrose E. Burnside, Commanding

Right Grand Division
Major General Edwin V. Sumner, Commanding

Corps and Divisions	Commanding Officer°	Killed	Wounded	Captured or Missing	Total
2d Corps	Darius N. Couch (staff)	...	1	...	1
1st Div.	Winfield S. Hancock	219	1,581	229	2,029
2nd Div.	Oliver O. Howard	104	718	92	914
3rd Div.	William H. French	89	904	167	1,160
		(412)	(3,204)	(488)	(4,104)
9th Corps	Orlando B. Willcox				
1st Div.	William W. Burns	1	24	2	27
2nd Div.	Samuel D. Sturgis	94	827	86	1,007
3rd Div.	George W. Getty	16	216	64	296
		(111)	(1,067)	(152)	(1,330)
Cav. Div.	Alfred Pleasonton	0	0	0	0
Total		523	4,271	640	5,434

Center Grand Division
Major General Joseph Hooker, Commanding

Corps and Divisions	Commanding Officer	Killed	Wounded	Captured or Missing	Total
3rd Corps	George Stoneman				
1st Div.	David B. Birney	114	655	181	950
2nd Div.	Daniel E. Sickles	12	85	3	100
3rd Div.	Amiel W. Whipple	19	92	18	129
		(145)	(832)	(202)	(1,179)
5th Corps	Daniel Butterfield (staff)	1	1		2
1st Div.	Charles Griffin	73	733	120	926
2nd Div.	George Sykes	17	163	48	228
3rd Div.	Andrew A. Humphreys	115	772	132	1,019
		(206)	(1,669)	(300)	(2,175)
Cav. Brig.	William A. Averell	1	0	0	1
Total		352	2,501	502	3,355

° Corps were commanded by major generals, except the 9th, 3rd and 5th, which were commanded by brigadier generals. All divisions by brigadier generals.

Left Grand Division
Major General William B. Franklin, Commanding

Corps and Divisions	Commanding Officer	Killed	Wounded	Captured or Missing	Total
1st Corps	John F. Reynolds (escort)		3		3
1st Div.	Abner Doubleday	31	164	22	217
2nd Div.	John Gibbon	141	1,024	102	1,267
3rd Div.	George G. Meade	175	1,241	437	1,853
		(347)	(2,432)	(561)	(3,340)
6th Corps	William F. Smith				
1st Div.	William T. H. Brooks	24	123	50	197
2nd Div.	Albion P. Howe	22	159	5	186
3rd Div.	John Newton	7	47	9	63
		(53)	(329)	(64)	(446)
Cav. Brig.	George D. Bayard	1	3	0	4
Total		401	2,764	625	3,790
Engineers	Daniel P. Woodbury	8	49	2	59
Artillery Reserve	Henry J. Hunt	0	8	0	8
	Arty. Res. with 2nd Corps	0	7	0	7
			(15)		(15)
Grand total		1,284	9,600	1,769	12,653

ARMY OF NORTHERN VIRGINIA
General Robert E. Lee, Commanding
FIRST CORPS—Lt. Gen. James Longstreet

Corps and Divisions	Commanding Officer	Killed	Wounded	Captured or Missing	Total
Divisions					
Anderson's	R. H. Anderson	20	106	44	170
McLaws'	Lafayette McLaws	101	697	66	864
Pickett's	George E. Pickett	3	50	1	54
Hood's	John B. Hood	54	188	11	253
Ransom's	Robert Ransom, Jr., Brig. Gen.	79	455	...	534
Total		257	1,496	122	1,875

SECOND CORPS—Lt. Gen. Thomas J. Jackson

Corps and Divisions	Commanding Officer	Killed	Wounded	Captured or Missing	Total
Divisions					
Jackson's	Wm. B. Taliaferro, Brig. Gen.	10	170	2	182
Ewell's	Jubal A. Early, Brig. Gen.	124	936	1	1,061
D. H. Hill's	D. H. Hill	17	125	0	142
A. P. Hill's	Ambrose P. Hill	183	1,300	528	2,011
Total		334	2,531	531	3,396
Cav. Div.	J.E.B. Stuart	3	29	...	32
Corps Artillery		4	34	...	38
Reserve Artillery	Brig. Gen. W. N. Pendleton	10	26	0	36
Grand total		608	4,116	653	5,377

Corps were normally commanded by lieutenant generals, divisions by major generals. Longstreet's corps included 5 divisions (20 brigades); Jackson had 4 divisions (19 brigades); Stuart's command was composed of 3 cavalry brigades, (Brig. Generals Wade Hampton, Fitzhugh Lee, and W. H. F. Lee) and Pelham's 5 artillery batteries. The corps and reserve artillery had 5 battalions aggregating 25 batteries.

NOTES

1. The strength return for the Army of the Potomac is not broken down below the grand divisions. In order to give an idea as to the relative numerical strength of the corps, there is also furnished under column (2) the unofficial data cited by Colonel Allan, CSA. If it may be assumed that Colonel Allan's figures do not include the organic divisional artillery and the attached cavalry, but only the infantry, it will be found that his strengths as shown for the several Federal corps agree fairly well with those summarized by General Burnside in his remarks on page 90, Vol. XXI, Series I, *Official Records of the Rebellion*. For example, Burnside gives in round figures the strength of the First Corps as being 18,500 and of the Sixth Corps 24,000; and he states that the aggregate for the three grand divisions is 113,000, which is not greatly different from Allan's 114,873. The reader will remember, also, that Civil War strength figures are often unreliable, or difficult to evaluate because of differ-

ences in the methods used in rendering returns. The totals may or may not include men absent sick, on leave, AWOL, or for other reasons.

2. Burnside's return for December 10 (p. 1121, *op. cit.*), also gives the following strengths for the infantry, cavalry, and artillery:

Infantry	104,903
Cavalry	5,884
Artillery	5,896
Total	116,683

3. The wide discrepancy between the data furnished in columns (3) and (4) for the Confederates may be partly explained as follows: Colonel Allan does not include in his total for the cavalry a part of Stuart's cavalry which was detached and operating in the Shenandoah Valley. However, the discrepancy of some 11,500 in the totals of the two corps is not explained; possibly Allan cites only the numbers actually present whereas the strength returns also include those absent for various causes.

BIBLIOGRAPHY

Alexander, Gen. E. P. *The Battle of Fredericksburg.* Southern Historical Society Papers, Vol. X, Richmond, Va., 1882.

Andrews, J. Cutler. *The North Reports the Civil War.* Pittsburgh: University of Pittsburgh Press, 1955.

Battles and Leaders of the Civil War, Vol. III. Contributions by Union and Confederate Officers. New York: The Century Company, 1884.

Catton, Bruce. *Glory Road.* Garden City: Doubleday & Co., 1952.

Carter, Capt. R. G., U.S.A. *Four Brothers in Blue, From Bull Run to Appomattox.* Washington: 1913.

Comte de Paris. *History of the Civil War in America,* Vol. II. Philadelphia: The John C. Winston Co., 1907.

Cox, Maj. Gen. Jacob D. *Military Reminiscences of the Civil War,* 2 volumes. Charles Scribner's Sons, 1900.

Cullum, Bvt. Maj. Gen. George W. *Register of the Officers and Graduates of the U.S. Military Academy,* 3 volumes. Houghton-Mifflin and Company, 1891.

Early, J. B. *Autobiography of Lt. Gen. Jubal A. Early C.S.A.* Philadelphia: J. B. Lippincott, 1912.

Freeman, Douglas Southall. *Lee's Lieutenants,* 3 volumes. New York: Charles Scribner's Sons, 1944.

Freeman, Douglas Southall. *R. E. Lee, Vol. II.* New York: Charles Scribner's Sons, 1935.

Henderson, Colonel G. F. R. *Stonewall Jackson and the American Civil War,* Vol. II. New York: Longmans, Green and Co., 1927.

The Campaign of Fredericksburg. London: Gale and Polden.

McClellan, H. B. *Major-General J. E. B. Stuart.* Boston: Houghton, Mifflin and Co., 1885.

Redway, Maj. G. W. *Fredericksburg.* London: Swan, Sonnenschein and Co., 1906.

Schenck, Martin. *Civil War History.* Iowa City: State University of Iowa, December 1956. Article entitled "Burnside's Bridge."

Steele, Matthew Forney. *American Campaigns,* 2 volumes. Washington: War Department Document No. 324.

War of the Rebellion: *Official Records of the Union and Confederate Armies.* Government Printing Office: 1882-1900.

West Point Alumni Foundation, The. *1954 Register of Graduates of the United States Military Academy,* 1802-1954.

Williams, Kenneth P. *Lincoln Finds a General,* Vol. II. New York: The MacMillan Company, 1949.

INDEX

285